Illustrated PFS:® First Publisher™

for Versions 2.0 and 3.0

John P. Mueller
and
Wallace E. Wang

Wordware Publishing, Inc.

Library of Congress Cataloging-in-Publication Data

Mueller, John (John P.)
Illustrated PFS:First publisher : for versions 2.0 and 3.0 / John P. Mueller and Wallace E. Wang.
p. cm.
Includes index.
ISBN 1-55622-201-7 : $21.95
1. Desktop publishing -- Computer programs. 2. PFS:First publisher (Computer program). I. Wang, Wally. II. Title.
Z286.D47M84 1991
686.2'25445369--dc20 90-27668
CIP

1506 Capital Avenue
Plano, Texas 75074

Printed in the United States of America

ISBN 1-55622-201-7
10 9 8 7 6 5 4 3 2 1
9103

All inquiries for volume purchases of this book should be addressed to Wordware Publishing, Inc., at the above address. Telephone inquiries may be made by calling:

(214) 423-0090

Contents

Contents (Cont.)

Recommended Learning Sequence

Recommended Learning Sequence (Cont.)

Module 1
ABOUT THIS BOOK

INTRODUCTION

This book describes Software Publishing Corporation's PFS: First Publisher desktop publishing program for IBM PC and compatible computers. PFS: First Publisher lets you mix text and graphics to create newsletters, reports, flyers, or magazines. You can import Write, Microsoft Word, WordPerfect, MultiMate, WordStar, PFS: First Choice, PC Paint Plus, PC Paintbrush, and Harvard Graphics. Or, you can create text and graphics using the PFS: First Publisher built-in word processor and graphics tools.

This book describes and demonstrates the features offered by PFS: First Publisher for creating printed or typeset-ready pages from start to finish. It describes such features as kerning, stylesheets, picture cropping, and letter spacing.

Illustrated PFS: First Publisher can appeal to a wide range of users. Beginners can use this book to learn about desktop publishing using PFS: First Publisher. Intermediate and advanced users can use this book as a quick reference to command examples that work. Finally, classroom instructors can use this book as a desktop publishing and PFS: First Publisher textbook.

PFS: First Publisher contains many features that may intimidate inexperienced computer or desktop publishing users. However, you will find PFS: First Publisher easy to use if you are willing to "play around" with the commands. The sample session in Module 3 shows how easy and powerful the program can be to use. PFS: First Publisher makes desktop publishing easy to use for everybody.

ORGANIZATION

We organized *Illustrated PFS: First Publisher* into small, easy-to-read modules to help readers use this book. The modules appear in alphabetical order for quick reference to specific commands. If you are learning PFS: First Publisher for the first time, the Recommended Learning Sequence lists the modules from simple to complex. By following the Recommended Learning Sequence, you can quickly learn how to use all the features of PFS: First Publisher.

This module describes how to use this book, its organization, and its contents. It also contains some information about your computer and what you should know.

Module 2 gives a brief overveiw of PFS: First Publisher. It describes how to use a desktop publishing program and the steps to follow before you start PFS: First Publisher.

Module 3 is a sample PFS: First Publisher session. Impatient users can follow this sample session to quickly see how they can use PFS: First Publisher for creating finished or typeset-ready pages. 73 Modules 73 4 through 40 give descriptions, applications, and examples for each of the PFS: First Publisher commands. Each module describes what a particular command does, why you would use it, and how the command works. This book provides hundreds of examples and illustrations in the Description, Applications, and Typical Operation sections of each module.

You can use the examples in the modules to learn how to use PFS: First Publisher. Working examples let you experiment with the program so you can see how the different commands work. As you will see, PFS: First Publisher is one of the easiest and most powerful desktop publishing programs for IBM PC and compatible computers.

Appendix A contains command terms and definitions used by the PFS: First Publisher manual. Each definition references a specific PFS: First Publisher command or tool.

Appendix B contains guidelines for using desktop publishing programs such as PFS: First Publisher. These guidelines can help you create and print professional- looking documents with a minimal amount of trial and error.

Appendix C contains graphic terms not mentioned in the PFS: First Publisher manual. It also contains guidelines for including graphics in your documents. These guidelines can help you design pages for including graphics from scanners, painting programs, or spreadsheets.

Appendix D contains publishing terms not mentioned in the PFS: First Publisher manual. These terms describe fonts and typefaces along with guidelines for using typefaces and fonts in your documents.

Appendix E contains explanations for using PFS: First Publisher with a mouse such as the Microsoft™ or Logitech™ mouse.

Appendix F describes how to bit-edit graphics for touching up pictures.

Appendix G explains how to use the PFS: First Publisher Font Move program for including additional fonts into a PFS; First Publisher document.

Appendix H describes how to capture screen images using the Snapshot and Snap2Art PFS: First Publisher programs.

Appendix I explains how to use the PFS: First Publisher printer utility program.

Appendix J describes how to transfer graphic images between an IBM PC using PFS: First Publisher and a Macintosh using MacPaint or FullPaint.

Appendix K provides you with some tips on using clip art plus a directory of the clip art provided in several First Publisher packages.

Appendix L shows you how to use the Business Template Kit. This is an add-on product specifically designed for business users of 73 First Publisher. It allows you to enhance the capabilities of First Publisher.

Appendix M contains exercises for charting your progress with PFS: First Publisher. If you are learning by yourself, you can use these exercises to test what you've learned from each module. If you are a classroom instructor, you can use these exercises for student assignments. When you can answer the questions in each module, you are ready to move on to the next module in the Recommended Learning Sequence.

HARDWARE AND SOFTWARE REQUIREMENTS

PFS: First Publisher runs on any IBM PC or compatible computer with a minimum of 512K of memory (RAM), DOS 2.0 or higher, and a Hercules™, CGA, EGA, or VGA video card and monitor. You can run PFS: First Publisher with two floppy disk drives but we recommend one floppy disk drive and one hard drive.

Module 2
PFS: FIRST PUBLISHER OVERVIEW

INTRODUCTION

PFS: First Publisher is a desktop publishing program that combines graphics and text on a single page. You can use PFS: First Publisher by itself or in combination with your favorite word processor or graphics program.

Beginnners can use PFS: First Publisher to create flyers and brochures. Advanced users can use PFS: First Publisher to design entire magazines and books. If you want to produce professional-looking documents, then PFS: First Publisher is for you.

WHAT IS DESKTOP PUBLISHING

In the past, word processors could only create text, while drawing and painting programs could only create graphics. To combine the two together required printing both files separately and manually pasting the two together on a page. A desktop publishing program like PFS: First Publisher removes that step. Rather than paste text and graphics together by hand, PFS: First Publisher lets you combine text and graphics electronically.

CREATING TEXT FOR PFS: FIRST PUBLISHER

You can create text using the PFS: First Publisher built-in word processor or using any number of word processors like Microsoft Word, WordStar, Professional Write, PFS: First Choice, or WordPerfect. You can even create text and graphics on another computer, such as an Apple Macintosh, and transfer the text and graphics file directly into PFS: First Publisher.

Once you have created text using PFS: First Publisher or a separate word processor, PFS: First Publisher lets you control the way your words look. You can arrange your words in columns and as double-sided pages. You can also change the size and style of individual letters. The choice is up to you.

CREATING GRAPHICS FOR PFS: FIRST PUBLISHER

You can create graphics using the PFS: First Publisher built-in graphics tools. You can also use any number of drawing, painting, or scanning programs such as PC Paint Plus, PC Paintbrush, or Harvard Graphics. Once you have created graphics using PFS: First Publisher or a separate graphics program, PFS: First Publisher lets you alter the way the graphics look. You can resize, crop, and touch up a picture.

DESKTOP PUBLISHING EQUIPMENT

Desktop publishing requires a printer. You can use a dot-matrix printer or a laser printer such as the Hewlett-Packard LaserJet.

Additional equipment you may find helpful includes optical character recognition (OCR) devices, image digitizers, or special drawing pads and tablets. An OCR electronically scans or "reads" printed text into the computer, eliminating the need for typing. An image digitizer electronically scans or "reads" photographs and pictures into the computer, eliminating the need for drawing the pictures yourself. If you want to draw your own pictures, you can use a drawing pad or tablet. Such special drawing devices let you draw pictures with a pen rather that with the mouse or the keyboard.

While equipment such as an OCR, image digitizer, or drawing pad or tablet can simplify desktop publishing, they are not necessary. As long as you have PFS: First Publisher and an IBM PC or compatible computer, you can start creating camera-ready pages in minutes.

DESKTOP PUBLISHING ADVANTAGES

Desktop publishing with PFS: First Publisher can save you time and money. To create a newsletter or catalog the old-fashioned way, you would first type the text. Then you would send the draft to a printer for typesetting.

After receiving the pages back from the printer, you would proof the pages for errors. If you found an error or needed to add more information, you would correct the page by hand. Then you would send the page back to the printer and have the entire page typeset all over again. If you found another error or needed to add another paragraph, sentence, word, or punctuation mark, you would have to repeat this process until the page looked perfect.

Next you would cut and paste blocks in the text for any photographs, drawings, or figures you wanted to include. After pasting all the pictures in the correct places and double-checking them for accuracy, you would be ready for the final printing.

Not only is the old-fashioned way of printing slower and more expensive than desktop publishing, it's also less flexible. Each time you find a mistake or add more information, you have to send the entire page back to the printer for typesetting.

Compare this to desktop publishing with PFS: First Publisher. First you create the text using the PFS: First Publisher built-in word processor. Next, you could add graphics by importing them from a drawing or painting program, or drawing them yourself using the PFS: First Publisher graphics tools.

When you're happy with the page layout, you can print the pages on a dot-matrix or laser printer for proofing. If a page needs corrections, you can make them yourself.

Desktop publishing gives you a choice. You can print the pages yourself on your own dot-matrix or laser printer, or you can send the pages to a typesetting machine for final output. In either case, the pages always remain in your control no matter how many changes you make. If you send your pages to a printer for typesetting, you need do this only once. If you print the pages yourself, you remove the cost of typesetting altogether.

BEFORE YOU START

Before you start using PFS: First Publisher, you should know how to use your IBM PC or compatible computer. You should understand how to copy and format disks and how to use the basic MS-DOS commands. If you have a hard disk, you should know how to create, select, and search through subdirectories containing documents.

USING THE MOUSE AND THE KEYBOARD

This book uses the keyboard for all typical operations. A table in each module contains any special mouse instructions for that command. Appendix E describes generic mouse usage.

COPYING THE PFS: FIRST PUBLISHER DISKS

PFS: First Publisher comes on five 5.25-inch floppy disks or three 3.5-inch floppy disks: two Program Disks, a Fonts Disk, a Sampler Disk, and a Laser Support Disk.

Single Floppy Disk Drive

To copy your PFS: First Publisher master disks using a single floppy disk drive, perform the following steps:

1. Insert the first PFS: First Publisher disk in drive A, type **DISKCOPY A: A:**, and press **Enter**.
2. Insert a blank disk in drive A when the computer prompts you for the target disk.
3. Repeat steps 1 and 2 until you have copies of all the PFS: First Publisher disks.

Dual Floppy Disk Drives

To copy your PFS: First Publisher master disks using dual floppy disk drives, perform the following steps:

1. Insert a blank disk in drive B.
2. Insert the first PFS: First Publisher disk in drive A.
3. Type **DISKCOPY A: B:** and press **Enter**.

Hard Disk Drive

To copy your PFS: First Publisher master disks on to a hard disk drive, perform the following steps:

1. From your hard disk drive prompt (C:\) type **MD FIRSTPUB** and press **Enter** to create the PFS: First Publisher directory on your hard disk.
2. Type **CD FIRSTPUB** and press **Enter** to change into the \FIRSTPUB subdirectory you just created.
3. Insert the first PFS: First Publisher disk into drive A, type **COPY A:*.***, and press **Enter**.
4. Repeat step 3 until you have copies of all the PFS: First Publisher disks on your hard disk.

UNDERSTANDING THE PFS: FIRST PUBLISHER SCREENS

Before beginning, you should know how to interpret the PFS: First Publisher screen displays. When you first start the program, PFS: First Publisher displays a blank document containing three parts: the menu bar, the tool bar, and the page scroll bar.

The menu bar displays seven different menus for choosing an option. You can choose a menu by pressing the appropriate function key, such as F1 for the File menu. If you have a mouse, you can click on the menu name. To remove a menu, press Esc.

Many menu options display alternate keystroke combinations. For example, to quit PFS: First Publisher, you can choose Exit from the File menu or press Alt-E. The pull-down menus also show the options you can use in boldface. Any options that you cannot use appear dimmed.

The tool bar contains the PFS: First Publisher tools for selecting blocks, creating text and graphics blocks, and drawing rectangles, circles, and lines.

The page scroll bars appear to the right of the window. These page scroll bars let you slide a document left and right or up and down. To slide a document in the window, you can click on the arrow at each end of the page scroll bars, or you can slide the box within the page scroll bar.

Module 3
A SAMPLE SESSION WITH PFS: FIRST PUBLISHER

INTRODUCTION

PFS: First Publisher can create pages by combining text and graphics on a page. To enhance the appearance of your pages, First Publisher lets you draw lines, circles, and boxes to divide a page into columns or to frame text and pictures.

SAMPLE SESSION (Version 2.0)

In this sample session you learn to modify text, import a graphic image, and wrap text around the graphic image. Use this procedure for version 2.0 of First Publisher only.

1. Type **FP** and press **Enter** to load First Publisher.
2. Press **F1** to display the File menu.

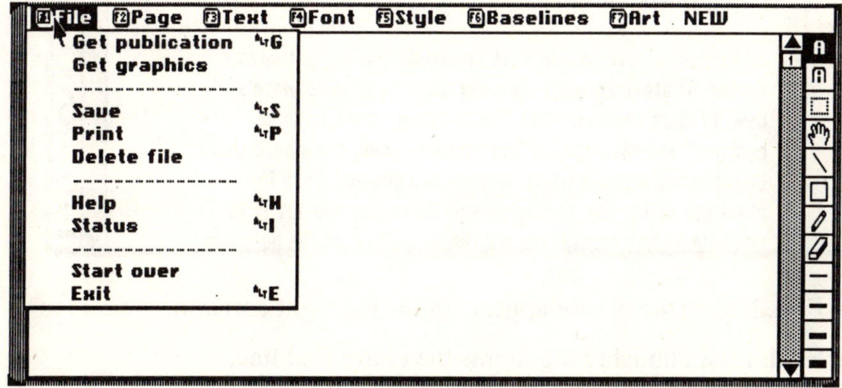

3. Select Get Publication by pressing **Down Arrow**. Press **Enter**. A dialogue box appears.

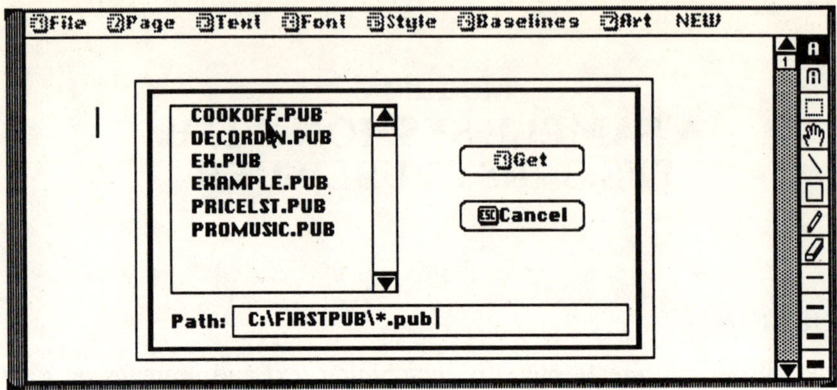

4. Press **Down Arrow** to scroll through the file list until the arrow points to the EXAMPLE.PUB file.
5. Press **F10** to highlight the file.
6. Press **F1** to open the file. First Publisher displays the file on screen.

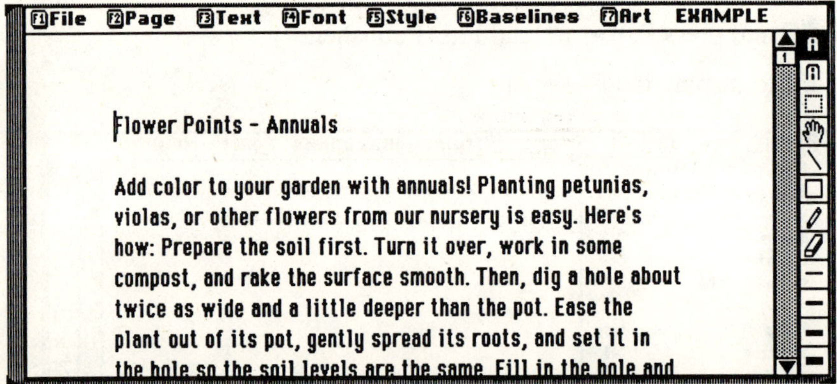

7. Press **F10**. Notice the mouse appears in the top right corner of the screen.
8. Press **End**. First Publisher highlights the entire first line.

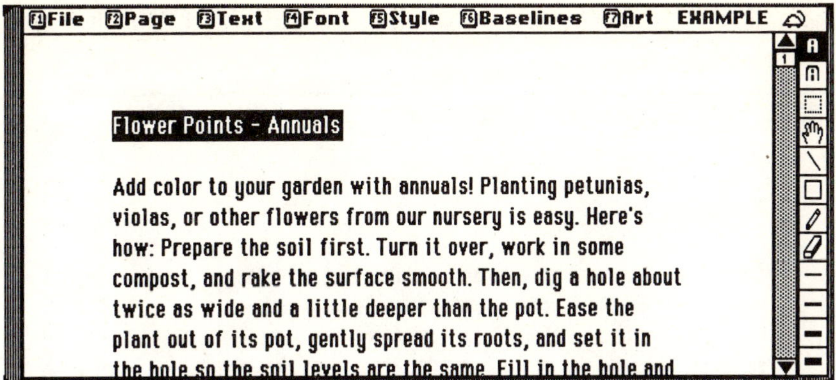

9. Press **F5** to choose the Style menu. First Publisher displays an error message.

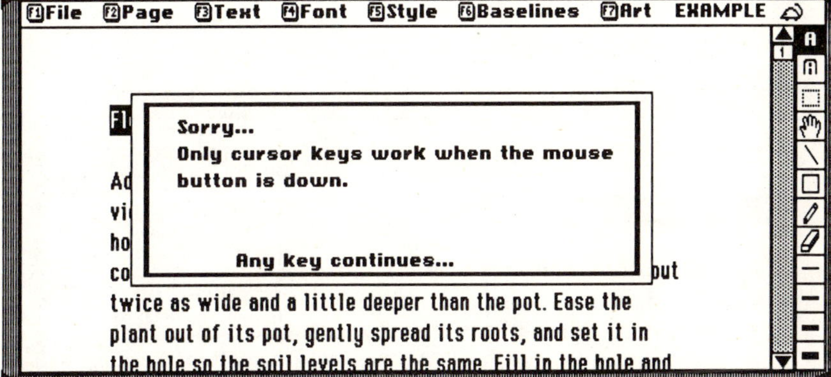

10. Press **Spacebar**.
11. Press **F10** to remove the mouse from the top right corner of the screen.
12. Press **F5** to choose the Style menu.

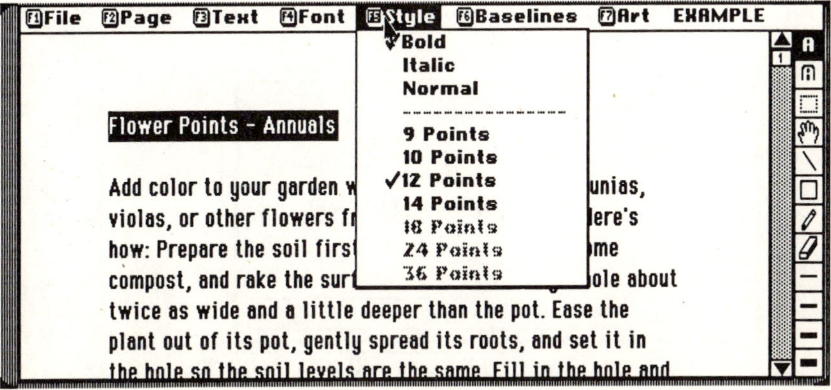

13. Choose Italic by pressing **Down Arrow**. Press **Enter**. First Publisher changes the highlighted text to italics.

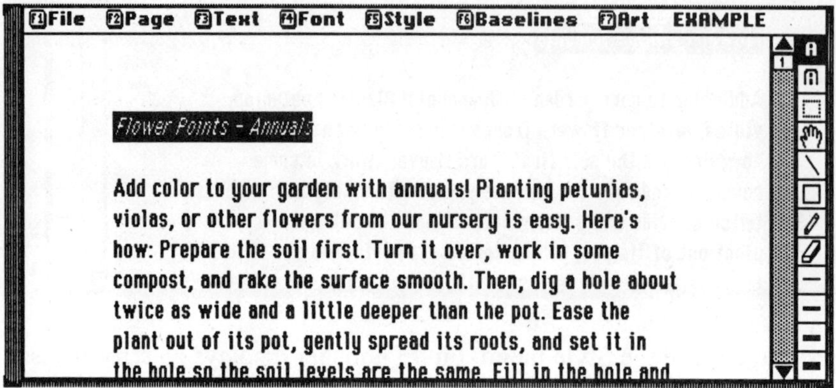

14. Press **F7** to choose the Art menu.

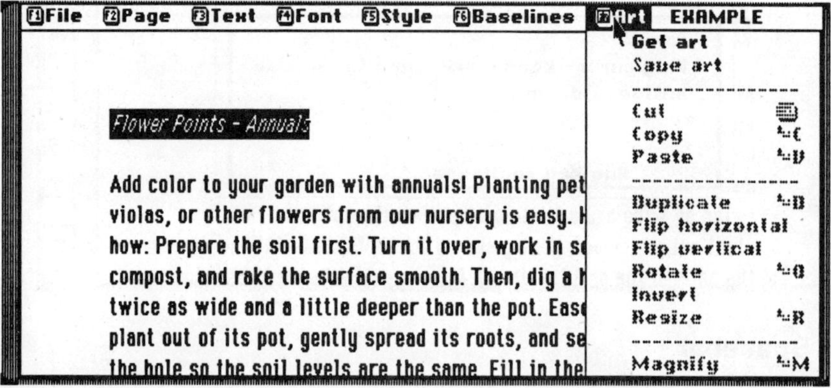

15. Choose Get Art by pressing **Down Arrow**. Press **Enter**. A dialogue box appears.

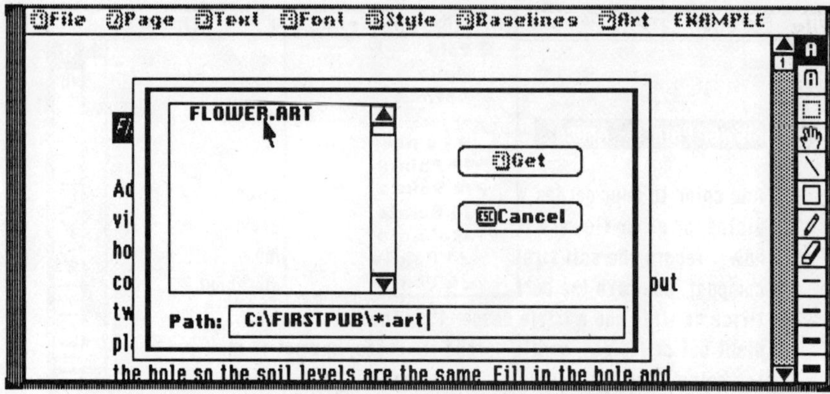

16. Press **F10**. Press **F1**. First Publisher dims the text and displays the hand tool on screen.

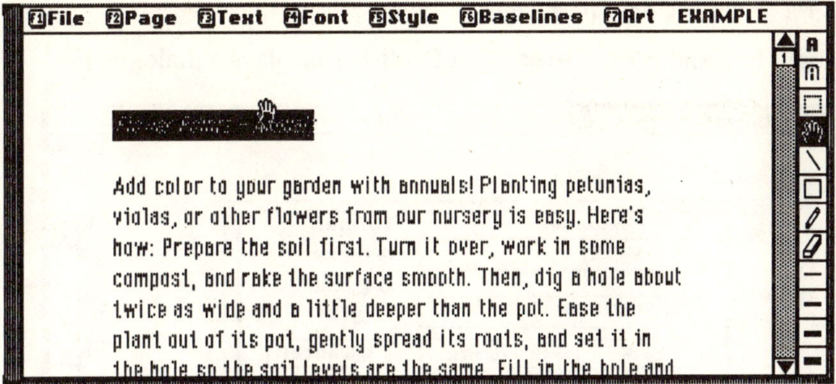

17. Move the hand tool over the word "little" using the arrow keys.
18. Press **F10**. First Publisher displays a flower on the page.

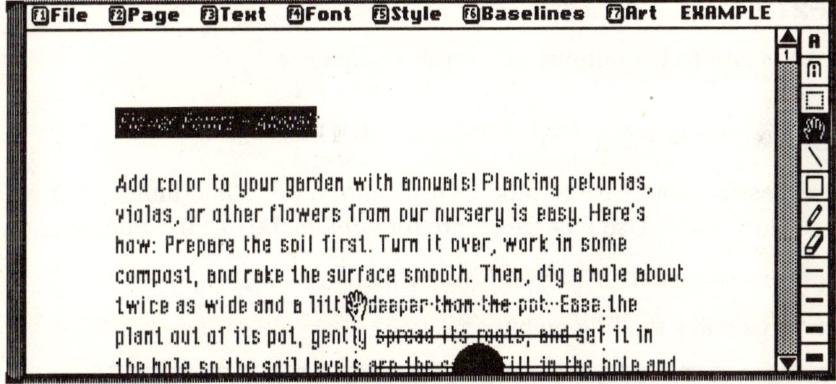

19. Press **F2** to choose the Page menu.

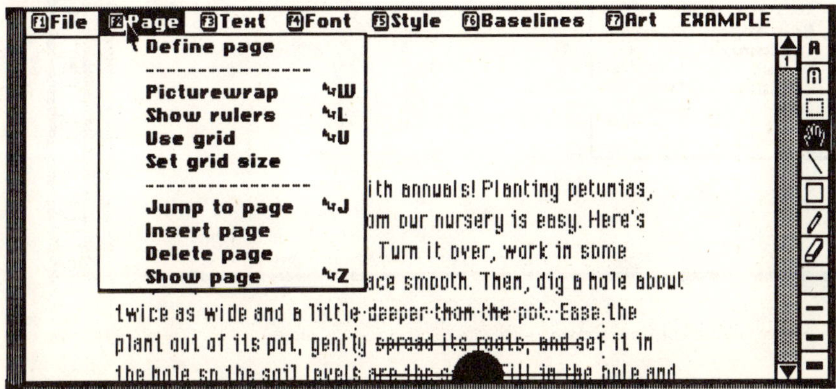

20. Choose Picturewrap by pressing **Down Arrow**. Press **Enter**. First Publisher wraps text around the flower graph.
21. Press **F1** to choose the File menu.
22. Highlight Exit and press **Enter**. First Publisher displays a dialogue box.

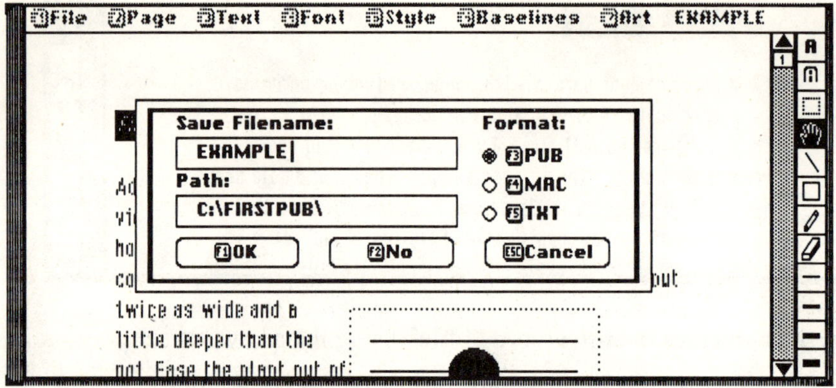

23. Press **F2** (No) to exit without saving.
24. Turn to Module 14 to continue the learning sequence.

SAMPLE SESSION (Version 3.0)

In this sample session you learn to modify text, import a graphic image, and wrap text around the graphic image. Use this procedure for version 3.0 of First Publisher only.

1. Type **FP** and press **Enter** to load First Publisher.
2. Press **F1** to display the File menu.

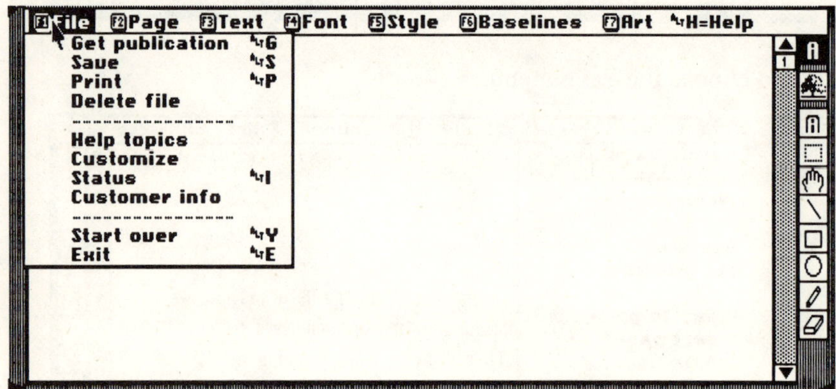

3. Select Get Publication by pressing **Down Arrow**. Press **Enter**. A dialogue box appears.

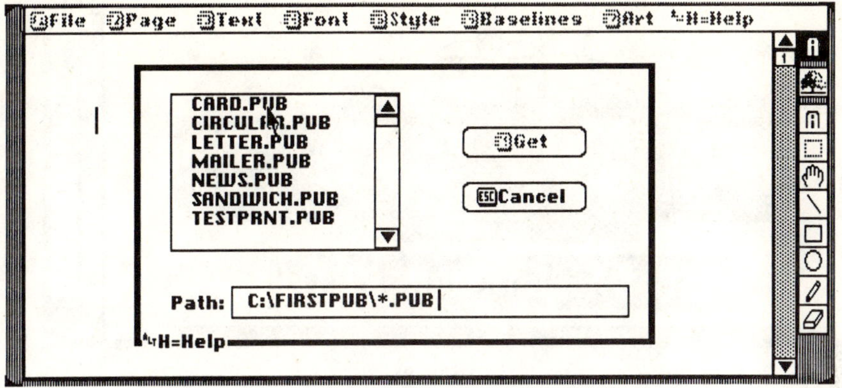

4. Press **Down Arrow** to scroll through the file list until the arrow points to the SANDWICH.PUB file.
5. Press **F10** to highlight the file.
6. Press **F1** to open the file. First Publisher displays several dialogue boxes saying it cannot find specific fonts. Press **F1** at each dialogue box. First Publisher displays the file on screen.

7. Press **F10**. Notice the mouse appears in the top right corner of the screen.

8. Press **End**. First Publisher highlights the entire first line.

9. Press **F5** to choose the Style menu. Notice that this version of First publisher does not display the error message displayed by previous versions.

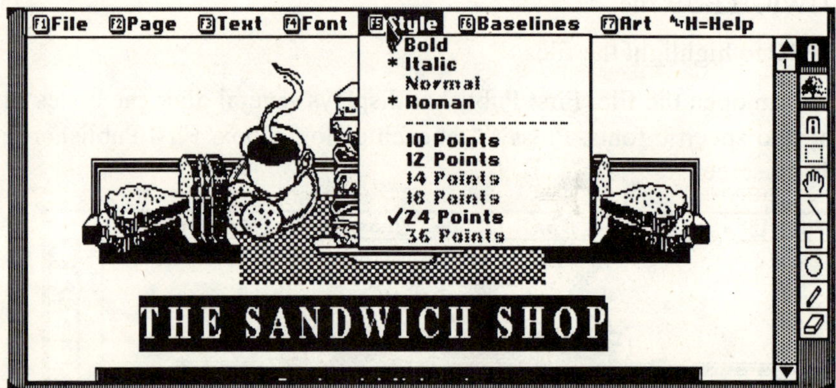

10. Choose Italic by pressing **Down Arrow**. Press **Enter**. First Publisher changes the highlighted text to italics. Notice that First Publisher also resized the font. When an asterisk appears next to the style selection, it means that the style is available in a different size only.

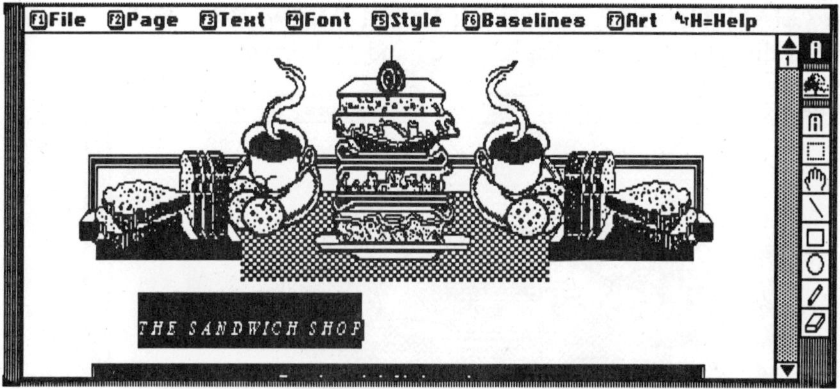

11. Press **F5** to choose the Style menu. Choose Bold by pressing **Down Arrow**. Press **Enter**. Press **F5**. Choose 24 Points by pressing **Down Arrow**. Press **Enter**. First Publisher returns the font to its original appearance.
12. Press **F7** to choose the Art menu.

13. Choose Get Art by pressing **Down Arrow**. Press **Enter**. A dialogue box appears.

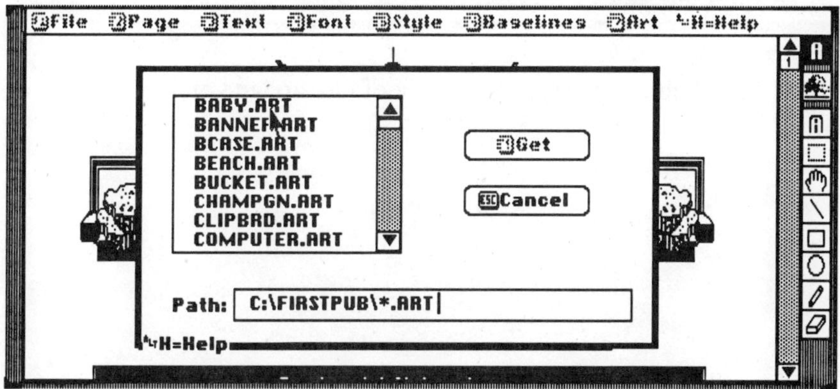

14. Select CHAMPGN.ART by pressing **Down Arrow**. Press **F10**. Press **F1**. First Publisher dims the text and displays the hand tool on screen.

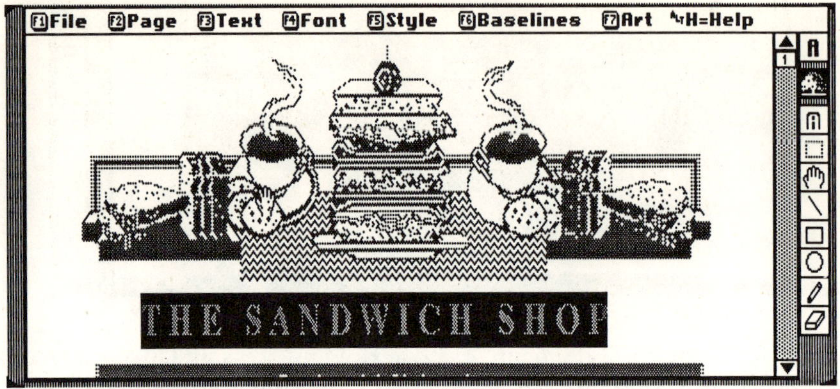

15. Press **PgDn** to display the lower half of the page. Move the hand tool between the two graphics of a fork and knife using the arrow keys.

16. Press **F10**. First Publisher displays a dotted-line box showing the size and exact position of the graphic. Use the arrow keys to position the graphic as shown in the following screen shot.

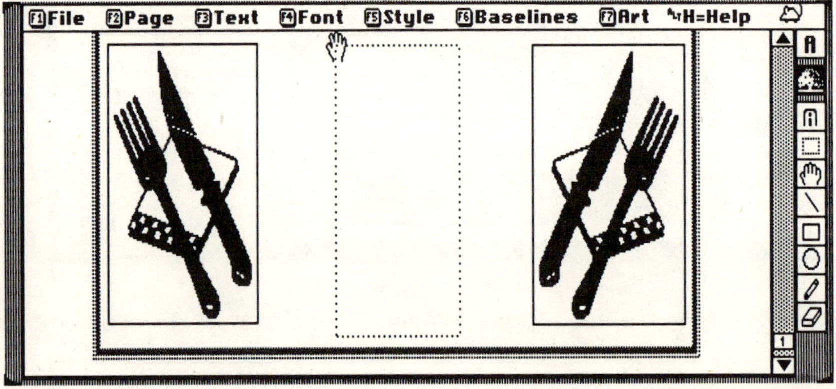

17. Press **F10**. First Publisher displays a bottle of champagne on the page.

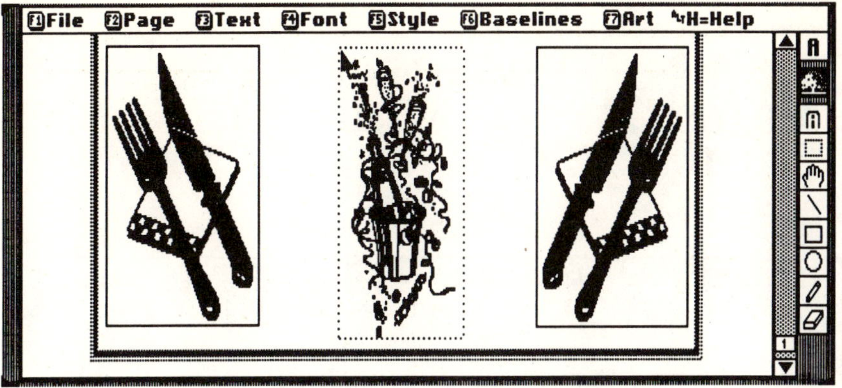

18. Press **F1** to choose the File menu.
19. Highlight Exit and press **Enter**. First Publisher displays a dialogue box.

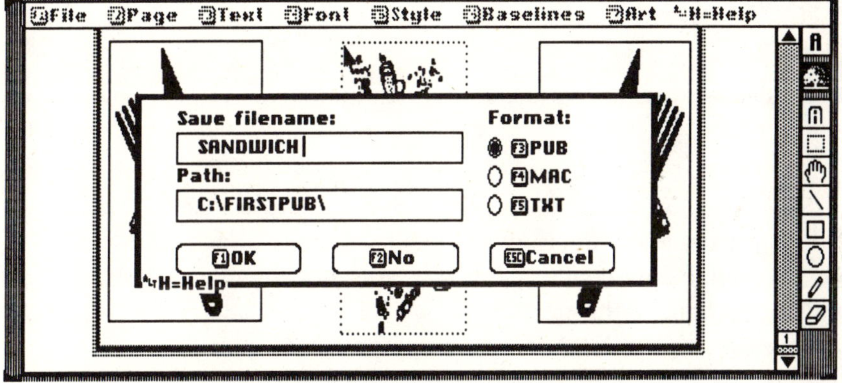

20. Press **F2** (No) to exit without saving.
21. Turn to Module 14 to continue the learning sequence.

Module 4
ADJUST SINGLE, ADJUST COLUMN, ADJUST ABOVE, ADJUST BELOW

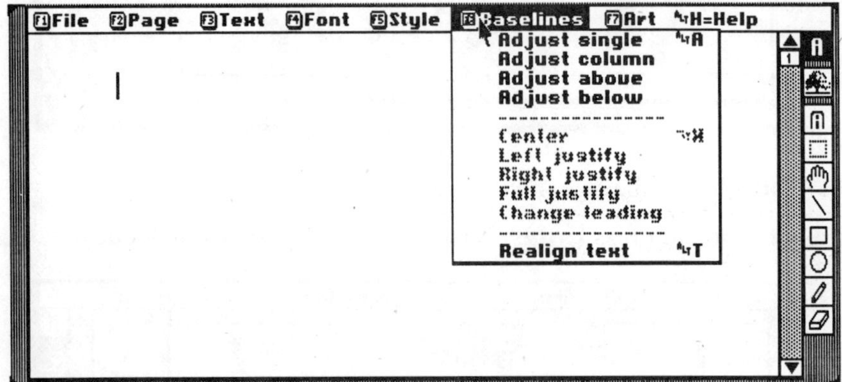

DESCRIPTION

The Adjust Single, Adjust Column, Adjust Above, and Adjust Below commands on the Baselines menu greatly affect the format of your document. Each command changes the vertical and horizontal alignment of the text in your document to a varying degree. You can access all the commands throughout the Baselines menu. The Adjust Single command also allows access using the Alt-A key combination.

All four commands use the same method to change text alignment. When you select a line to change, First Publisher places three adjustment blocks on the line. By selecting the right block you can adjust the right margin. By selecting the left block you can change the left margin. Selecting the middle block allows vertical movement of the line.

The Adjust Single command changes the alignment of the selected line only. First Publisher does not allow you to move the line past boundaries set by the software (0.5 inches on each margin) or above/below any other lines.

The Adjust Column command changes the alignment of an entire column. When you adjust any element of the selected line, all other lines change as well. This command does not affect the spacing between lines (leading).

The Adjust Above command changes the alignment of the lines above the selected line only. The lines below the selected line remain the same. This command changes the leading as well as all other factors for the affected lines. As the leading between the selected line and the line directly below it changes, the leading changes by the same amount for the other lines as well.

The Adjust Below command changes the alignment of the lines below the selected line only. The lines above the selected line remain the same. This command changes the leading between all the affected lines in the same manner as the Adjust Above command.

APPLICATIONS

Use the Adjust Single command to adjust titles and other single line text entries. Also use it to adjust columns of text around graphic images when the square outline produced by the Picturewrap command is unacceptable.

Use the Adjust Column command to change the physical positioning of columns of text. For example, you can change the distance between a column of text and a title.

Use the Adjust Above and Adjust Below commands to change the leading between columns of text uniformly. These commands provide a means of exactly filling a page with text, so the top and bottom margins remain even and the margins remain the same on each page of a multipage document. The Adjust Below or Adjust Above commands also repair gutter margins left ragged by adjustments to a page with graphics.

TYPICAL OPERATION

In this example you learn how to use the Adjust Column, Adjust Single, Adjust Below, and Adjust Above commands. You also learn how to repair a gutter margin damaged due to column adjustments around a graphic image. This example begins at the First Publisher Main menu with EXAMPLE.PUB loaded.

1. Press **Alt-U**, **Alt-W**, then **Alt-L**. The rulers appear.
2. Press **F6**. The Baselines menu appears.
3. Select the Adjust Column command using the **Down Arrow**. Press **Enter**. First Publisher changes the text color to gray and displays lines under each line of text. The graphics cursor and grid appear.

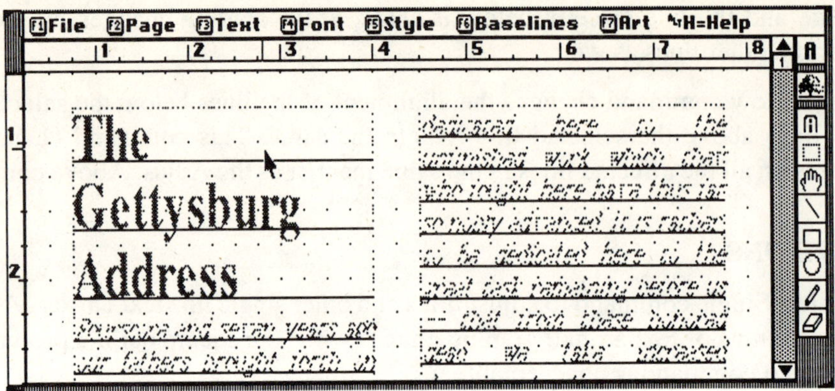

4. Point to the middle of the first line of right column text with the graphics cursor using the arrow keys. Press **F10**. The cursor flashes.
5. Press the arrow keys to align the cursor with the vertical position block. The cursor stops blinking when aligned.

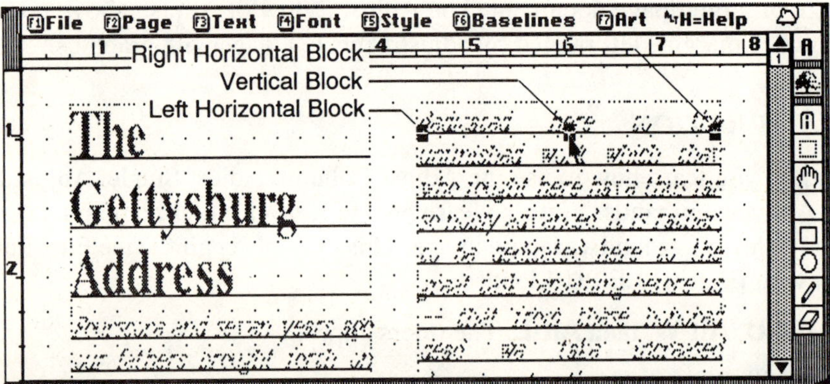

6. Align the right column of text with the left column using the **Down Arrow**. The line directly across from the left column start position disappears.

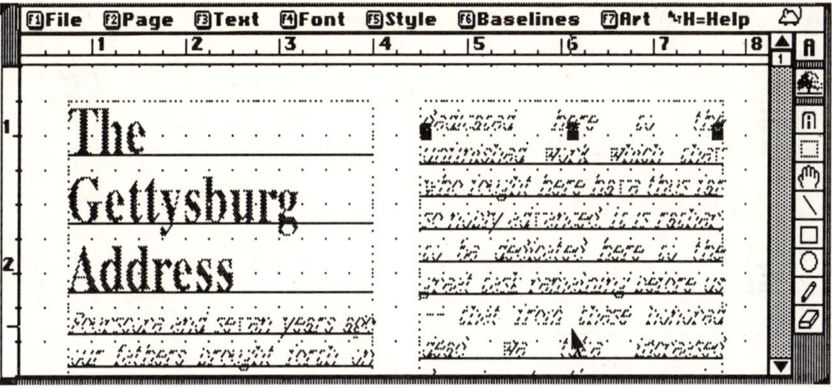

7. Press **F10**. First Publisher realigns the text.
8. Press **F6**. Select the Adjust Single command using the **Down Arrow**. Press **Enter**. First Publisher clears the previous line selection.

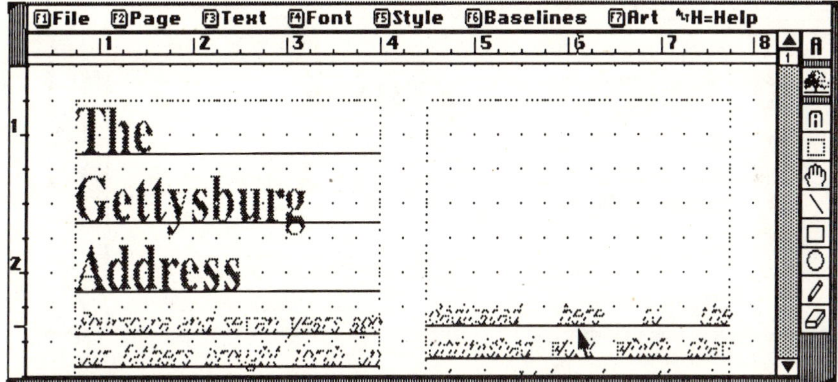

9. Position the graphics cursor on the right side of the first title line using the arrow keys. Press **F10**. First Publisher selects the line. The cursor flashes.
10. Press the arrow keys to align the cursor with the right horizontal position block. The cursor stops blinking when aligned.
11. Align the right horizontal position block with the right margin using the **Right Arrow**. First Publisher extends the line as the cursor moves.

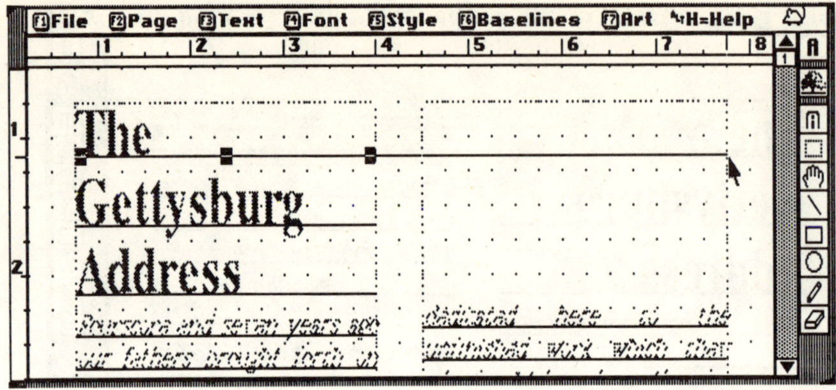

12. Press **F10** then **Alt-A**. First Publisher extends the line. The text appears the normal color, the grid disappears, and the right column is below the left column.

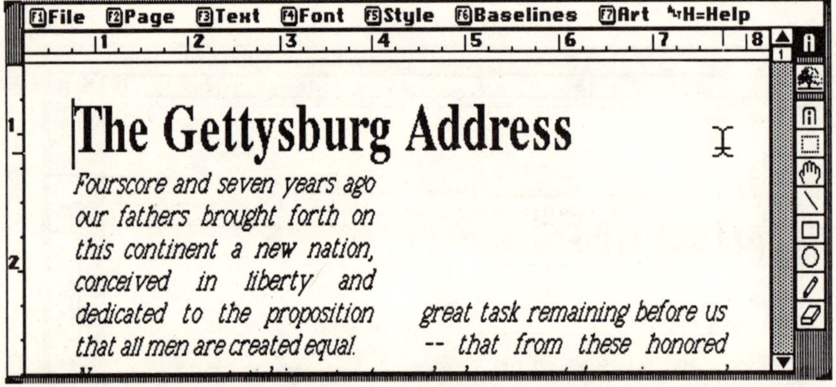

13. Press **F6**. Select the Adjust Column command using the **Down Arrow**. Press **Enter**. First Publisher changes the text color to gray and displays lines under each line of text. The graphics cursor and grid appear.
14. Position the graphics cursor in the middle of the first line of the right column. Press **F10**. First Publisher selects the line. The cursor flashes.
15. Press the arrow keys to align the cursor with the right horizontal position block. The cursor stops blinking when aligned.

16. Align the right and left columns using the arrow keys. Press **F10**. First Publisher aligns the left and right columns.

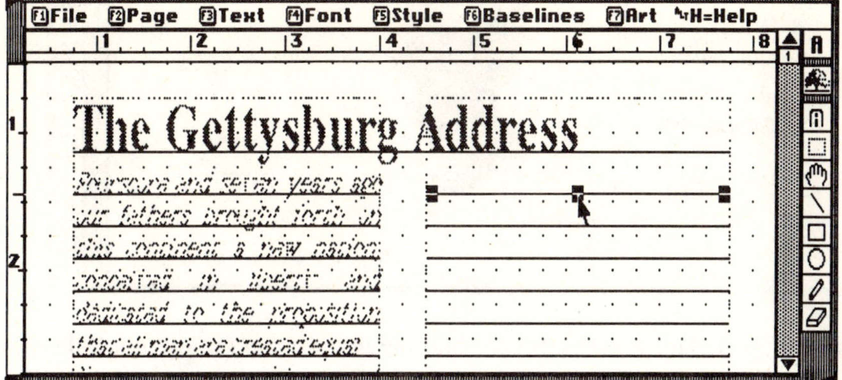

17. Press **F6**. Select the Adjust Column command using the **Down Arrow**. Press **Enter**. The graphics cursor and grid disappear. The text appears in the normal color.

18. Press **Alt-Z**. First Publisher displays a reduced view of the page. Notice the gutter margin distortion. This occurred during the movement of the right and left columns.

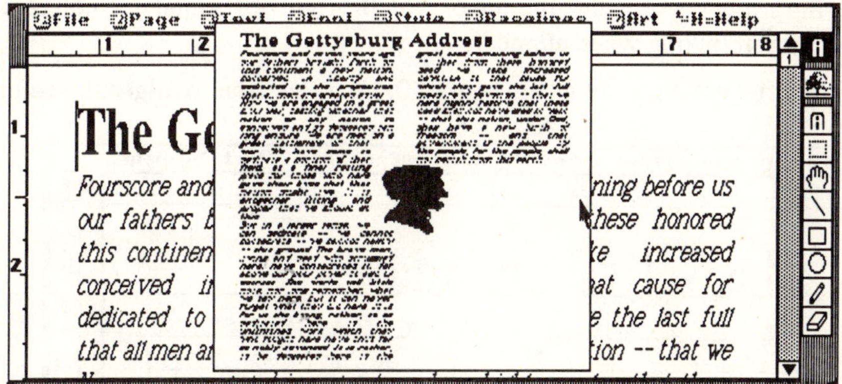

19. Press **Enter**. Press **PgDn** twice and the **Down Arrow** four times to reveal the graphic image. Press **F9** until the Selection Tool is highlighted. First Publisher displays the grid and turns the text gray.

20. Position the cursor to the top left corner of the silhouette of Lincoln. Press **F10**. Outline the silhouette of Lincoln. Press **F10**. First Publisher selects the graphic image.

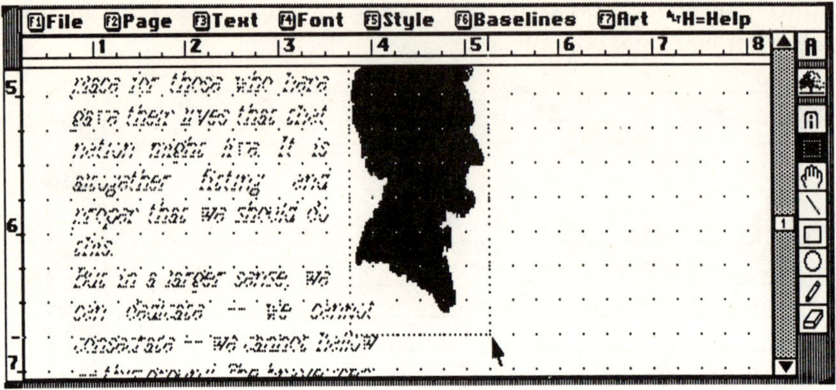

21. Press **Shift-F9**. The grid disappears and the text appears in the normal color.
22. Press **Ctrl-Home** then **F6**. The Baselines menu appears.
23. Select the Adjust Below command using the **Down Arrow**. Press **Enter**. The graphics cursor and grid appear.
24. Position the graphics cursor on the right side of the first line of the left column using the arrow keys. Press **F10**. First Publisher selects the line. The cursor flashes.
25. Press the arrow keys to align the cursor with the right horizontal position block. The cursor stops blinking when aligned.
26. Press **Shift-Left Arrow** twice. Press **F10**. First Publisher realigns the column.

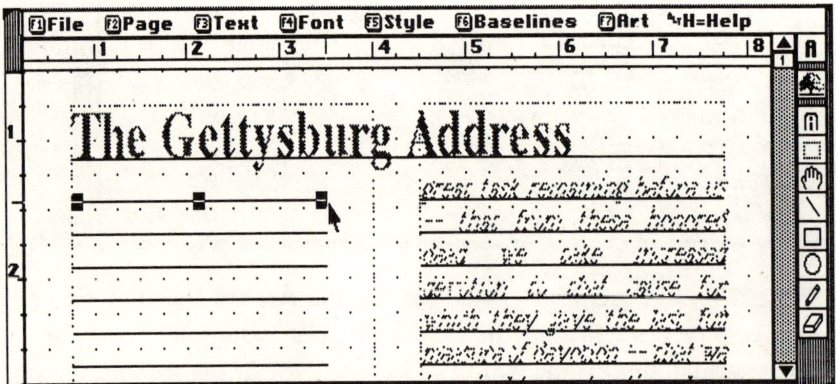

27. Press **F10** then **Shift-Right Arrow** twice. Press **F10**. First Publisher realigns the column.
28. Position the graphics cursor on the left side of the first line of the right column using the arrow keys. Press **F10**. First Publisher selects the line. The cursor flashes.

29. Press the arrow keys to align the cursor with the left horizontal position block. The cursor stops blinking when aligned.
30. Press **Shift-Right Arrow** twice. Press **F10**. First Publisher realigns the column.
31. Press **F10** then **Shift-Left Arrow** twice. Press **F10**. First Publisher realigns the column.
32. Press **F6**. The Baselines menu appears.
33. Select Adjust Below using the **Down Arrow**. Press **Enter**. Press **Alt-Z**. First Publisher displays a reduced view of the page. Notice the gutter and graphic margins appear normal.

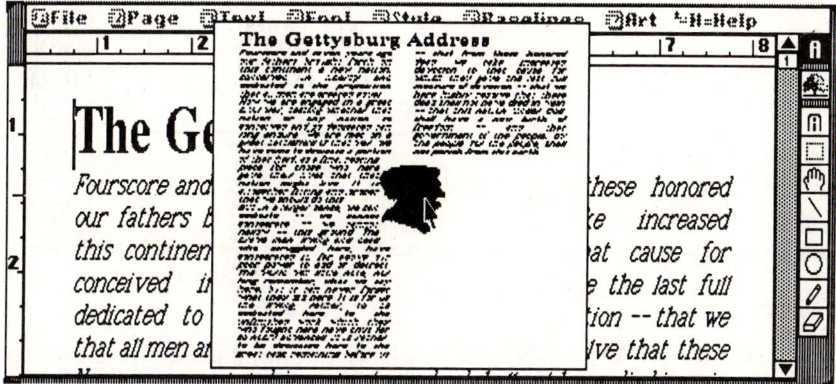

34. Press **Esc** to erase the reduced view. Press **Alt-E** then **F1**. First Publisher asks if you want to overwrite the old copy of EXAMPLE.PUB.
35. Press **F1**. First Publisher displays a saving file message.
36. Turn to Module 5 to continue the learning sequence.

Module 5
CENTER, LEFT JUSTIFY, RIGHT JUSTIFY, FULL JUSTIFY

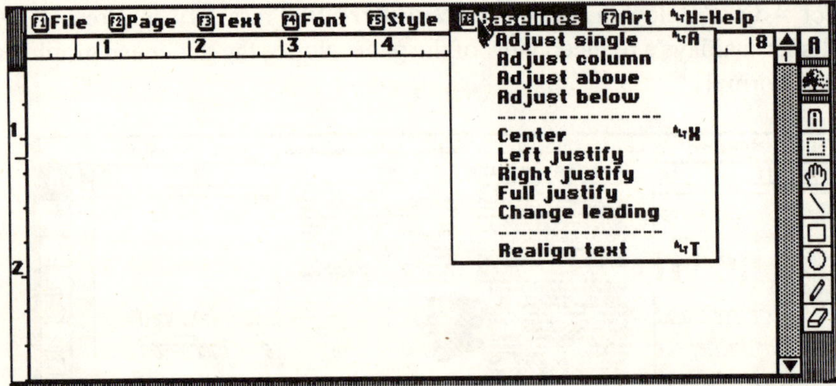

DESCRIPTION

The Center, Left Justify, Right Justify, and Full Justify commands on the Baselines menu allow you to change the position of each line of text on a page. You can access all the commands using the Baselines menu; the Center command also uses the Alt-X key combination.

The Center command tells First Publisher to align the text with the center of the line. Both the right and left margins are ragged (uneven).

The Left Justify command tells First Publisher to align the text with the left margin of a page/column. The right margin is ragged.

The Right Justify command tells First Publisher to align the text with the right margin of a page/column. The left margin is ragged.

The Full Justify command tells First Publisher to align the text with both the right and left margin of a page/column. To do this, First Publisher inserts spaces between each word on the line.

APPLICATIONS

Use the Center, Left Justify, Right Justify, and Full Justify commands to align text in your document. You normally use centered text for document, table, and figure titles. For text using monospaced fonts or the left side of a table, use left justification. This prevents uneven spacing between words in text using a monospaced font. This also allows the entries in a table to align easier. Use right justification for the right side of a table. This is especially useful for a table of contents, where the page numbers should line up on the right side of the page. Finally, use full justification for text using proportionally spaced fonts. This usually enhances the appearance of the page and makes the document easier to read.

TYPICAL OPERATION

In this example, you use the Center, Left Justify, Right Justify, and Full Justify commands to change the appearance of a document. You begin this example at the First Publisher Main menu with EXAMPLE.PUB loaded.

1. Press **Alt-U**, **Alt-L**, then **Alt-W**. First Publisher displays the rulers.
2. Press **Alt-A**. First Publisher displays the grid and baseline adjustment lines.
3. Press **Shift-Down Arrow** then **F10**. If the cursor flashes, use the arrow keys to align the cursor with the left horizontal position block of the title. Press **F10**. First Publisher selects the title line.

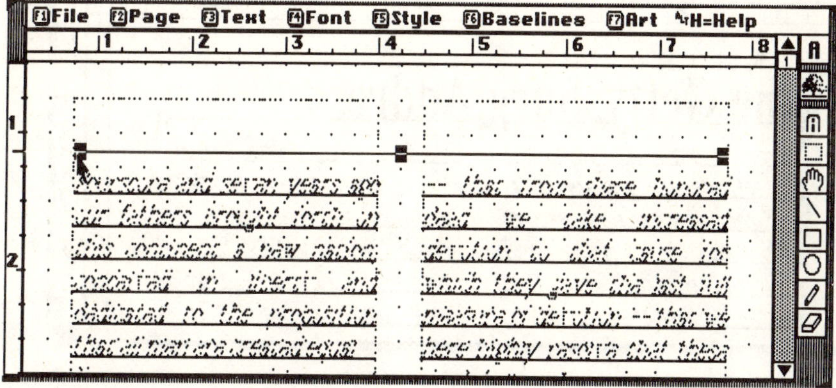

4. Press **F6**. The Baselines menu appears.

5. Select the Center command using the **Down Arrow**. Press **Enter**. First Publisher centers the title text.

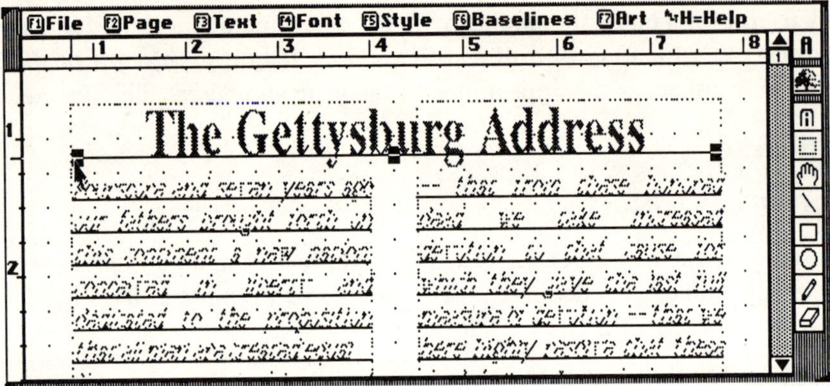

6. Press **F6**. The Baselines menu appears.
7. Select the Left Justify command using the **Down Arrow**. Press **Enter**. First Publisher left-justifies the title text.

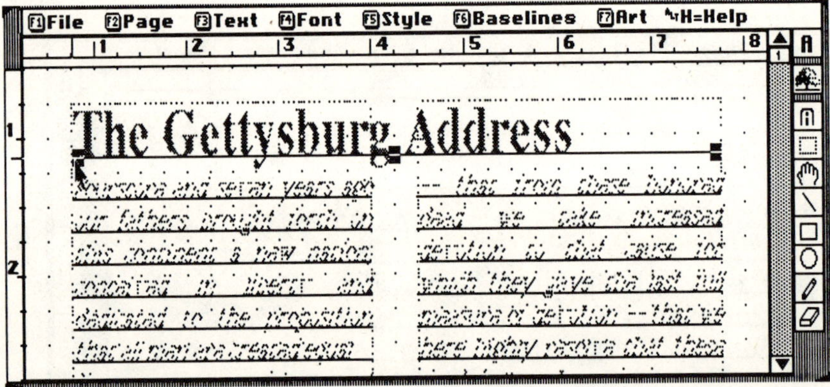

8. Press **F6**. The Baselines menu appears.
9. Select the Right Justify command using the **Down Arrow**. Press **Enter**. First Publisher right-justifies the title text.

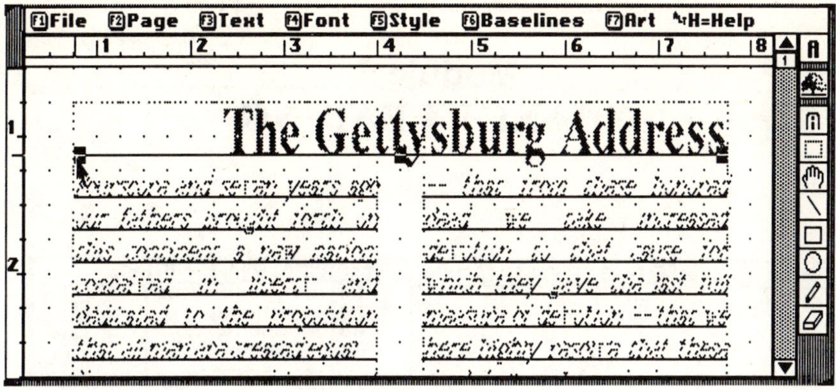

10. Press **F6**. The Baselines menu appears.
11. Select the Full Justify command using the **Down Arrow**. Press **Enter**. First Publisher full-justifies the title text.

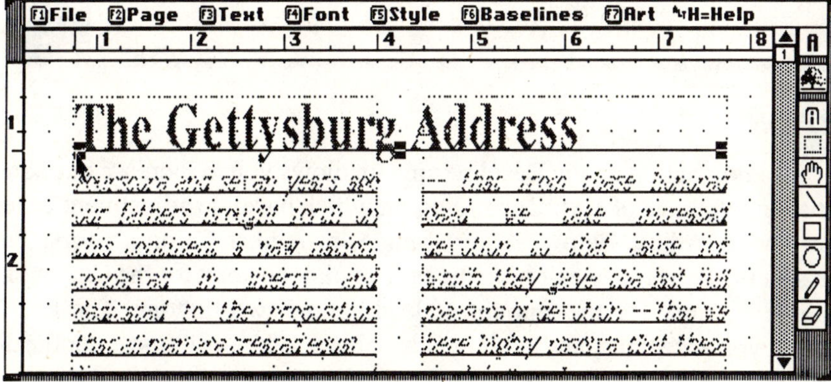

12. Press **Alt-X**. First Publisher centers the title.
13. Press **Alt-E** then **F1**. First Publisher asks if you want to overwrite the old copy of EXAMPLE.PUB.
14. Press **F1**. First Publisher displays a saving file message.
15. Turn to Module 6 to continue the learning sequence.

Module 6
CHANGE LEADING

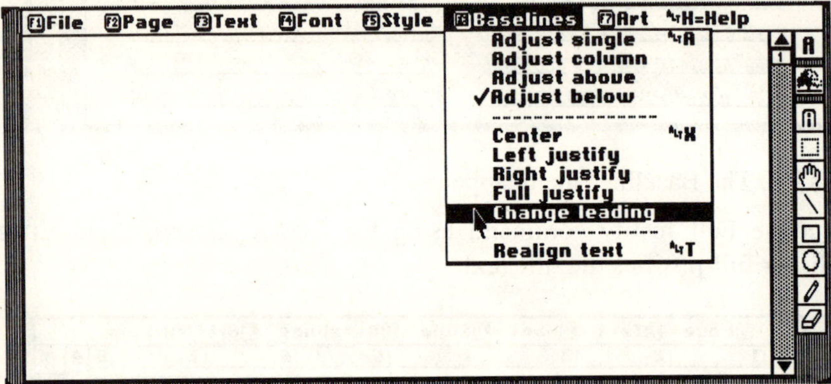

DESCRIPTION

The Change Leading option on the Baselines menu allows you to increase or decrease the spacing between two lines of text. Depending on which baseline adjustment criteria you use (Adjust Above, Adjust Below, Adjust Single, or Adjust Column), First Publisher changes the spacing between one or more lines. The dialogue box for the Change Leading option contains an entry for the amount of leading and two buttons. The two buttons control whether you accept the new leading value or not. When you first enter the dialogue box, the leading entry contains the current amount of leading for the selected line in points. You use this reading for any calculations required to compute the new amount of leading to use.

APPLICATIONS

Use the Change Leading option whenever you need to change the leading between two or more lines, but not all the lines on a page. If you need to change the leading between all the lines, use the Define Page option of the Page menu. Examples of times when this is necessary include filling out a page with text (instead of having a gap at the bottom of the page). The Change Leading option also provides a convenient means of changing the distance between columns of text and a title.

TYPICAL OPERATION

In this example you learn how to use the leading command. This example also shows how to calculate the leading required to fill an entire page with text when the default leading leaves it partially blank. You begin this example at the First Publisher Main menu with EXAMPLE.PUB loaded.

NOTE

To perform this example, you need a current printout of the sample document. Use the procedure in Module 27 to create a printout if you don't have one.

1. Press **Alt-W** then **F6**. The Baselines menu appears.
2. Select the Adjust Below command using the **Down Arrow**. Press **Enter**. The baseline adjustment lines and graphics cursor appear.
3. Press **Shift-Down Arrow** then **F10**. If the cursor blinks, use the arrow keys to select the vertical position block on the first line of text in the left column. Press **F10**. First Publisher selects the first text line.

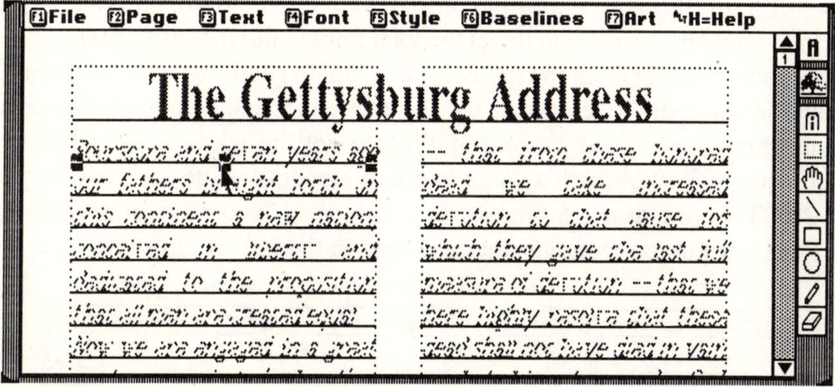

4. Press **F6**. The Baselines menu appears.
5. Select the Change Leading option using the **Down Arrow**. Press **Enter**. The Change Leading dialogue box appears.

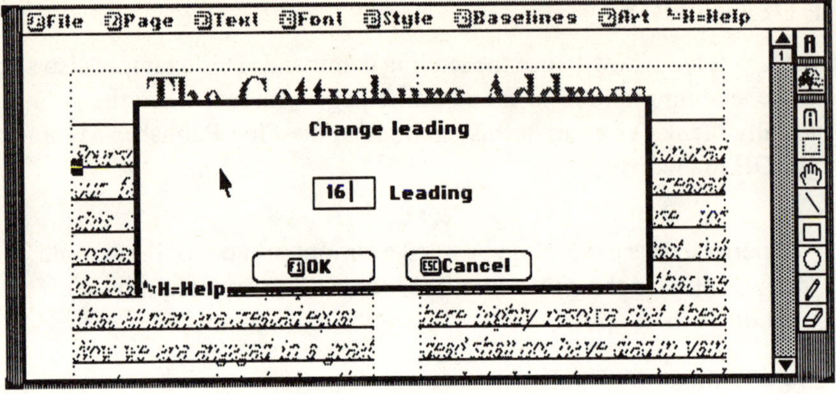

NOTE

The mathematic procedure below provides an estimate of how much to change the leading to fill a page with text. The document may still require minor adjustment.

6. Count the number of lines of text in the left column (should equal 37). Count the number of lines of text in the right column (should equal 16). Add the left column count to the right column count to get the total lines count (should equal 53). Subtract the right column count from the left column count to get the extra lines (should equal 21). Divide the extra lines count by the total lines count (should equal 0.396). Multiply this value by the current leading to get the additional leading required (should equal 6.339). Add this value to the old leading value and round up (should equal 23). Type the new leading value, **23**, in the Change Leading dialogue box. Press **F1**. First Publisher moves the text lines in the left column down.

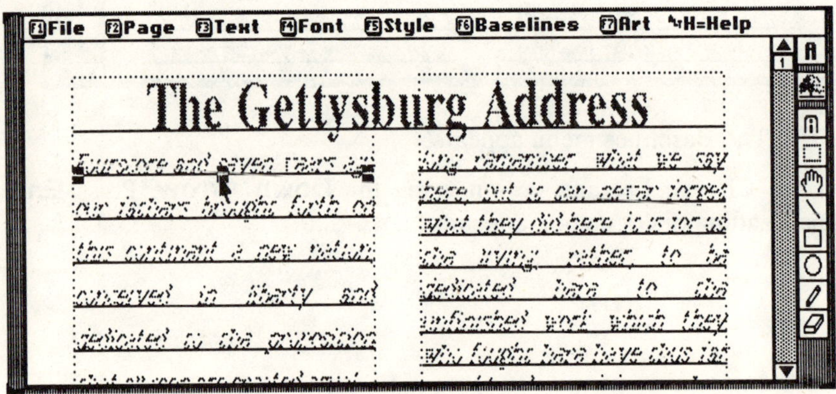

7. Select the second line of the right text column using the arrow keys. Press **F10**. If the graphics cursor blinks, use the arrow keys to align the cursor with the vertical position block. Press **F10**. First Publisher selects the second line of the right column.

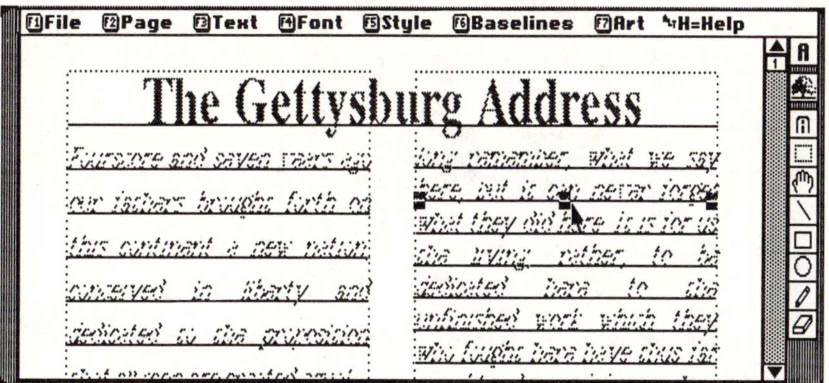

8. Press **F6**. The Baselines menu appears.
9. Select the Change Leading option using the **Down Arrow**. Press **Enter**. The Change Leading dialogue box appears.
10. Type **23** and press **F1**. First Publisher changes the leading between the lines of text in the right column.

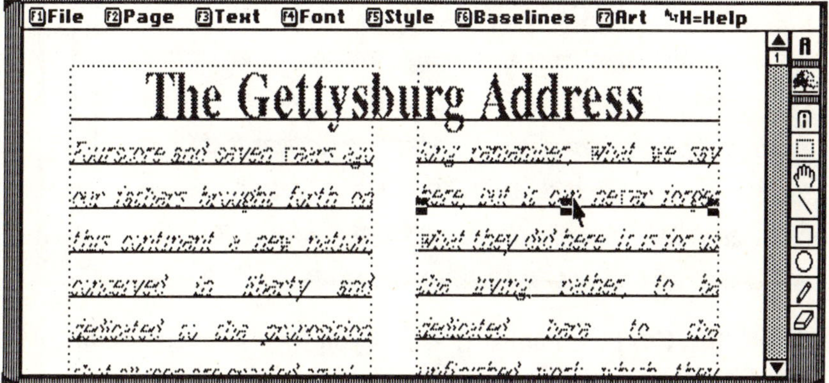

11. Press **Alt-Z**. First Publisher shows a reduced view of the page. Notice both columns of text end near the bottom of the page.

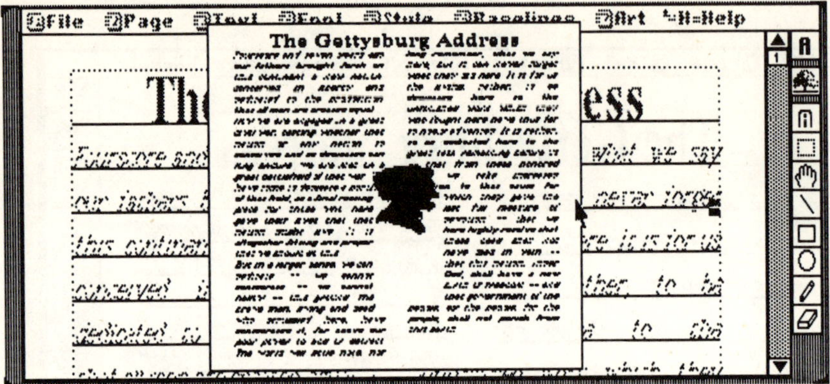

12. Press **Esc**. Press **F6**. The Baselines menu appears.
13. Select the Adjust Below command using the **Down Arrow**. Press **Enter**. First Publisher displays the text normally. The baseline adjustment lines and graphics cursor disappear.

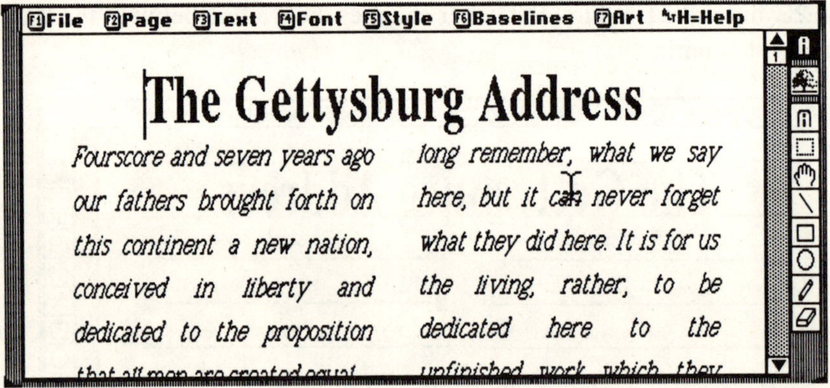

14. Press **Alt-E** then **F1**. First Publisher asks if you want to overwrite the old copy of EXAMPLE.PUB.
15. Press **F1**. First Publisher displays a saving file message.
16. Turn to Module 28 to continue the learning sequence.

Module 7
CUT, COPY, PASTE (ART)

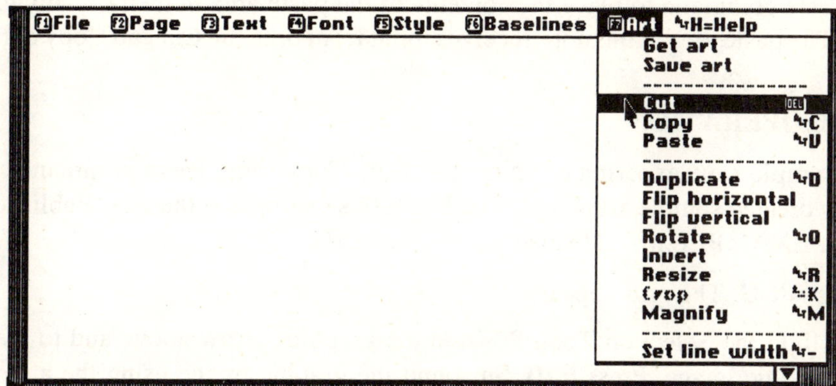

DESCRIPTION

The Cut, Copy, and Paste commands on the Art menu do the same thing for graphic images as the corresponding commands for text. The difference between the two is that the Art menu commands work on graphic images and the Text menu commands work on ASCII text. Because of their different environments, the Art menu commands use the Selection Tool to identify the graphic images to operate on. Beside using the Art menu, you can access the Cut command using the Del key, the Copy command by pressing Alt-C, and the Paste command by pressing Alt-V.

The Cut command removes the graphic image area surrounded by the dashed line produced by the Selection Tool. First Publisher moves the graphic from the display area to the paste area in memory. If another graphic gets cut before the Paste command restores the image, First Publisher discards it.

The Copy command creates a duplicate of the selected graphic image area and places it in memory. By using this command, you can make copies of a graphic without removing the original image.

The Paste command places the contents of the paste area in memory in the display area pointed to by the graphics cursor. First Publisher indicates the position of the graphic using the Hand Tool. To see the graphic, put the mouse button down by pressing F10. You may then move the graphic anywhere on the page.

APPLICATIONS

Use the Cut command to remove large areas of unwanted graphic images quickly. In most cases using the Cut command requires less time than the Eraser Tool for large areas. If you removed too much, then you can restore the graphic by using the Paste command.

Use the Copy command to quickly duplicate a graphic image. First Publisher places the selected image in memory for use by the Paste command.

Use the Paste command to place the contents of the paste area in memory anywhere on the page. The paste area in memory receives input from both the Cut and Copy command.

TYPICAL OPERATION

In this example you experiment using the Cut, Copy, and Paste commands on the previously created sample art image. You begin this example at the First Publisher Main menu with EXAMPLE.MAC loaded.

1. Press **Alt-U**. The grid appears.
2. Highlight the Selection Tool. Position the graphics arrow above and to the left of the graphic image. Press **F10**. Surround the graphic image using the arrow keys. Press **F10**. First Publisher selects the graphic image.

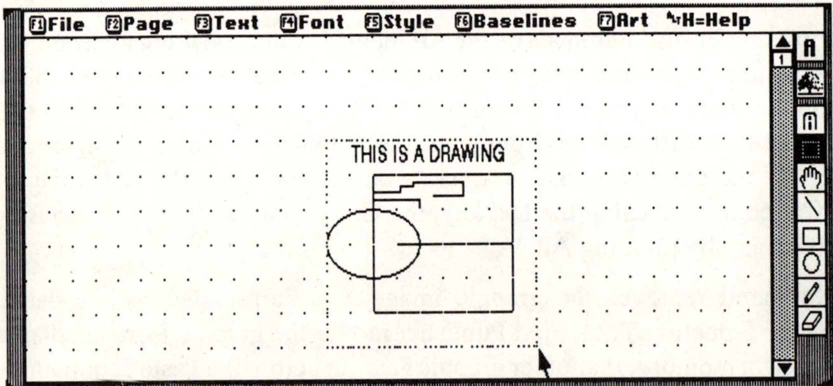

3. Press **Del**. First Publisher removes the graphic image.

4. Press **Alt-V**. The Hand Tool appears.
5. Press **F10**. Press the **Up Arrow** six times, the **Left Arrow** 20 times. Press **F10**. First Publisher restores the graphic image and places it in the desired location.

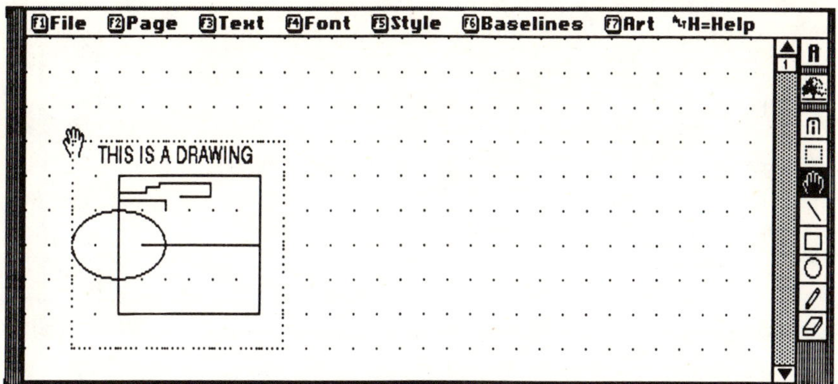

6. Press **Alt-C**. First Publisher creates a copy of the graphic image in memory.
7. Press **Alt-V** then **F10**. The graphic image disappears, but the dashed box remains.

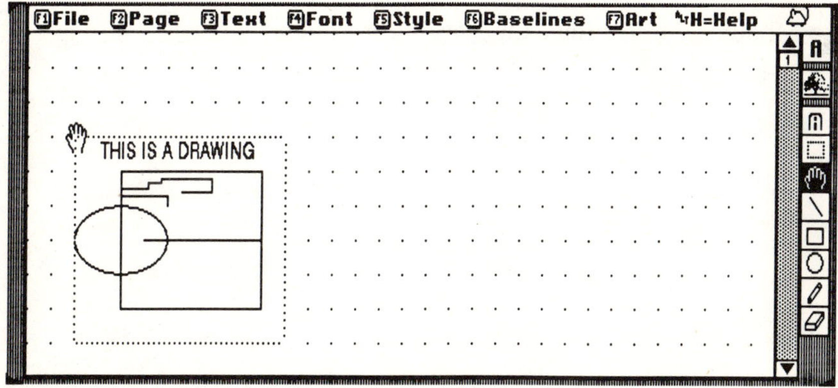

8. Press the **Right Arrow** ten times. Press **F10**. Two copies of the graphic image appear.

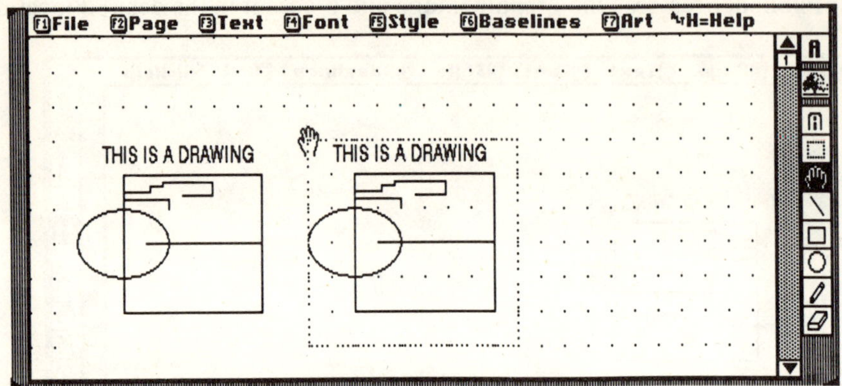

9. Press **Alt-S**, **F4** (Mac), type **EXAMPLE** as the filename, then press **F1** (Ok). First Publisher asks if you want to overwrite the existing file.
10. Press **F1**. First Publisher displays a saving file message.
11. Press **Alt-E** then **F2** to exit First Publisher.
12. Turn to Module 29 to continue the learning sequence.

Module 8
CUT, COPY, PASTE (TEXT)

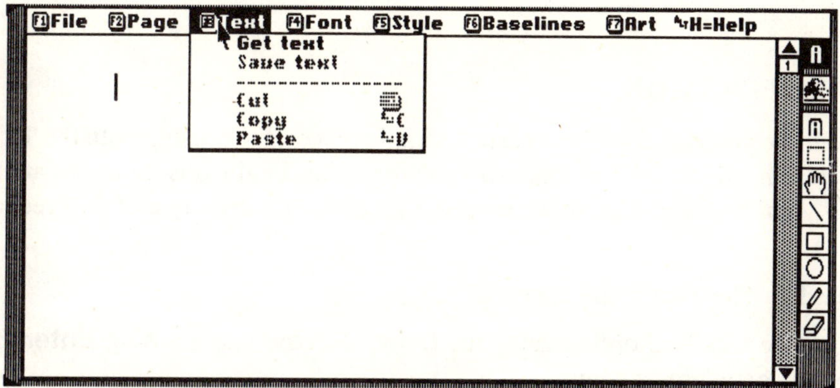

DESCRIPTION

The three commands Cut, Copy, and Paste for text appear on the Text menu. The Cut command removes a highlighted piece of text and places it in memory. The Copy command makes a copy of the highlighted piece of text and places it in memory. The Paste command places the text stored in memory into the document starting at the position pointed to by the cursor.

You can access all three commands through the Text menu or by using key combinations. To Cut a piece of text use the Del key. To Copy a piece of text use the Alt-C key combination. To Paste the contents of memory into the document, use the Alt-V key combination.

These three commands allow you to make rapid modifications to a document when using First Publisher. They allow you to do this by using the pc's memory to temporarily store sections of text for you. This way you can avoid the multiple keystrokes involved in removing or adding text to the document.

APPLICATIONS

Use the Cut command to remove unwanted text or to move the text to another location. Always highlight the text you want cut before using the Cut command.

Use the Copy command to add the same piece of text to other areas of the document. This is especially useful for repetitive information in tables, headers, and footers. You can also use the Copy command to copy a piece of information contained in one document and place it in another. Always highlight the text you want to copy before using the Copy command.

Use the Paste command to place the text in memory into the document. Always make sure the cursor is at the position you want to start placing the text before using the Paste command.

TYPICAL OPERATION

In this example you cut, copy, and paste a sample piece of text using both the Text menu and key commands for the associated function. You begin this example at the First Publisher Main menu with nothing loaded. (To clear the display exit and reenter First Publisher.)

1. Press **F3**. The Text menu appears.
2. Select the Get Text option using the **Down Arrow** and pressing **Enter**. The Get Text dialogue box appears.
3. Select EXAMPLE.TXT using the **Down Arrow**. Press **F10** then **F1**. The Text Type dialogue box appears.
4. Select ASCII using the **Down Arrow**. Press **F10** then **F1**. The Gettysburg Address appears.
5. Press **F10** then **End**. First Publisher highlights the title.

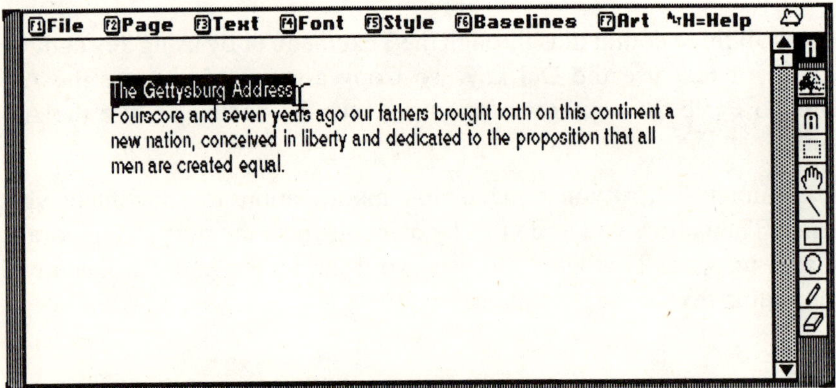

6. Press **F10** then **F3**. The Text menu appears. Notice the Cut and Copy commands are active. The Paste command is gray, indicating it is not available.

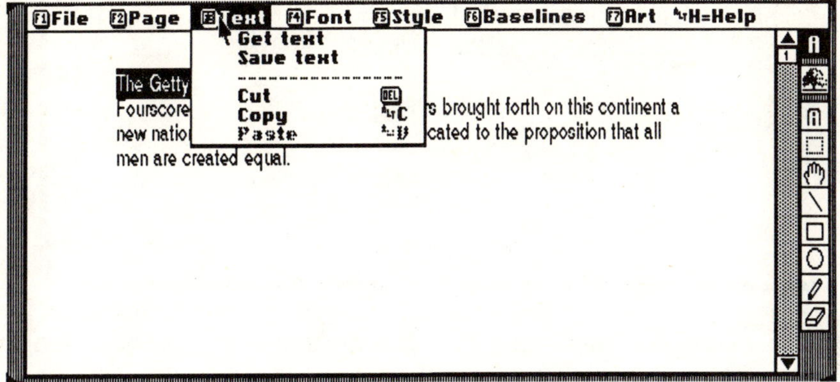

7. Select the Cut command using the **Down Arrow** and pressing **Enter**. First Publisher removes the title.

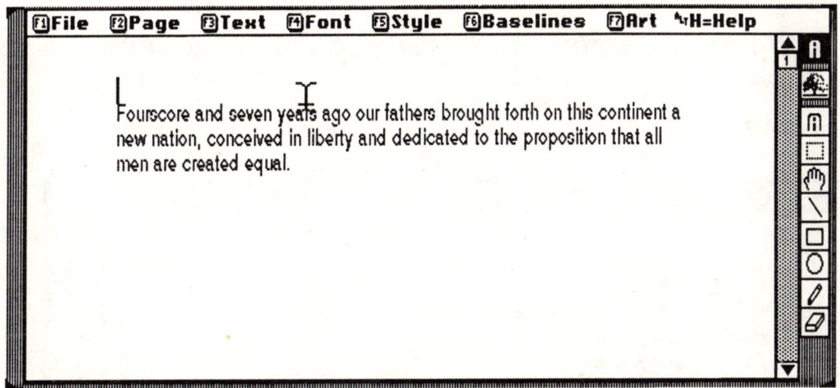

8. Press **F3**. The Text menu appears. Notice the Paste command is active. The Cut and Copy commands are gray, indicating they are not available.

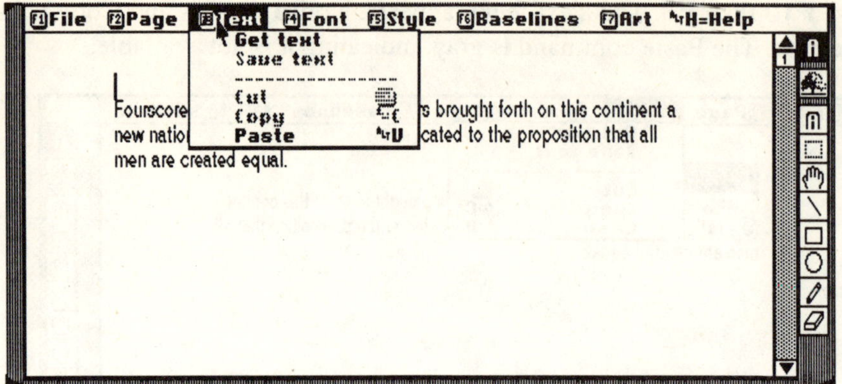

9. Select the Paste command using the **Down Arrow** and pressing **Enter**. First Publisher replaces the previously cut title.
10. Press **F10** then **End**. First Publisher highlights the title.
11. Press **F10** then **Alt-C**. First Publisher copies the title into memory and removes the highlight.
12. Press **Ctrl-End** then **Enter**. First Publisher goes to the end of the document and adds a new line.
13. Press **Alt-V**. First Publisher inserts a copy of the title at the new line.

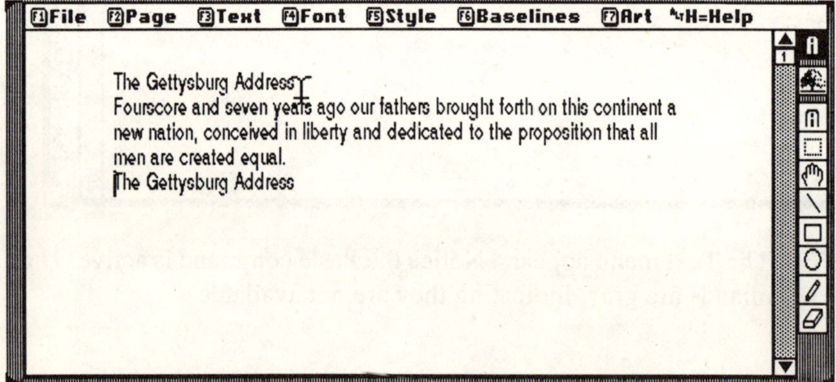

14. Press **F10** then **End**. First Publisher highlights the copy of the title.
15. Press **F10** then **Del**. First Publisher removes the copy of the title.
16. Press **Alt-E** then **F2** to exit First Publisher.
17. Turn to Module 34 to continue the learning sequence.

Module 9
DEFINE PAGE, CHOOSE LAYOUT, ADJUST LAYOUT

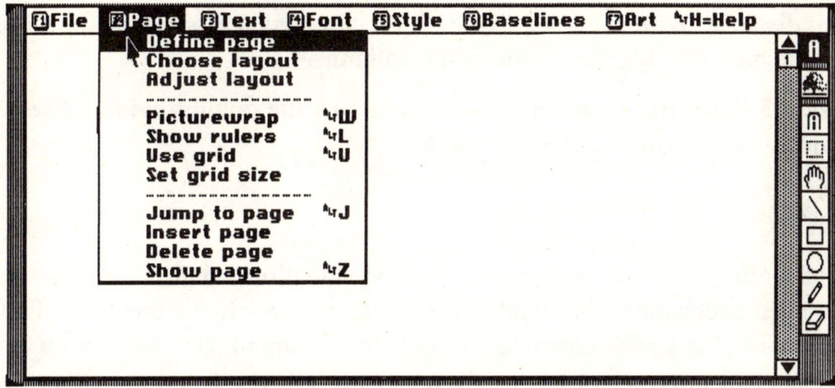

DESCRIPTION

The Define Page option of the Page menu changes the physical characteristics of your document. By changing these characteristics, you decide how your document looks and how much text will fit on a page. The characteristics include margins, text justification, leading, and gutter width.

In version 2.0 of PFS: First Publisher, the characteristics include margins, text justification, leading, and gutter width.

In version 3.0 of PFS: First Publisher, the characteristics include margins, paper size, and paper orientation. To adjust the text justification, leading, number of columns, and column width, use the Choose Layout and Adjust Layout commands.

(Version 3.0 only) The Choose Layout command lets you choose from one of 21 predefined page layout designs.

(Version 3.0 only) The Adjust Layout command lets you modify a page layout by adding, resizing, duplicating, and adjusting columns.

Margins adjust how much white space appears between the end of your text and the edge of the paper. Adjusting the top, bottom, right, and left margins affects the amount of text that fits on the page and the readability of your document.

First Publisher supports four different justifications: right, left, centered, and full justification. Using right justification gives you an even right margin, left gives you an even left margin, centered gives you centered text with both margins ragged, and full justification gives you even right and left margins.

Leading (pronounced ledding) is the distance between one line of text and the next. First Publisher adds the leading entry to the point size of the type used to determine line height.

A gutter is the white space between two columns of text. The gutter entry allows you to change this distance. With version 2.0 of PFS: First Publisher, you adjust the gutter width. The wider the gutter width, the narrower the columns.

With version 3.0 of PFS: First Publisher, you adjust the column width. The wider the column width, the narrower the gutter width.

APPLICATIONS

You use the Define Page option to globally change the physical characteristics of a page. When you need to change the amount of text on a page to achieve the desired effect on a document, change the global characteristics of the document. Use this option before you create any special page effects since these special effects disappear when the global characteristics change.

With version 3.0 of PFS: First Publisher you use the Choose Layout and Define Layout commands to change the physical characteristics of a document.

To make page designing easier, version 3.0 of PFS: First Publisher includes 21 common page layout designs that you can choose through the Choose Layout command. Rather than design a page from scratch, you can use one of these predefined page layouts and modify it using the Adjust Layout command.

TYPICAL OPERATION

This example shows you how to change the global characteristics of a document. Use this setup for the rest of the examples in this book. Begin this example at the DOS prompt.

The following steps are for version 2.0 of PFS: First Publisher only:

1. Type **FP** and press **Enter**. The First Publisher Main menu appears.
2. Press **F2**. The Page menu appears.
3. Select the Define Page option using the **Down Arrow**. Press **Enter**. The Define Page dialogue box appears.
4. Type **2** and press **Enter**. The number of columns changes to 2 and the cursor advances to the left margin entry.

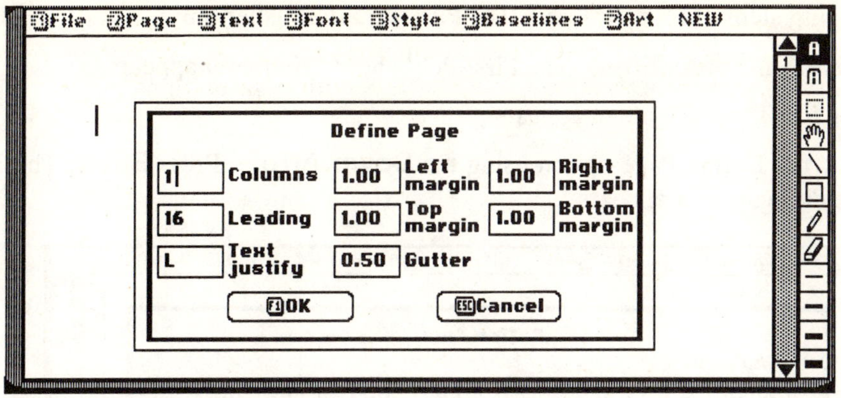

5. Type **.75** and press **Enter**. The left margin changes to .75 and the cursor advances to the right margin entry.

6. Type **.75** and press **Enter**. The right margin changes to .75 and the cursor advances to the leading entry.

7. Press **Enter**. The cursor advances to the top margin entry.

8. Type **.75** and press **Enter**. The top margin changes to .75 and the cursor advances to the bottom margin entry.

9. Type **.75** and press **Enter**. The bottom margin changes to .75 and the cursor advances to the text justification entry.

10. Type **J** and press **Enter**. The text justification entry changes to J and the cursor advances to the gutter entry.

11. Press **F1**. The Define Page menu disappears.

12. Press **Alt-S**. The File Save dialogue box appears.

13. Type **EXAMPLE** and press **Enter**. Press **F1**. The screen flashes a saving file message, then the edit area clears.

13. Press **Alt-E**. The File Save menu appears.

14. Press **F1**. First Publisher asks if you want to replace the original document.

15. Press **F1**. First Publisher saves the document. The DOS prompt appears.

16. Turn to Module 19 to continue the learning sequence.

The following steps are for version 3.0 of PFS: First Publisher only:

1. Type **FP** and press **Enter**. The First Publisher Main menu appears.
2. Press **F2**. The Page menu appears.
3. Select the Define Page option using the **Down Arrow**. Press **Enter**. The Define Page dialogue box appears.

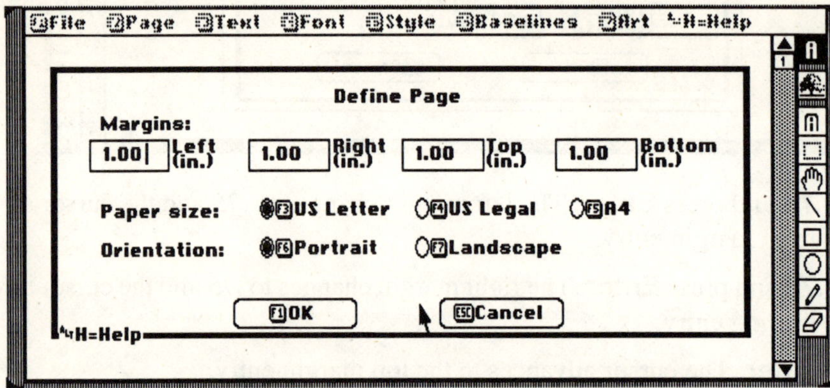

4. Type **.75** and press **Enter**. The left margin changes to .75 and the cursor advances to the right margin entry.
5. Type **.75** and press **Enter**. The right margin changes to .75 and the cursor advances to the top margin entry.
6. Type **.75** and press **Enter**. The top margin changes to .75 and the cursor advances to the bottom margin entry.
7. Type **.75** and press **Enter**. The bottom margin changes to .75 and the cursor advances back to the left margin entry.
8. Press **F1** to choose OK.
9. Press **F2** to choose the Page menu.
10. Select the Choose Layout option using the **Down Arrow**. Press **Enter**. The Choose Layout dialogue box appears.

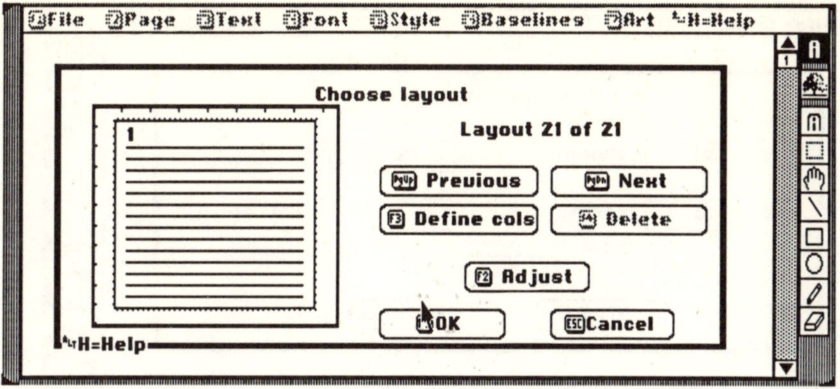

11. Press **PgDn** to choose Layout 1 of 21.

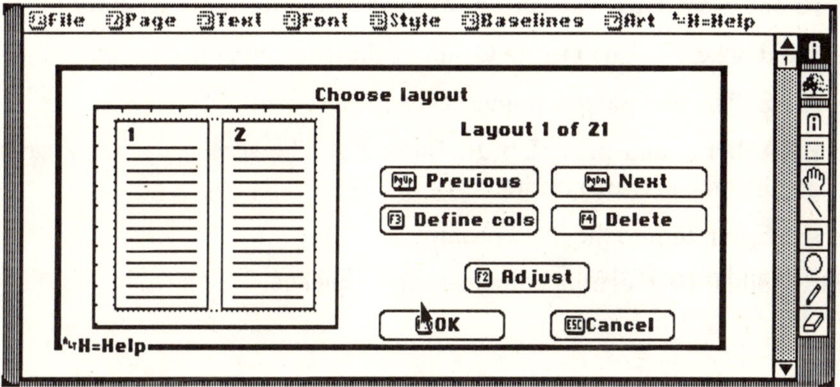

12. Press **F1** to choose OK.
13. Press **F2** to choose the Page menu.
14. Select the Choose Layout option using the **Down Arrow**. Press **Enter**.
15. Press **F3** to choose the Define Columns option. The Define Columns dialogue box appears.

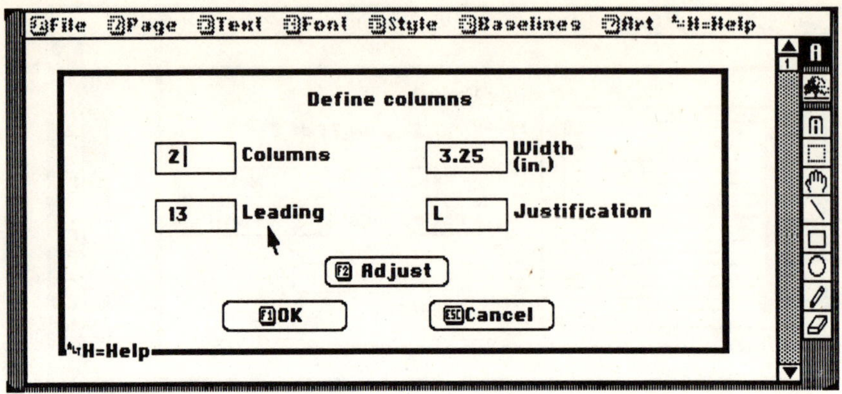

16. Press **Tab** twice. The cursor advances to the leading entry.
17. Type **16** and press **Tab**. The cursor advances to the justification entry.
18. Type **J** and press **F1**. The Define Columns dialogue box disappears.
19. Press **Alt-S**. The File Save dialogue box appears.
20. Type **EXAMPLE** and press **Enter**. Press **F1**. The screen flashes a saving file message, then the edit area clears.
21. Press **Alt-E** to return to the DOS prompt.
22. Turn to Module 19 to continue the learning sequence.

Module 10
DELETE FILE

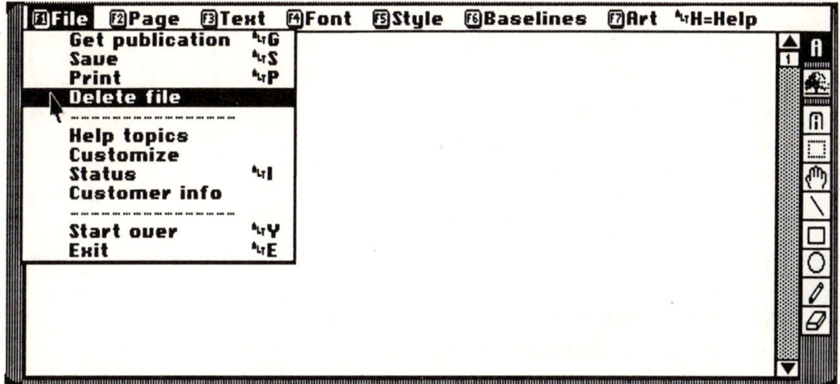

DESCRIPTION

The Delete File option on the File menu allows you to remove old files from your hard or floppy disk drive. First Publisher always displays two different dialogue boxes when using the option. The first dialogue box contains a file selection menu, a path entry, and two buttons. The buttons determine if First Publisher executes the command. The second dialogue box offers you a choice of deleting the selected file or going back to the Main menu (Esc).

APPLICATIONS

Use the Delete File option when you want to remove old files from your hard or floppy disk drive to make room for new ones. First Publisher always double-checks to make sure you want to delete the selected file. By doing this, First Publisher reduces the chance that you will inadvertently remove a much needed file.

TYPICAL OPERATION

In this example you delete EXAMPLE.TXT from your hard or floppy disk drive (the illustration uses drive C). Begin this example at the First Publisher Main menu with nothing loaded.

1. Press **F1**. The File menu appears.
2. Select the Delete File option using the **Down Arrow**. Press **Enter**. The Delete File dialogue box appears.

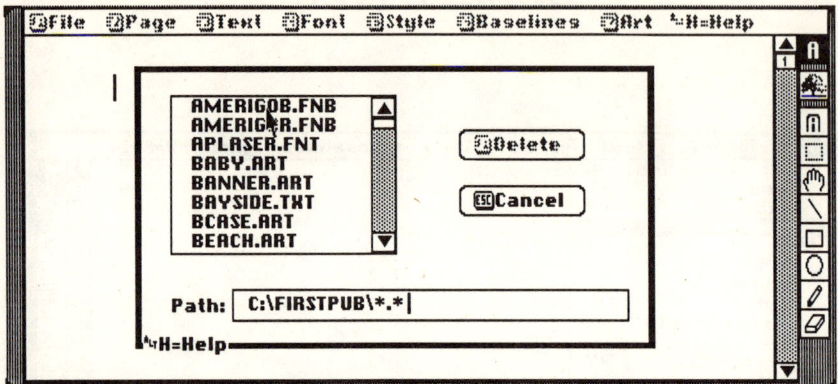

3. Select EXAMPLE.TXT using the **Down Arrow**. Press **F10** then **F1**. First Publisher displays a warning message dialogue box.

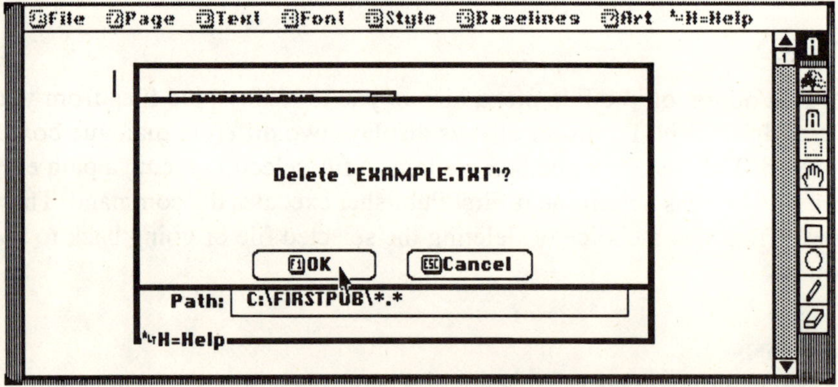

4. Press **F1**. The First Publisher Main menu appears.
5. Turn to Module 25 to continue the learning sequence.

Module 11
DELETE PAGE

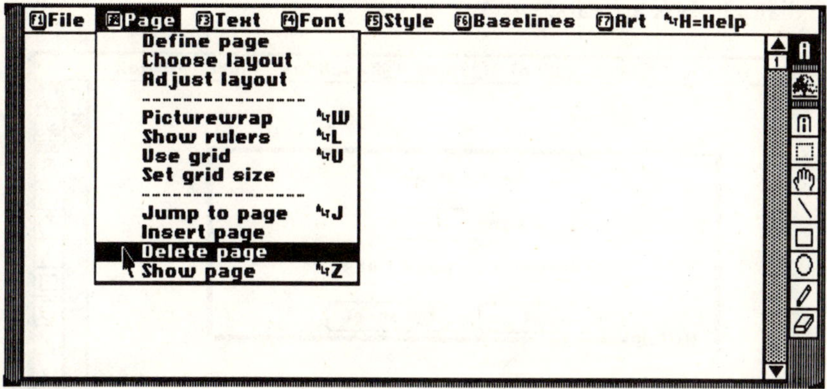

DESCRIPTION

The Delete Page option on the Page menu removes a page from a document permanently. The Delete Page dialogue box consists of three items. The first item is the page number indicator. This shows the current page as well as the total number of pages in the document. First Publisher displays an error message if you try to delete a page that doesn't exist. The second item is the page number entry. The third item is two buttons. The buttons determine if First Publisher executes the option.

APPLICATIONS

Use the Delete Page to remove any unwanted page from the document. Always exercise extreme care when using this command since it removes the pages permanently. You cannot recover a deleted page except by starting over and using an unaltered original disk file.

TYPICAL OPERATION

In this example you see what happens if you try to delete a page that doesn't exist. Then you delete the two previously added pages. Begin this example at the First Publisher Main menu with EXAMPLE.PUB loaded.

1. Press **F2**. The Page menu appears.
2. Select the Delete Page option using the **Down Arrow**. Press **Enter**. The Delete Page dialogue box appears.

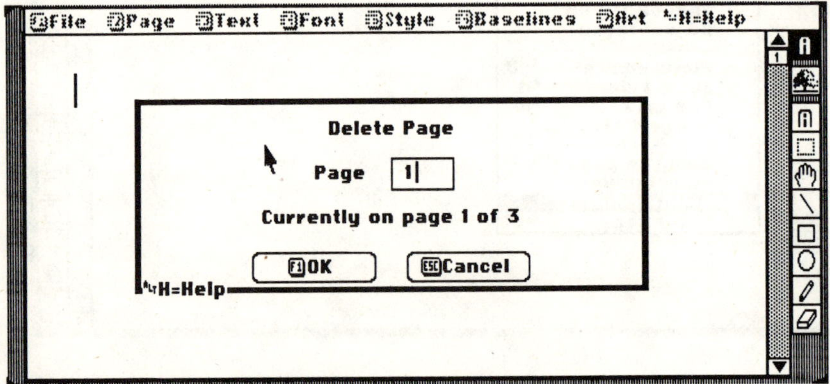

3. Type **4** then press **F1**. First Publisher displays an error message.

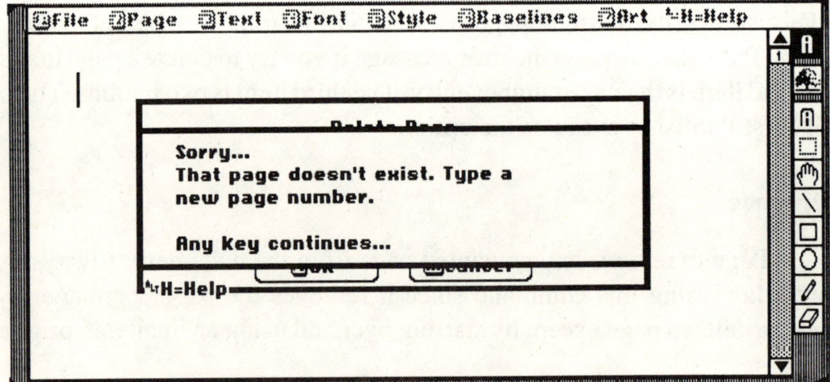

4. Press **Enter**. The error message disappears.
5. Type **1** then press **F1**. The Gettysburg Address appears.

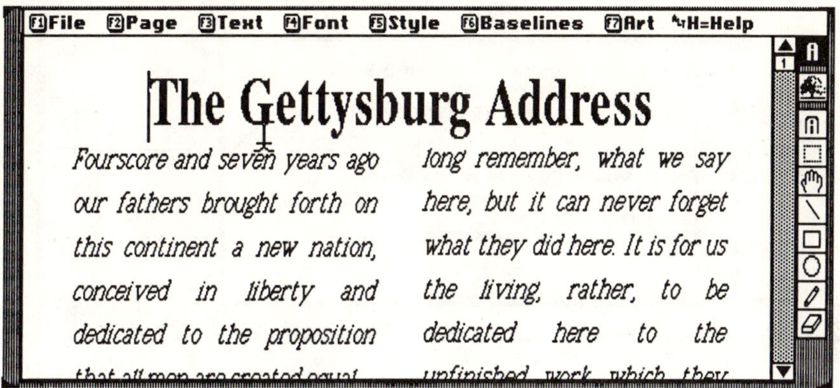

6. Press **F2**. The Page menu appears.
7. Select the Delete Page option using the **Down Arrow**. Press **Enter**. The Delete Page dialogue box appears. Notice First Publisher updated the display to show the new total number of pages.

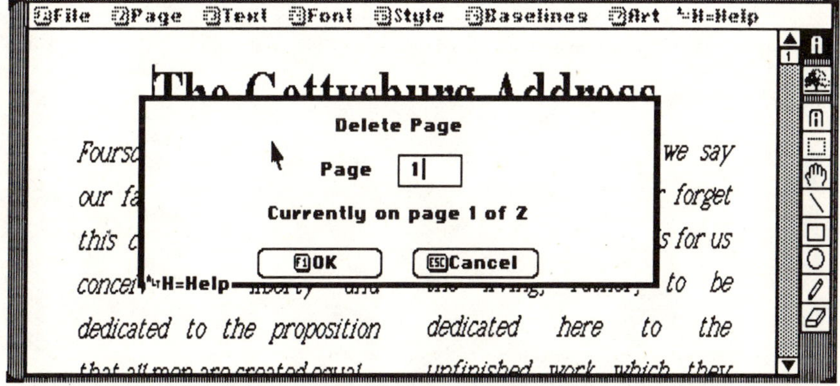

8. Type **2** then press **F1**. Press **Alt-I**. First Publisher shows that only one page exists.

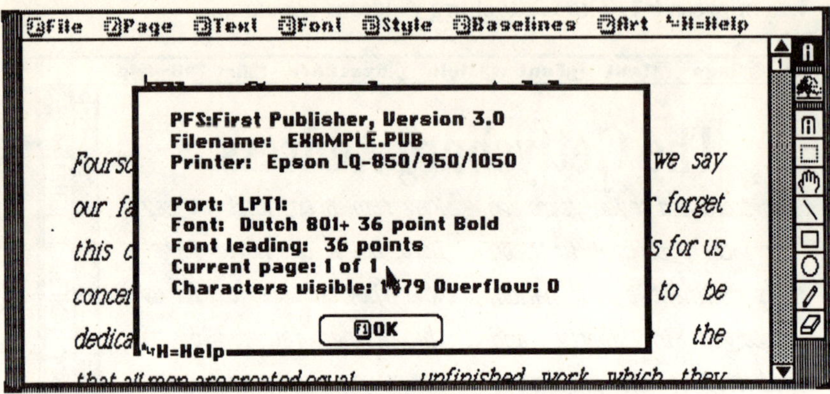

9. Press **F1**. The Status dialogue box disappears.
10. Press **Alt-E** then **F1**. First Publisher asks if you want to overwrite the old copy of EXAMPLE.PUB.
11. Press **F1**. First Publisher displays a saving file message.
12. Turn to Module 10 to continue the learning sequence.

Module 12
DRAWING TOOLS

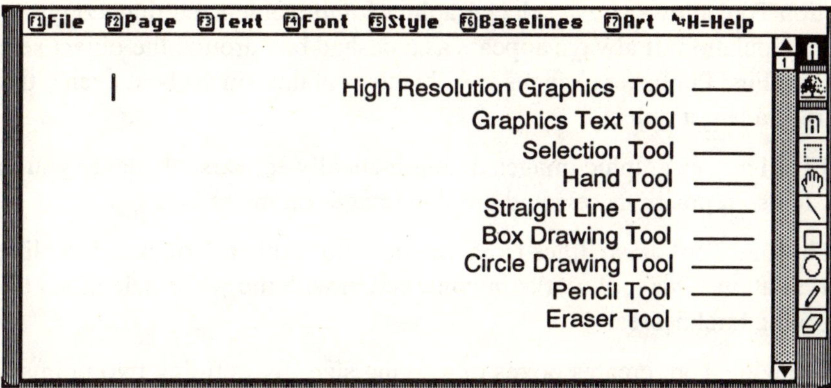

DESCRIPTION

First Publisher provides three different types of drawing tools on the Side Tools menu. The first type, text tools, consists of the Graphics Text Tool. The second type, manipulation tools, consists of the Selection Tool and Hand Tool. The third type, graphic tools, consists of the Straight Line Tool, Box Drawing Tool, Pencil Tool, and Eraser Tool. The Width Tools on the Side Tools menu work with the graphics tools to allow different thicknesses of the graphic images. In most cases (except the Graphics Text Tool), you activate the drawing tool by pressing F10 to lower the mouse button. To deactivate the drawing tool, press F10 a second time.

Version 3.0 only. The High Resolution Graphics Tool allows you to manipulate high resolution graphics in First Publisher. If a graphic image uses a resolution greater than the 75 dpi supported in versions prior to 3.0, then you use this tool instead of the Hand Tool to manipulate it. In all respects this tool looks and acts like the Hand Tool described below.

The Graphics Text Tool produces text that you can easily manipulate using the other drawing tools. The difference between graphics text and standard text is the way First Publisher stores them in memory. First Publisher stores standard text as ASCII characters and graphics text as bit-mapped images. The only disadvantage to graphics text is that once placed, you cannot easily change it like standard text. However, graphics text is much easier to place and manipulate. For instance, you can stretch graphics text to exactly fit in an area normally too large or small for standard text.

The Selection Tool allows you to select graphics for movement, cutting, copying, or other forms of manipulation. It always appears as a dashed box around the object selected for manipulation. First Publisher changes any objects contained in the box, even if the graphic is only part of a larger object.

The Hand Tool moves graphic images. It automatically appears whenever you import an art image. It also repositions selected graphic images on the screen.

The Straight Line Tool draws lines from one point to another. You can draw lines in any angular orientation. This tool works in conjunction with the width selections to produce lines of varying thicknesses.

The Box Drawing Tool creates boxes of varying sizes by defining two points. The two points are always nonadjacent (upper right and lower left corners, or upper left and lower right corners). You use the width selections to define the thickness of the lines composing the box.

The Pencil Tool creates freehand images. Wherever you direct the pencil using the direction arrows, First Publisher places a line. The width selections determine line thickness.

The Erase Tool removes any graphic image created by the other tools. First Publisher removes only the portion of the image actually touched by the Eraser Tool. The width selections determine the erase size.

APPLICATIONS

You use the drawing tools to create original art or enhance graphic images created using other programs. The drawing tools also provide the means of creating text enhancements like rule lines and shaded side bars on news letters. By using the drawing tools to their full potential, you can make ordinary text and graphics look extraordinary.

TYPICAL OPERATION

In this example you experiment using the various drawing tools. You also see the effect of creating graphics text instead of using standard text. This Version 2.0 example also shows the error message that appears when you forget to raise the mouse button before performing a nonmovement related function. Begin this example at the First Publisher Main menu with nothing loaded.

The following steps work with version 2.0 of First Publisher only:

1. Press **F9** four times. Press **Alt-L** then **Alt-U**. The grid and rulers appear.

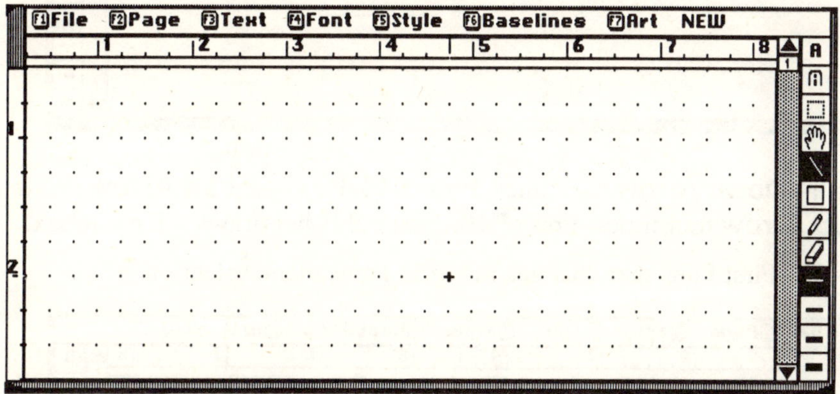

2. Press **F10**. Press the **Right Arrow** five times. First Publisher draws a 1-point line.
3. Press **F9**. First Publisher displays an error message.

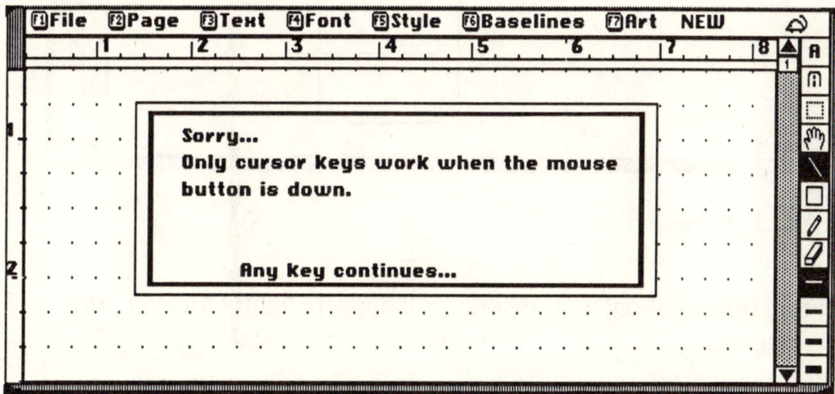

4. Press **Enter**. First Publisher clears the error message.

5. Press **F10** to raise the mouse button. Press **F9**. First Publisher changes the Side Tools menu selection.

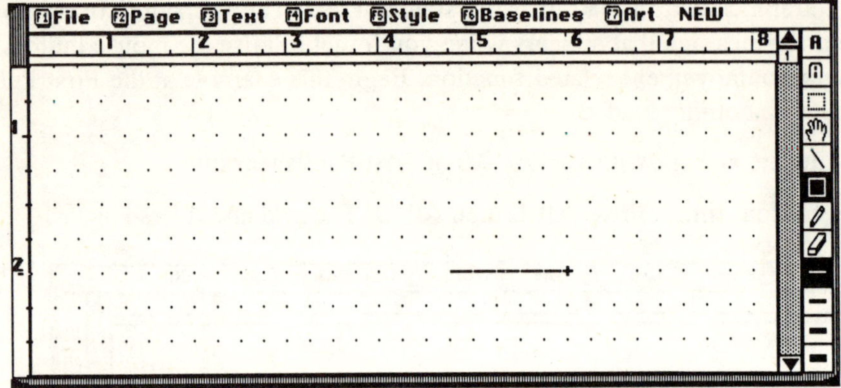

6. Press the **Down Arrow** two times. Press **F10**. Press the **Left Arrow** six times and the **Up Arrow** four times. Press **F10**. First Publisher draws a 1-point box.
7. Press **F9**. First Publisher changes the Side Tools menu selection.

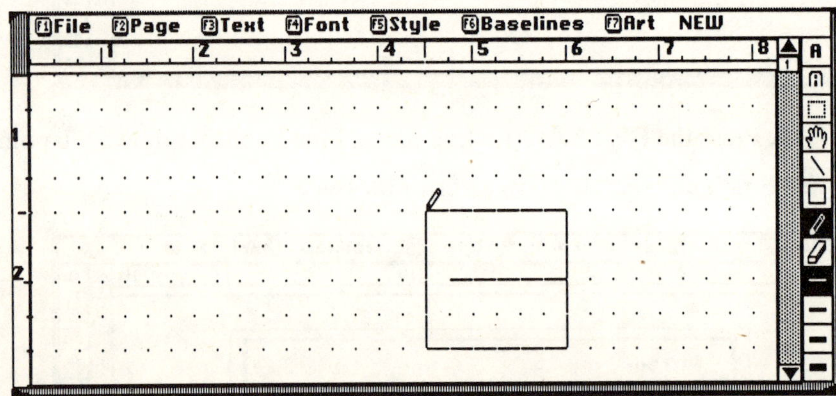

8. Press **Alt-U**. The grid disappears.

NOTE

From this point on, your display will appear slightly different than the figures appearing in this section.

9. Press **F10**. Press the arrow keys to draw a pattern on the display. Place part of the pattern outside the box and part inside. Press **F10**. Notice First Publisher places a free-form line wherever you place the Pencil Tool.

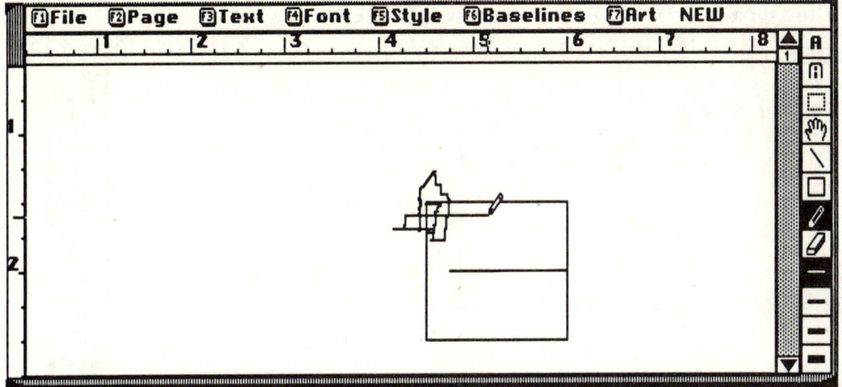

10. Press **Alt-U**. The grid reappears.
11. Press **F9**. First Publisher changes the Side Tools menu selection.
12. Press the **Right Arrow** until the Eraser Tool appears outside the box. Press **F10**. Press the arrow keys to remove any lines outside the box. Press **F10**. First Publisher removes the unwanted lines.

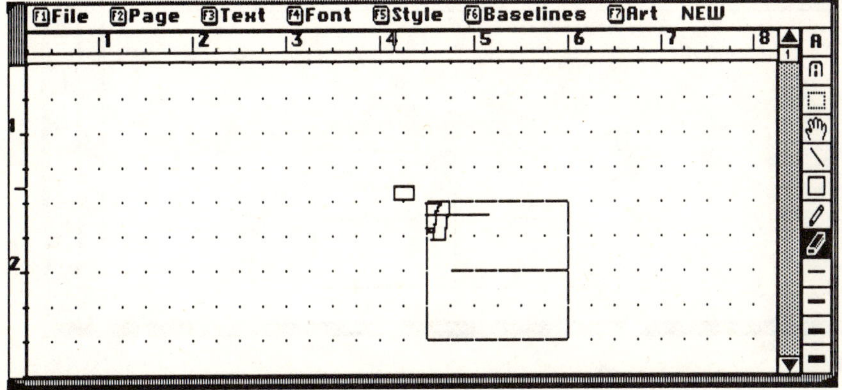

13. Press **F9** twice. First Publisher changes the Side Tools menu selection.
14. Type **THIS IS A DRAWING**. Press **F9**. First Publisher changes the Side Tools menu selection.

15. Position the graphics arrow above and to the right of the text. Press **F10**. Surround the text using the arrow keys. Press **F10**. First Publisher places a dashed box around the text.

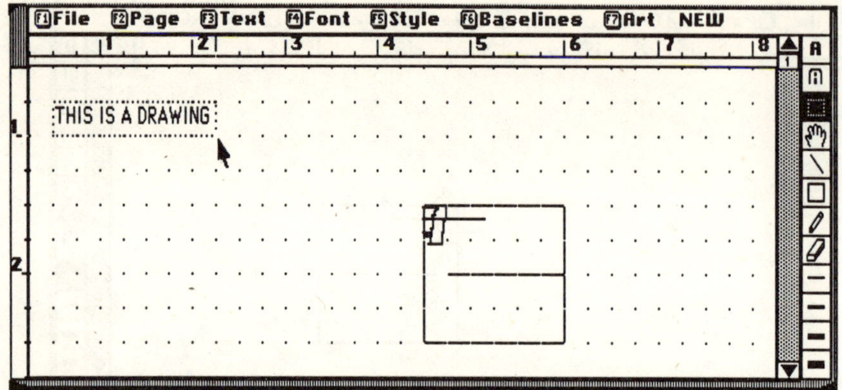

16. Press **F9**. First Publisher changes the Side Tools menu selection.
17. Place the Hand Tool in the middle of the dashed box using the arrow keys. Press **F10**. Place the text directly over the solid box using the arrow keys. Press **F10**. First Publisher places the text over the drawing.

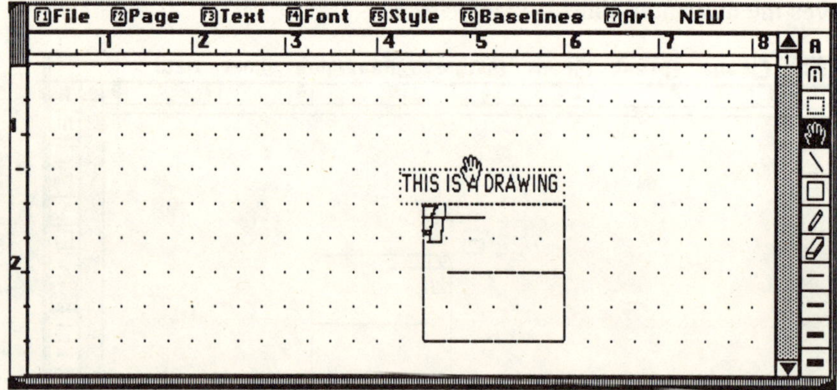

18. Press **F9** seven times. Press the **Up Arrow** twice. Press **F10** twice. First Publisher removes the dashed line from around the graphics text.

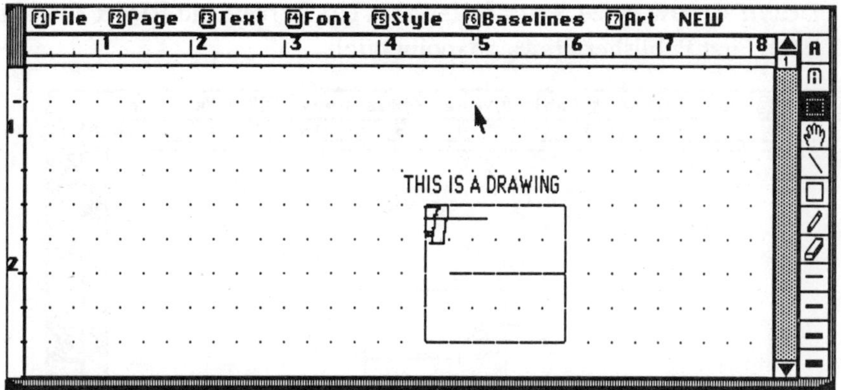

19. Press **Alt-S** then **F4** to save the example as a graphics file. Type **EXAMPLE**. Press **F1**. First Publisher displays a saving file message.
20. Turn to Module 18 to continue the learning sequence.

The following steps work with version 3.0 of First Publisher only:

1. Press **F9** five times. Press **Alt-L** then **Alt-U**. The grid and rulers appear.

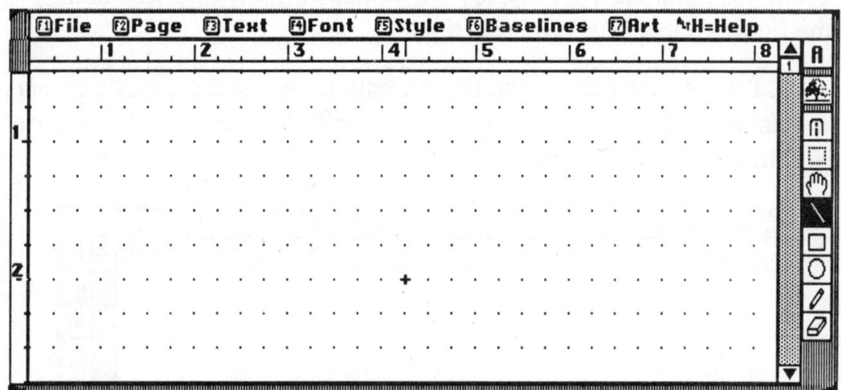

2. Press **F10**. Press the **Right Arrow** five times. First Publisher draws a 1-point line.
3. Press **F9**. Notice that, unlike version 2.0, First Publisher does not display an error message. The program automatically raises the mouse and selects the next graphics tool.
4. Press the **Down Arrow** two times. Press **F10**. Press the **Left Arrow** six times and the **Up Arrow** four times. Press **F10**. First Publisher draws a 1-point box.
5. Press **F9**. First Publisher changes the Side Tools menu selection.

6. Press **Down Arrow** twice. Press **F10**. Press **Up Arrow** and **Right Arrow** twice. Press **F10**. First Publisher draws a 1-point circle.

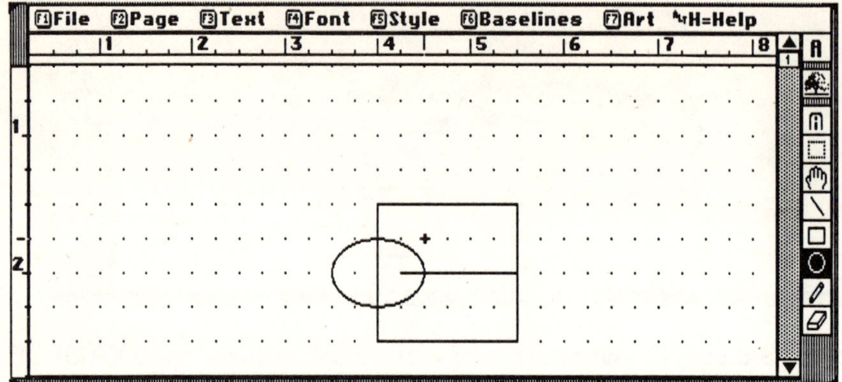

7. Press **F9**. First Publisher changes the Side Tools menu selection.
8. Press **Alt-U**. The grid disappears.

NOTE

From this point on, your display will appear slightly different than the figures appearing in this section.

9. Press **F10**. Press the arrow keys to draw a pattern on the display. Place part of the pattern outside the box and part inside. Press **F10**. Notice First Publisher places a free-form line wherever you place the Pencil Tool.

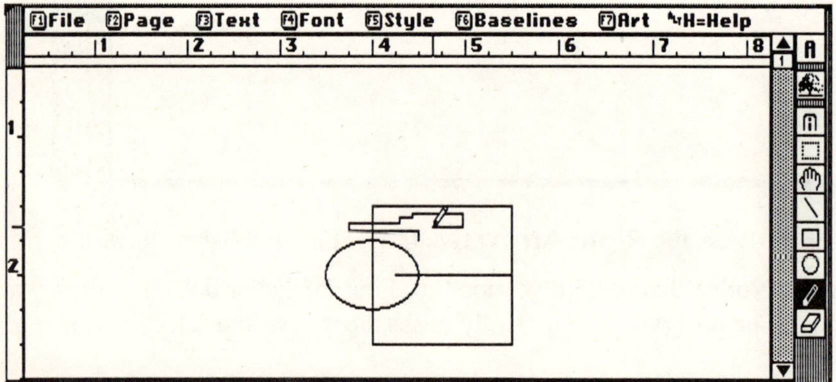

10. Press **Alt-U**. The grid reappears.
11. Press **F9**. First Publisher changes the Side Tools menu selection.

12. Press the **Left Arrow** until the Eraser Tool appears outside the box. Press **F10**. Press the arrow keys to remove any lines outside the box. Press **F10**. First Publisher removes the unwanted lines.

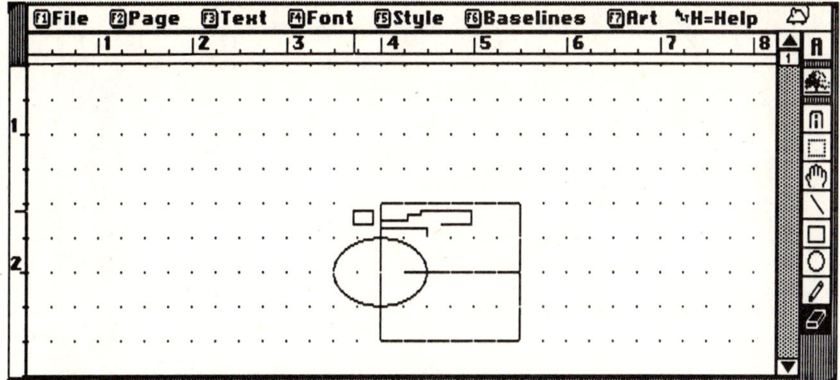

13. Press **F9** three times. First Publisher changes the Side Tools menu selection.
14. Type **THIS IS A DRAWING**. Press **F9**. First Publisher changes the Side Tools menu selection.
15. Position the graphics arrow above and to the right of the text. Press **F10**. Surround the text using the arrow keys. Press **F10**. First Publisher places a dashed box around the text.

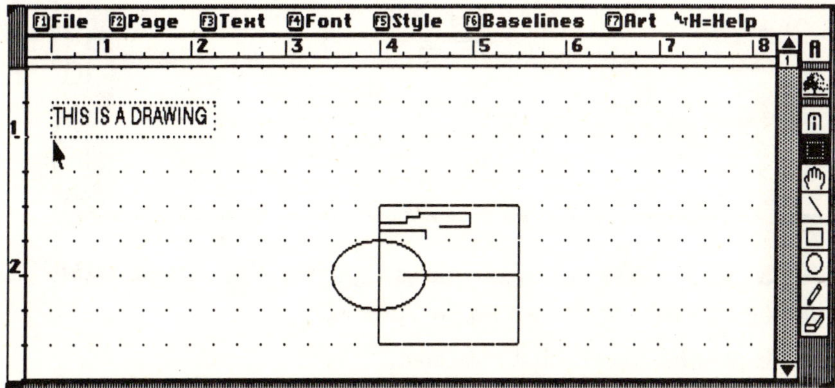

16. Press **F9**. First Publisher changes the Side Tools menu selection.

17. Place the Hand Tool in the middle of the dashed box using the arrow keys. Press **F10**. Place the text directly over the solid box using the arrow keys. Press **F10**. First Publisher places the text over the drawing.

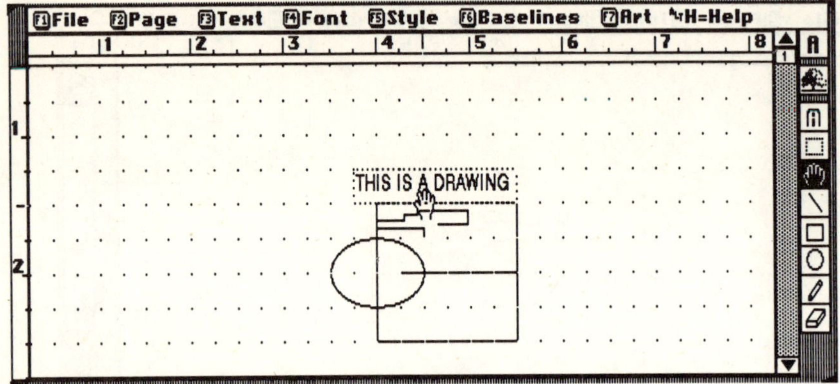

18. Press **F9** nine times. Press the **Up Arrow** twice. Press **F10** twice. First Publisher removes the dashed line from around the graphics text.

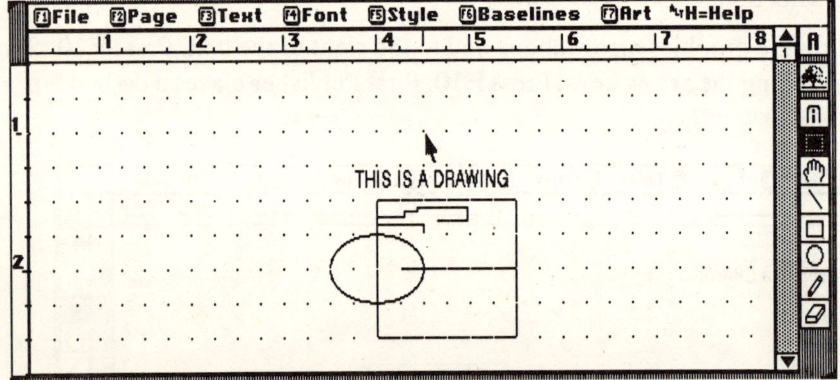

19. Press **Alt-S** then **F4** to save the example as a graphics file. Type **EXAMPLE**. Press **F1**. First Publisher displays a saving file message.

20. Press **Alt-E** then **F2** to exit First Publisher.

21. Turn to Module 18 to continue the learning sequence.

Module 13
DUPLICATE

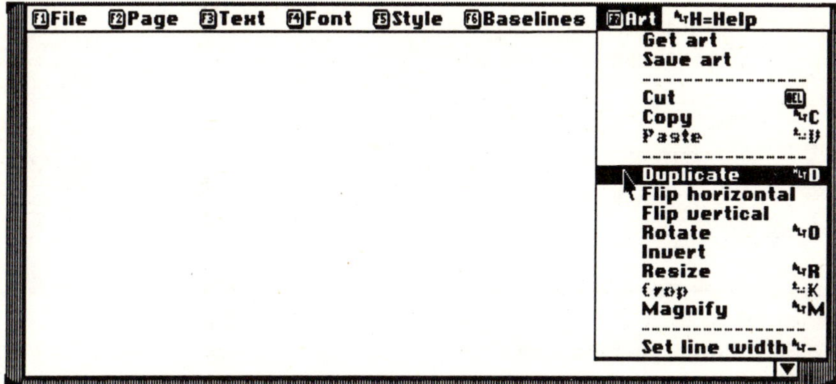

DESCRIPTION

The Duplicate command on the Art menu copies and pastes a graphic image in one step. This makes it faster to use than the copy command which requires two steps (one to copy, one to paste). You can access this command either from the Art menu or by pressing Alt-D.

APPLICATIONS

You use the Duplicate command to quickly make copies of a graphic when both images reside on the same page. If you want to copy a graphic on one page to another page, use the Copy command described in Module 7.

TYPICAL OPERATION

In this example you use the Duplicate command to create a copy of an existing graphic image. Begin this example at the First Publisher Main menu with EXAMPLE.MAC loaded.

1. Press **Alt-U**. The grid appears.
2. Activate the Selection Tool. Position the graphics arrow above and to the left of the first graphics image using the arrow keys. Press **F10**. Surround the graphic image using the arrow keys. Press **F10**. First Publisher selects the first graphic image.

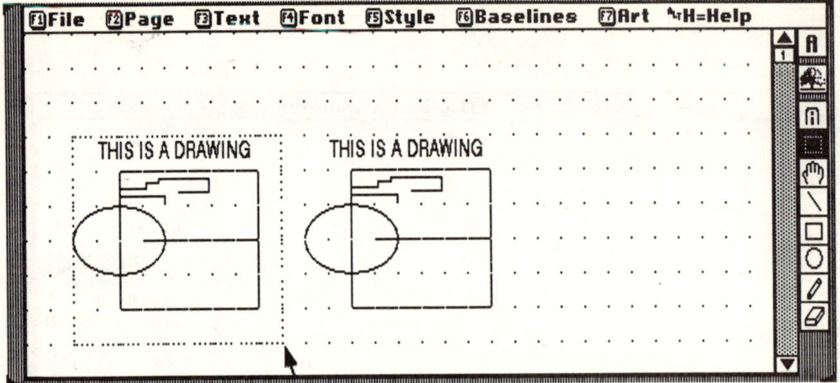

3. Press **F7**. The Art menu appears.
4. Select the Duplicate command using the **Down Arrow**. Press **Enter**. The Hand Tool appears.

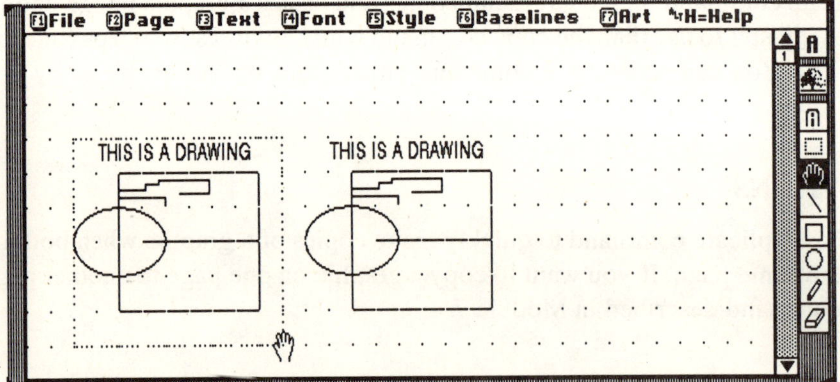

5. Press **F10**. Press the **Up Arrow** six times and the **Right Arrow** eleven times. Press **F10**. First Publisher places the graphic image in the requested position.

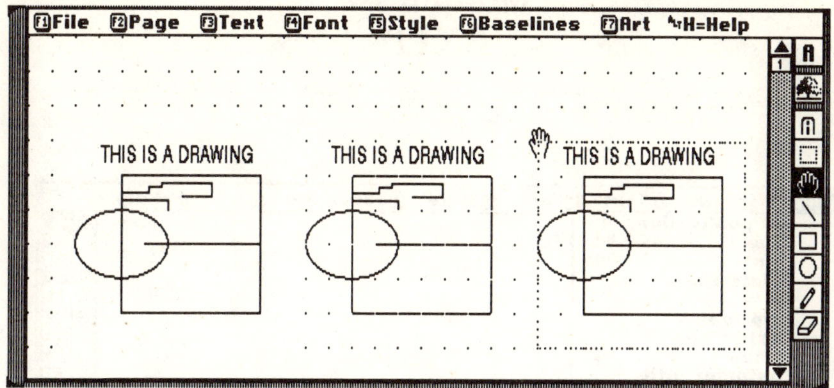

6. Press **Alt-S, F4**, type **EXAMPLE** as the filename, then press **F1**. First Publisher asks if you want to overwrite the existing file.
7. Press **F1**. First Publisher displays a saving file message.
8. Press **Alt-E** then **F2** to exit First Publisher.
9. Turn to Module 23 to continue the learning sequence.

Module 14
EXIT

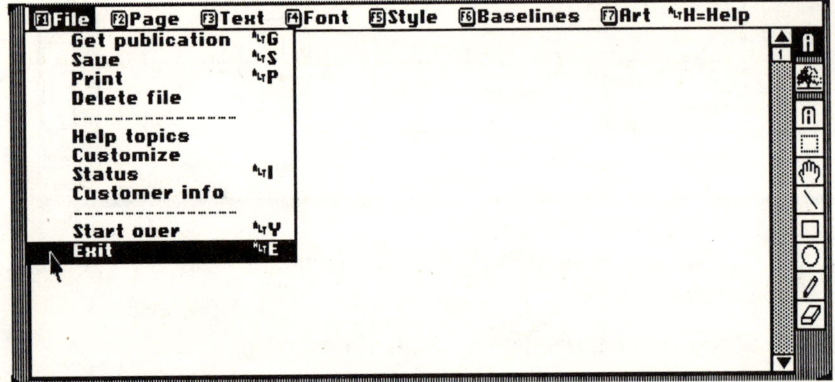

DESCRIPTION

The Exit command allows you to leave First Publisher when you complete work on your document. This command is accessed through the File menu (F1).

When you use the Exit command, First Publisher asks if you want to save your document. After you answer yes or no, it closes all files, then returns you to the DOS prompt.

APPLICATIONS

Use Exit command to leave First Publisher before turning your computer off or using another application.

TYPICAL OPERATION

In this example you use the Exit command to leave First Publisher. Begin at the DOS prompt.

1. Type **FP** and press **Enter**. The First Publisher Main menu appears.
2. Type **HELLO** in the edit area.

3. Press **Alt-E**. First Publisher asks if you want to save the file.

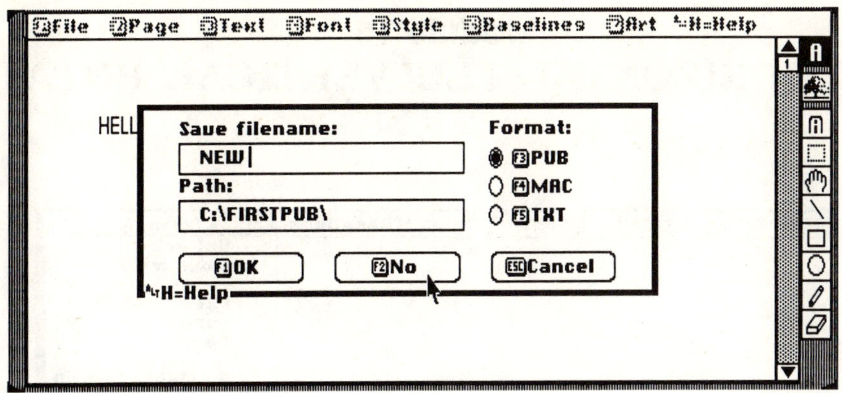

4. Press **F2** (No). The DOS prompt appears.
5. Turn to Module 21 to continue the learning sequence.

Module 15
FLIP HORIZONTAL, FLIP VERTICAL, ROTATE

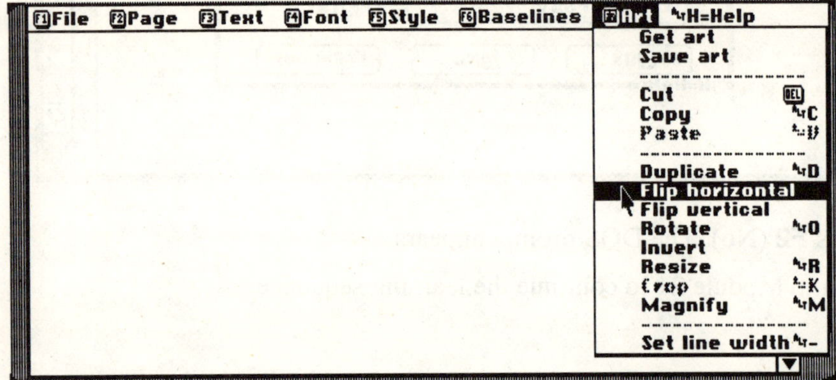

DESCRIPTION

The Flip Horizontal, Flip Vertical, and Rotate command on the Art menu provide the means for changing the orientation of your graphic. You can access the Rotate command using the Art menu or by pressing Alt-O. First Publisher allows access to the other two commands using the Art menu only.

The figure below shows how First Publisher changes the orientation of a graphic in response to one of the three commands. Even though all three commands manipulate the graphic image, all three are very different in effect. First Publisher provides a total of 64 different orientations using these three commands.

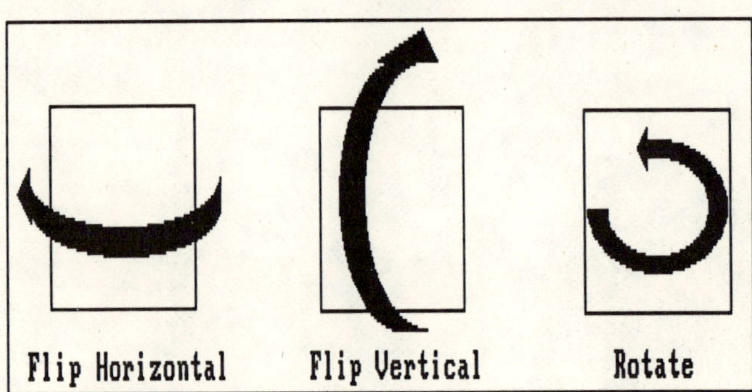

The Flip Horizontal command rotates the graphic image 180 degrees horizontally along the Z (or depth) axis. Selecting the command twice reverses the original effect.

The Flip Vertical command rotates the graphic image 180 degrees vertically along the Z (or depth) axis. Selecting the command twice reverses the original effect.

The Rotate command rotates the graphic image 90 degrees along the X (horizontal) and Y (vertical) axis. Selecting the command four times reverses the original effect.

APPLICATIONS

Use the Flip Horizontal, Flip Vertical, and Rotate commands to change the orientation of a graphic image. Since the three commands perform completely different functions, make sure you know which way you actually want to change the orientation before using them.

TYPICAL OPERATION

In this example you change the orientation of the three previously saved graphic images using a different command on each one. This allows you to see how the commands perform different tasks on the same graphic image. Begin this example at the First Publisher Main menu with EXAMPLE.MAC loaded.

1. Press **Alt-U**. The grid appears.
2. Activate the Selection Tool. Position the graphics arrow above and to the left of the first graphic image using the arrow keys. Press **F10**. Press the **Down Arrow** six times and the **Right Arrow** nine times. Press **F10**. First Publisher selects the first graphic image.
3. Press **F7**. The Art menu appears.
4. Select the Flip Horizontal command using the **Down Arrow**. Press **Enter**. First Publisher flips the graphic image horizontally.

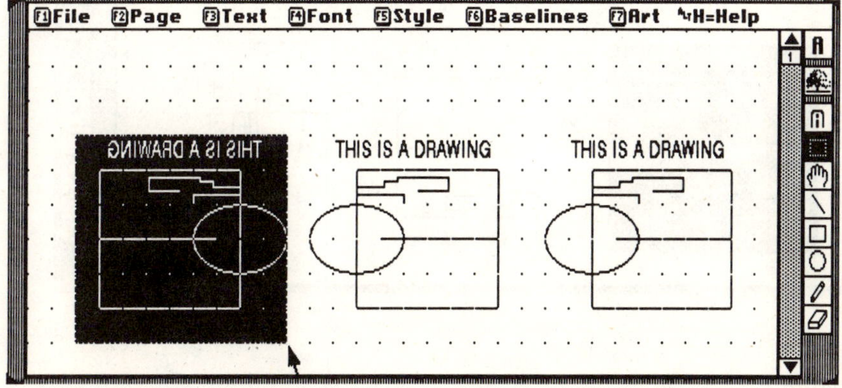

5. Position the graphic arrow above and to the left of the second graphic image using the arrow keys. Press **F10**. Press the **Down Arrow** six times and the **Right Arrow** nine times. Press **F10**. First Publisher selects the second graphic image.
6. Press **F7**. The Art menu appears.
7. Select the Flip Vertical command using the **Down Arrow**. Press **Enter**. First Publisher flips the graphic image vertically.

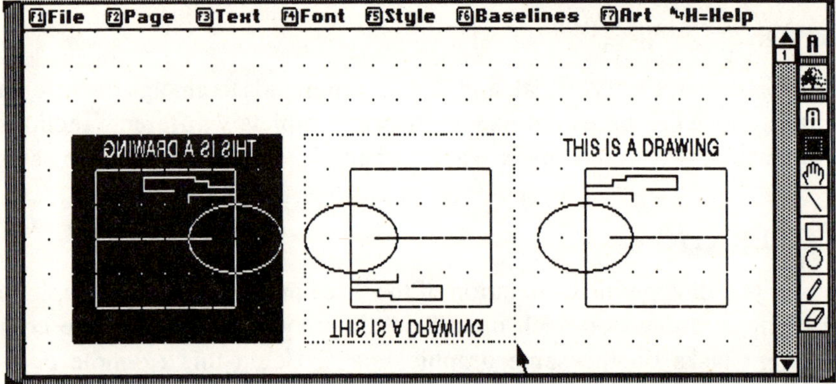

8. Position the arrow above and to the left of the third graphic image using the arrow keys. Press **F10**. Press the **Down Arrow** six times and the **Right Arrow** eight times. Press **F10**. First Publisher selects the third graphic image.
9. Press **F7**. The Art menu appears.
10. Select the Rotate command using the **Down Arrow**. Press **Enter**. First Publisher rotates the graphic image 90 degrees.

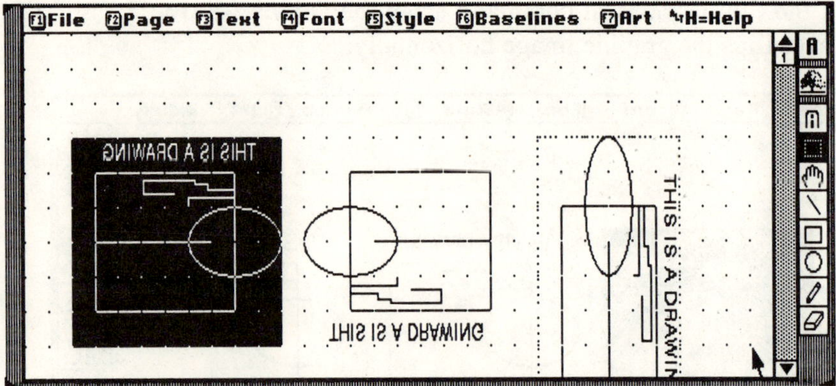

11. Press **Alt-O**. First Publisher rotates the graphic 90 degrees.

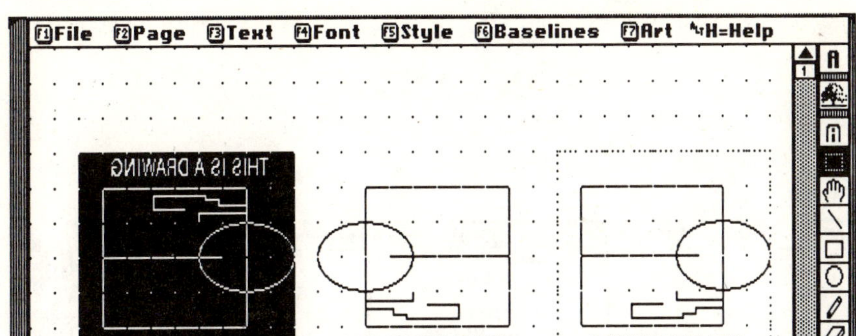

12. Press **Alt-E**, **F4**, type **EXAMPLE** as the filename, then press **F1**. First Publisher asks if you want to overwrite the existing file.
13. Press **F1**. First Publisher displays a saving file message.
14. Turn to Module 4 to continue the learning sequence.

Module 16
FONT MENU

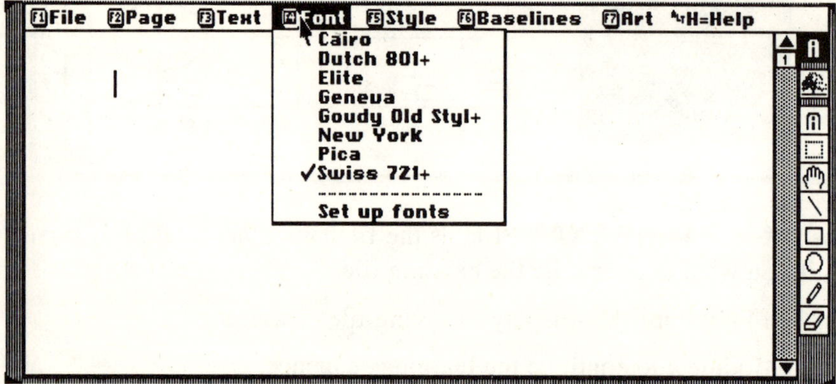

DESCRIPTION

The Font menu changes the appearance of the fonts used for display and printing in First Publisher. You access the Font menu by pressing F4 at the Main menu. First Publisher includes several fonts located in the .FNT files on your distribution disks. Appendix C of your First Publisher manual shows the general purpose fonts; Appendix E shows the laser printer specific fonts included with First Publisher.

(Version 2.0 only) First Publisher only displays the fonts located in the MASTER.FNT file on the Font menu. There are two methods of using the fonts contained in the other .FNT files. The first method is to rename the MASTER.FNT file (for example TEMP.FNT), then rename the font file you want to use MASTER.FNT. The second method is to use the fontmove utility described in Appendix G to move the desired fonts from one .FNT file to the MASTER.FNT file.

(Version 3.0 only) First Publisher includes a Set Up Fonts option located on the Font menu. This command lets you list, add, delete, or copy fonts to an .FNT file.

APPLICATIONS

Use the Font menu whenever you need to change the current font or the font used by text already contained in the document. Whenever you change the font, the page space used by the affected text will change. Also, remember that using too many different or contrasting fonts on a page detracts from rather than enhances the document.

TYPICAL OPERATION

In this example you experiment with several ways of using the Font menu to change your text. You also see the effect of making a font change on text following the change. Begin this example at the DOS prompt.

The following steps work with version 2.0 of First Publisher only:

1. Type **FP** and press **Enter**. The First Publisher Main menu appears.
2. Press **F4**. Notice that First Publisher places a check mark next to the Geneva font. This is the default font when you begin a new document (if present).
3. Press **Esc** then **Alt-G**. The Get Publication dialogue box appears.
4. Select EXAMPLE.PUB using the **Down Arrow**. Press **F10** then **F1**. First Publisher display a getting document message. The Gettysburg Address appears.
5. Press **F10** then **End**. First Publisher highlights the title.

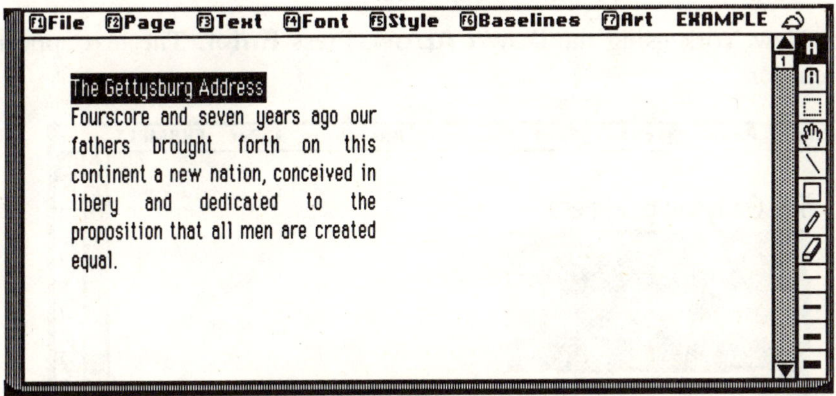

6. Press **F10** then **F4**. The Font menu appears.
7. Select Helvetica using the **Down Arrow**. Press **Enter**. The title appears in a different font.

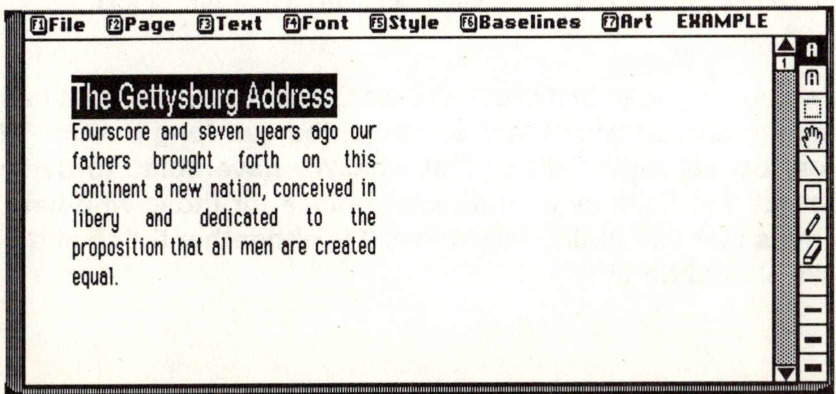

8. Press **Down Arrow** then **Home**. Press **F10** then **Ctrl-End.** First Publisher highlights the text.

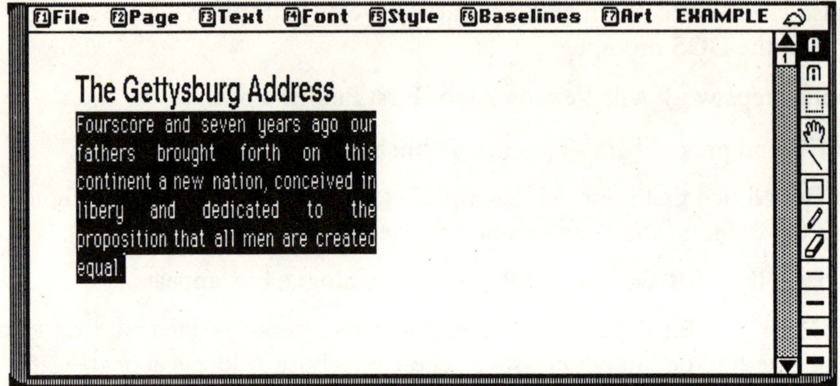

9. Press **F10** then **F4**. The Font menu appears.
10. Select New York using the **Down Arrow**. Press **Enter**. The text appears in a different font.

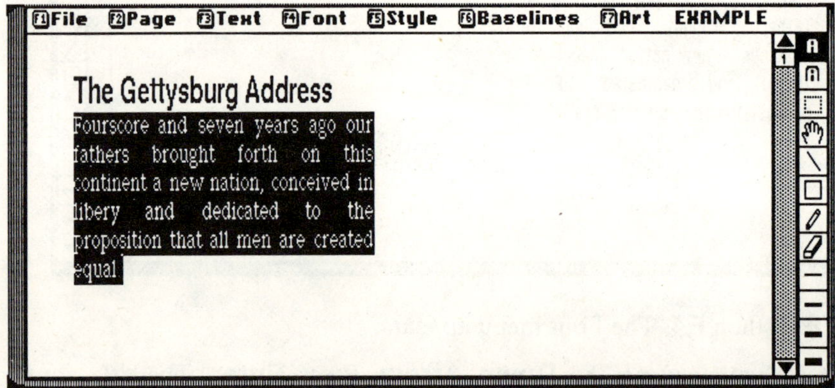

11. Press **F10** twice then **Enter**. First Publisher starts a new line of text.
12. Type the following:

    Now we are engaged in a great civil war, testing whether that nation or any nation so conceived and so dedicated can long endure. We are met on a great battlefield of that war. We have come to dedicate a portion of that field, as a final resting place for those who here gave their lives that that nation might live. It is altogether fitting and proper that we should do this.

13. Select the beginning of the paragraph using the arrow keys. Press **F10** then **Ctrl-End**. First Publisher highlights the second paragraph.

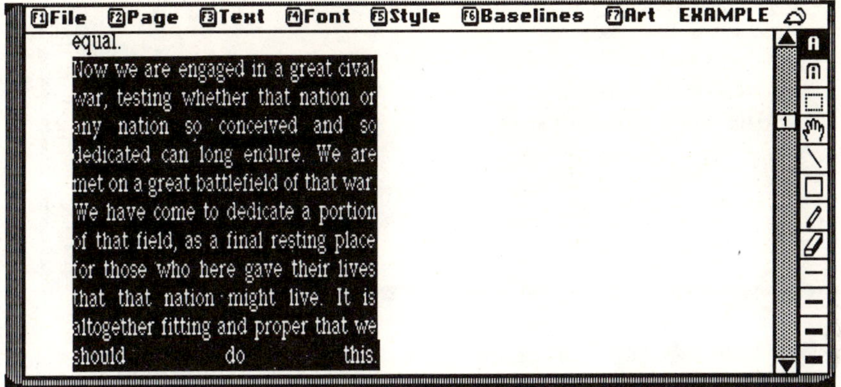

14. Press **F10** then **F4**. The Font menu appears. Notice First Publisher used the New York font instead of the Geneva font for the new text.
15. Press **Esc** then **F10** twice. First Publisher removes the highlight from the second paragraph.
16. Press **Alt-S** then **F1**. First Publisher asks if you want to replace the old copy of EXAMPLE.PUB.
17. Press **F1**. First Publisher displays a saving publication message.
18. Turn to Module 38 to continue the learning sequence.

The following steps work with version 3.0 of First Publisher only:

1. Type **FP** and press **Enter**. The First Publisher Main menu appears.
2. Press **F4**.
3. Select the Geneva font using the **Down Arrow** and pressing **Enter**.
4. Press **Alt-G**. The Get Publication dialogue box appears.
5. Select EXAMPLE.PUB using the **Down Arrow**. Press **F10** then **F1**. First Publisher displays a getting document message. The Gettysburg Address appears.
6. Press **F10** then **End**. First Publisher highlights the title.

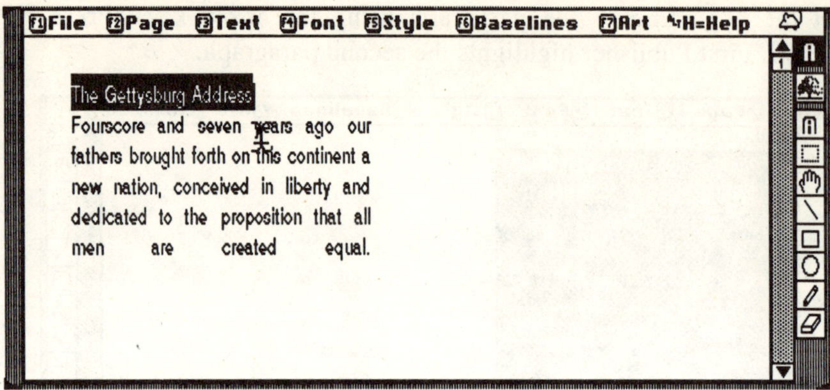

7. Press **F10** then **F4**. The Font menu appears.
8. Select Dutch 801+ using the **Down Arrow**. Press **Enter**. The title appears in a different font.

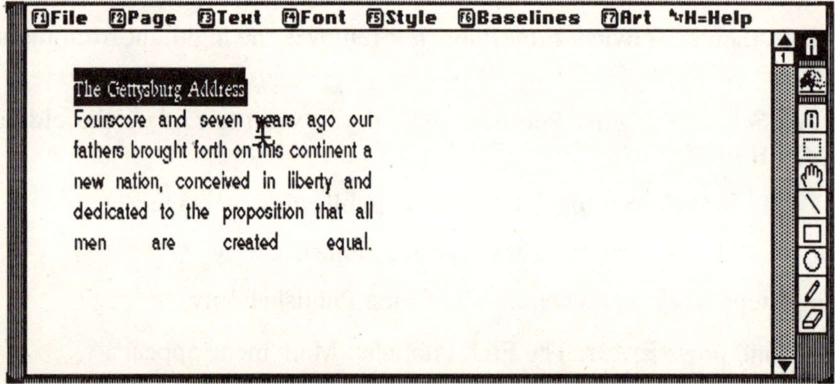

9. Press **Down Arrow** then **Home**. Press **F10** then **Ctrl-End**. First Publisher highlights the text.
10. Press **F10** then **F4**. The Font menu appears.
11. Select New York using the **Down Arrow**. Press **Enter**. The text appears in a different font.

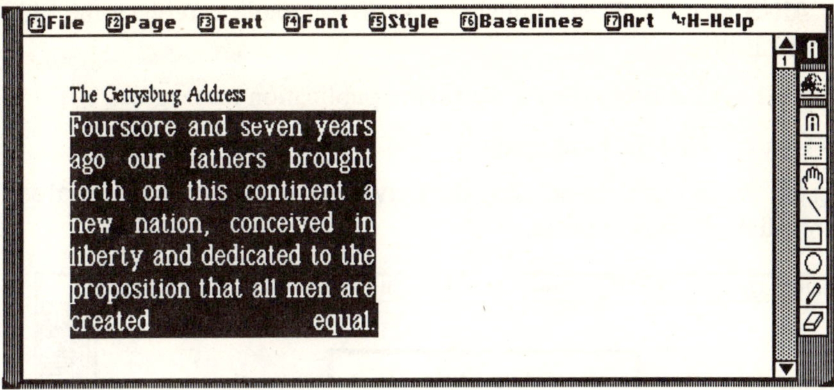

12. Press **F10** twice then **Enter**. First Publisher starts a new line of text.

13. Type the following:

    Now we are engaged in a great civil war, testing whether that nation or any nation so conceived and so dedicated can long endure. We are met on a great battlefield of that war. We have come to dedicate a portion of that field, as a final resting place for those who here gave their lives that that nation might live. It is altogether fitting and proper that we should do this.

14. Select the beginning of the paragraph using the arrow keys. Press **F10** then **Ctrl-End**. First Publisher highlights the second paragraph.

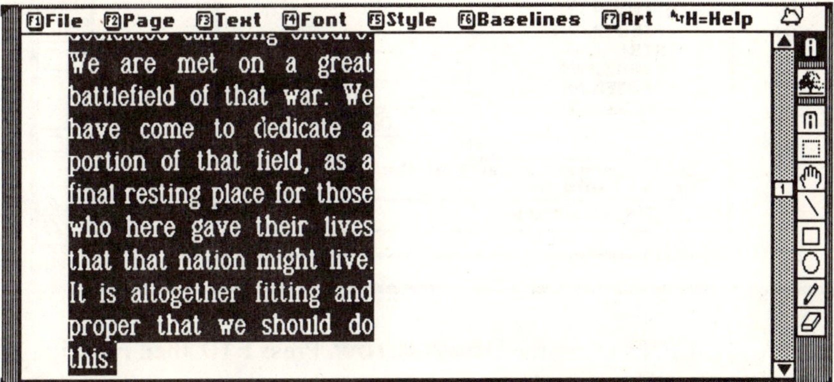

15. Press **F10** then **F4**. The Font menu appears. Notice First Publisher used the New York font instead of the Geneva font for the new text.

16. Press **Esc** then **F10** twice. First Publisher removes the highlight from the second paragraph.

17. Press **Alt-S** then **F1**. First Publisher asks if you want to replace the old copy of EXAMPLE.PUB.
18. Press **F1**. First Publisher displays a saving publication message.
19. Press **F4** to display the Font menu.
20. Select the Set up fonts option using the **Down Arrow** and pressing **Enter**. The Set up fonts dialogue box appears.

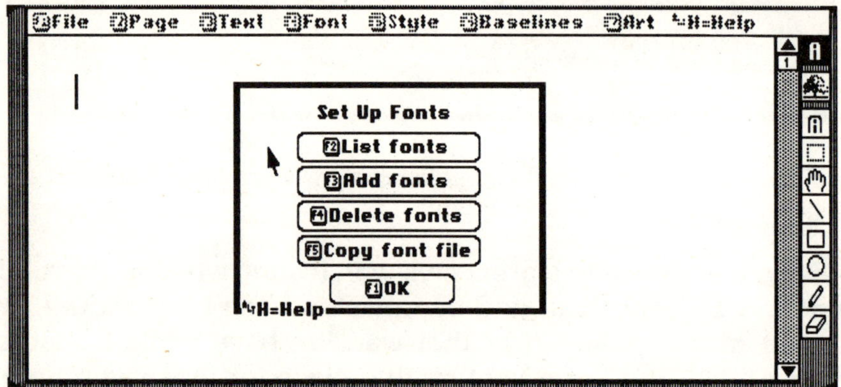

21. Press **F3** to add a new font. First Publisher displays a list of target font files.

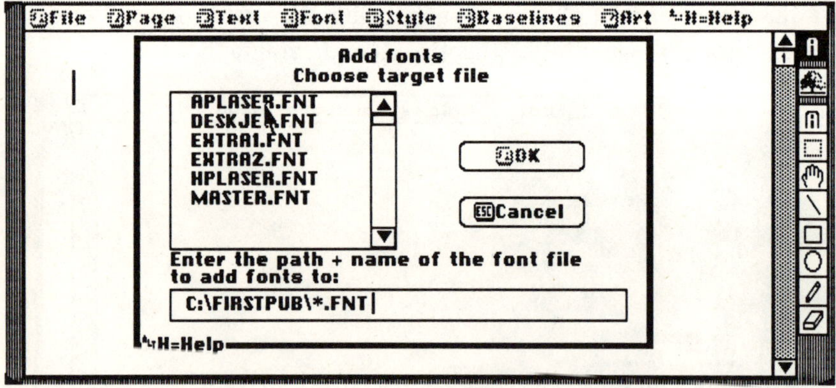

22. Select MASTER.FNT using the **Down Arrow**. Press **F10**, then **F1**. First Publisher displays a list of source font files.

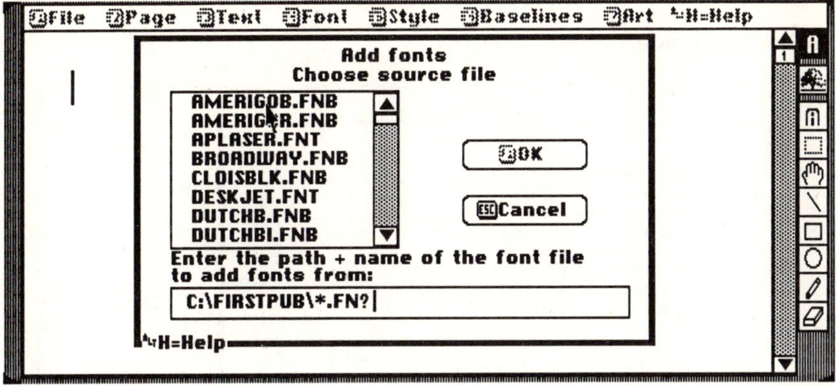

23. Select DUTCHB.FNB using the **Down Arrow**. Press **F10**, then **F1**. First Publisher displays the Add Scaled Font dialogue box.

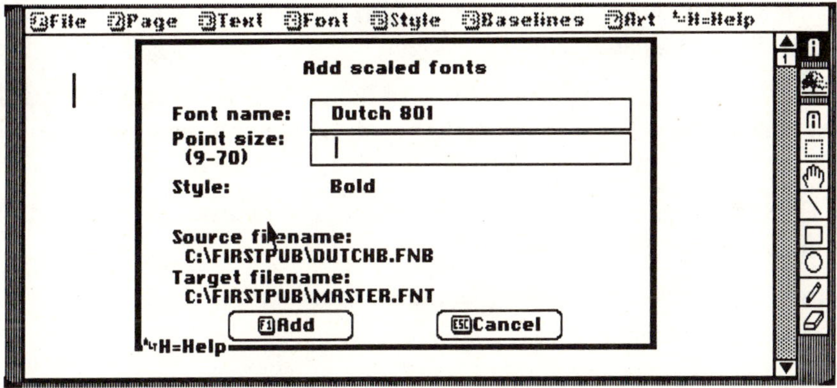

24. Type **36**, then press **F1**. First Publisher displays a series of three messages. First, reading scaled font. Second, making first publisher font. Finally, adding font.

25. Press **Esc**. First Publisher returns you to the Source Font File dialogue box. Notice that you can no longer see the .FNT files displayed.

26. Press **Backspace** to erase the B at the end of the path listing. Type **?** and press **Enter**. First Publisher displays the full list of source font files.

27. Select EXTRA1.FNT using the **Down Arrow**. Press **F10**, then **F1**. First Publisher displays the Add Fonts dialogue box.

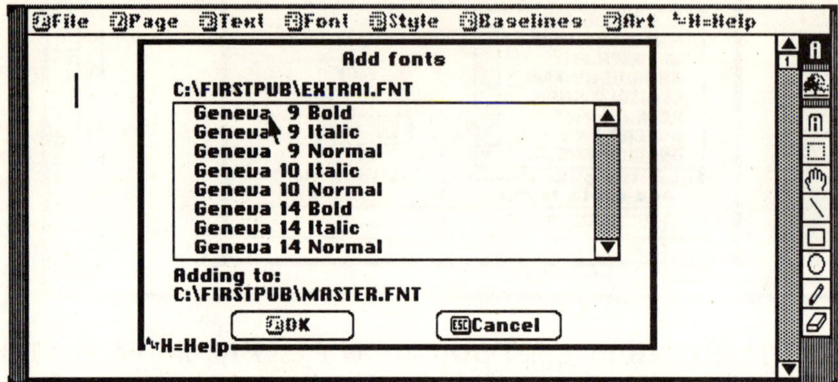

28. Select New York 14 Bold using the **Down Arrow**. Press **F10**, then **F1**. First Publisher displays an adding font message.
29. Press **Down Arrow** to select New York 14 Italic. Press **F10** then **F1**. Press **Down Arrow** to select New York 14 Normal. Press **F10**, then **F1**. First Publisher displays the adding font message for each font.
30. Press **Esc** twice, then **F1**. First Publisher displays a message about reinitializing fonts, then displays a clear edit area.
31. Turn to Module 38 to continue the learning sequence.

Module 17
GET ART

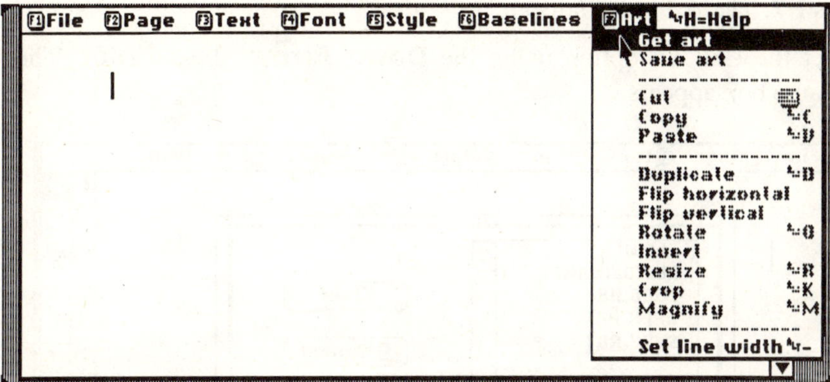

DESCRIPTION

The Get Art option of the Art menu allows you to retrieve previously saved .ART files. First Publisher provides two methods of producing art files. The first method is to convert graphic files produced by other programs (see Module 31). The second method is to use screen shots obtained using the Snap2art utility program discussed in Appendix H. The Get Art dialogue box contains the file selection window, path entry, and command buttons contained in all the file-related dialogue boxes discussed so far.

(Version 3.0 only) The Get Art option of the Art menu lets you retrieve both .ART and .MAC graphic files.

APPLICATIONS

You use the Get Art option to retrieve previously saved art for use in documents. Saving graphic images in .ART format allows you to create several versions of the same graphic on disk without disturbing the original. The Get Art option will not read graphic images created using other programs.

(Version 2.0 only) Use the Get Graphics option discussed in Module 18 to read graphic images created using other programs.

TYPICAL OPERATION

In this example you learn how to retrieve an art image using the Get Art option. This example also shows how to move the art image to the desired position on the document after retrieving it. Begin this example at the First Publisher Main menu with nothing loaded. (To clear the display exit and reenter First Publisher.)

The following steps work with version 2.0 of First Publisher only:

1. Press **F7**. The Art menu appears.
2. Select the Get Art option using the **Down Arrow**. Press **Enter**. The Get Art dialogue box appears.

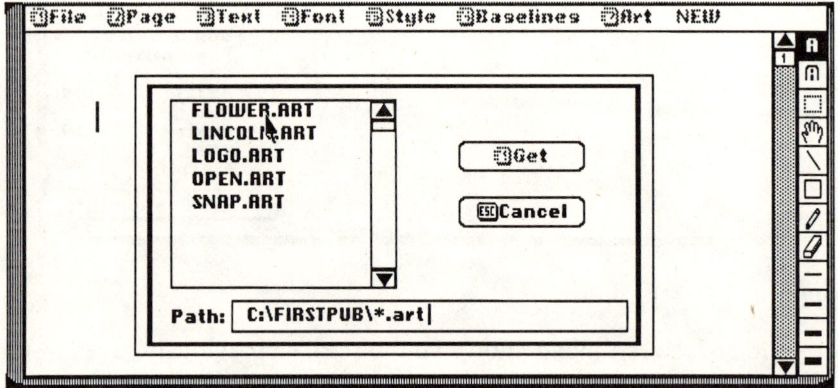

3. Select LINCOLN.ART using the **Down Arrow**. Press **F10** then **F1**. The Hand Tool appears.

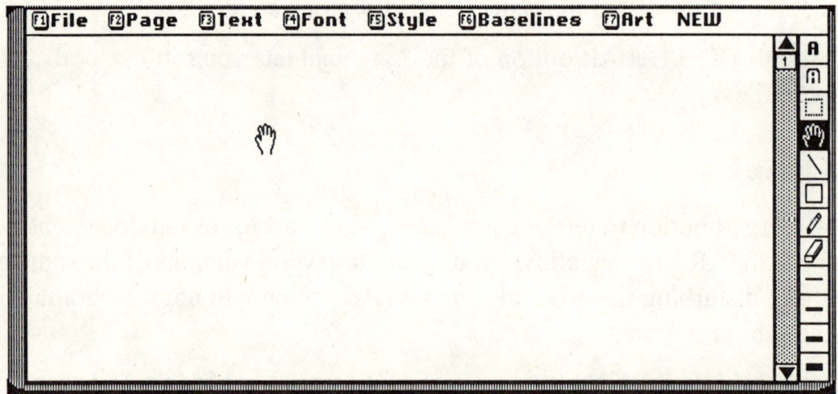

4. Press **F10**. The previously saved silhouette of Lincoln appears.

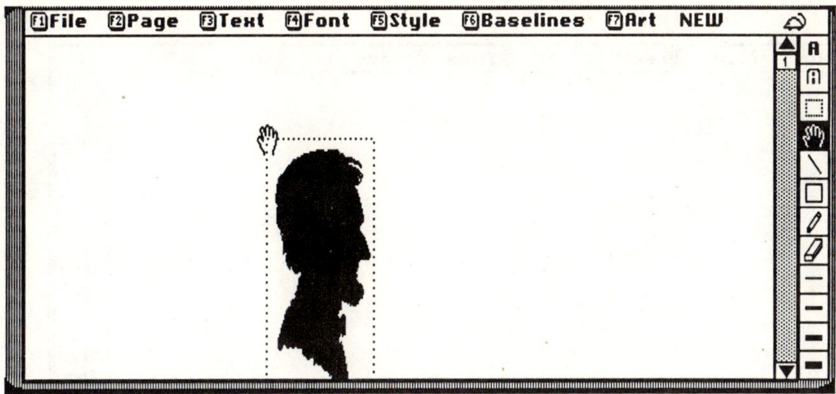

5. Position the art using the arrow keys. Press **Shift** with the arrow keys to move the art in larger increments. First Publisher places the art in the desired position.
6. Press **F10**. Press the arrow keys. First Publisher does not move the art.
7. Turn to Module 26 to continue the learning sequence.

The following steps work with version 3.0 of First Publisher only:

1. Press **F7**. The Art menu appears.
2. Select the Get Art option using the **Down Arrow**. Press **Enter**. The Get Art dialogue box appears.

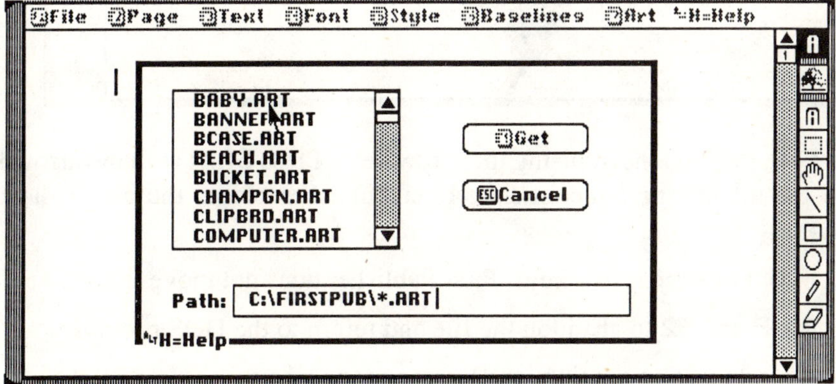

3. Select LINCOLN.ART using the **Down Arrow**. Press **F10** then **F1**. The Hand Tool appears.

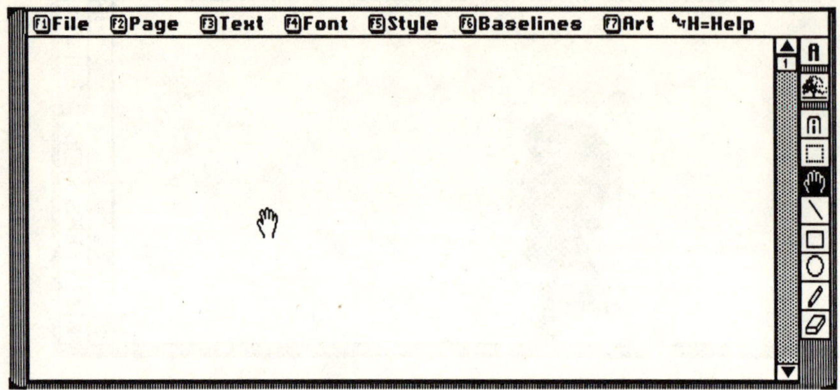

4. Press **F10** twice. The previously saved silhouette of Lincoln appears.

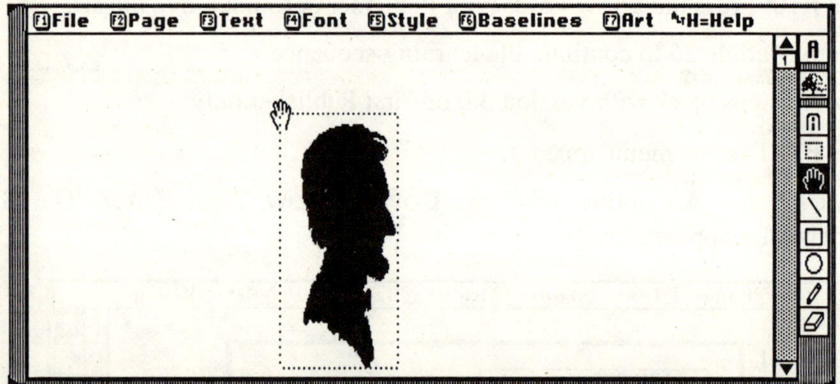

5. Press **F10**. Position the art using the arrow keys. Press **Shift** with the arrow keys to move the art in larger increments. First Publisher places the art in the desired position.
6. Press **F10**. Press the arrow keys. First Publisher does not move the art.
7. Press **Alt-E** and **F2** to abandon the file and return to the DOS prompt.
8. Turn to Module 26 to continue the learning sequence.

Module 18
GET GRAPHICS

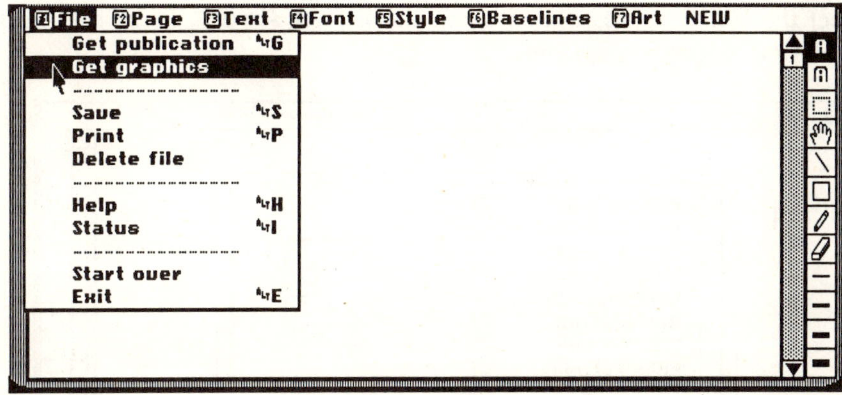

DESCRIPTION

The Get Graphics option of the File menu allows you to import graphic images into First Publisher. This means that you can use images created by spreadsheets, paint programs, and any other program producing images saved in a format acceptable to First Publisher. Appendix J tells you how to import graphics from the Macintosh as well.

NOTE

> The Get Graphics command does not appear in version 3.0 or greater of PFS: First Publisher. Instead, use the Get Art command (also see Module 17).

APPLICATIONS

Use the Get Graphics option when you want to use graphics produced by other programs in your document. First Publisher allows you to manipulate the image and save it in a First Publisher specific .ART file or export it as a .MAC file.

TYPICAL OPERATION

This example shows you how to import graphic images into First Publisher using the Get Graphics option. Begin this example at the First Publisher Main menu with nothing loaded.

The following steps work with version 2.0 of First Publisher only:

1. Press **F1**. The File menu appears.
2. Select the Get Graphics option using the **Down Arrow**. Press **Enter**. The Get Graphics dialogue box appears.

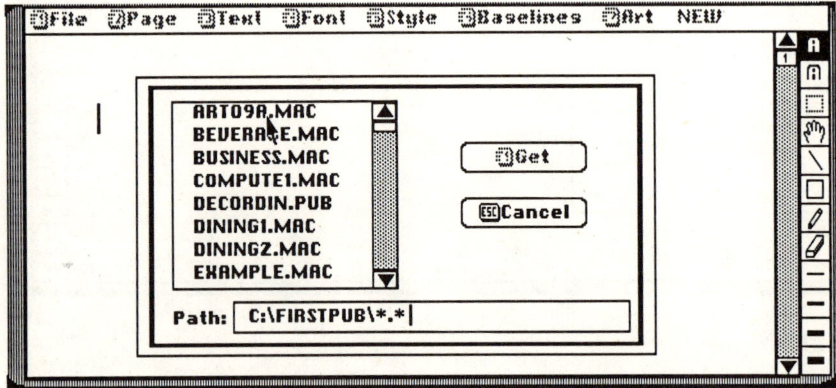

3. Press **Backspace** once then type **MAC**. Press **Enter**. First Publisher displays only files with a .MAC extension.
4. Select HOLIDAYS.MAC using the **Down Arrow**. Press **F10** then **F1**. First Publisher displays a getting document message, then a formatting page message. Notice First Publisher automatically highlights the Selection Tool.

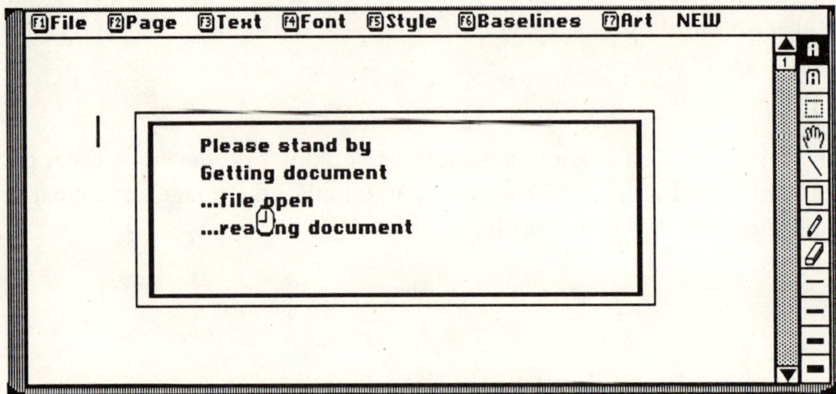

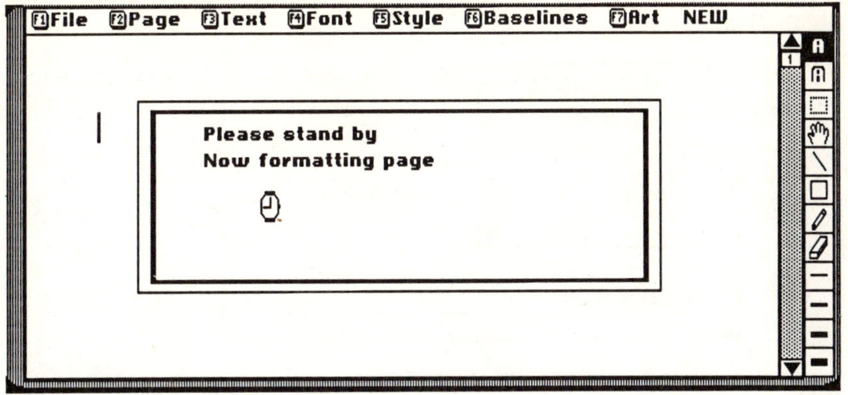

5. Turn to Module 31 to continue the learning sequence.

The following steps work with version 3.0 of First Publisher only:

1. Press **F7**. The Art menu appears.
2. Select the Get Art option using the **Down Arrow**. Press **Enter**. The Get Art dialogue box appears.

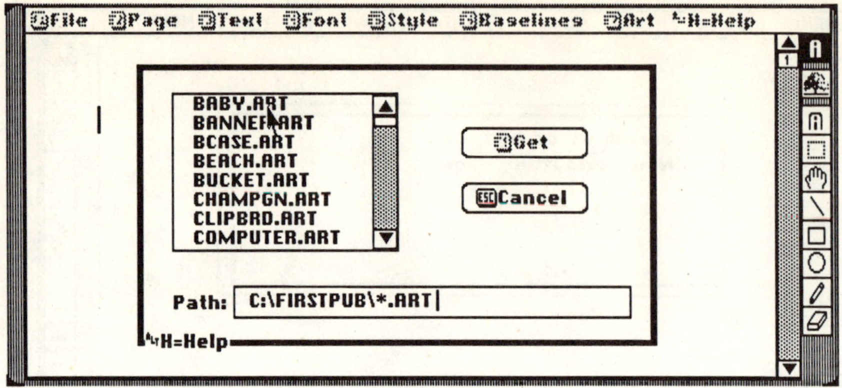

3. Press **Backspace** three times to remove the ART extension. Type **MAC** and press **Enter**.
4. Select HOLIDAYS.MAC using the **Down Arrow**. Press **F10** then **F1**. First Publisher displays the message, "The MAC file may overwrite any text or art on this page. Do you want to get the file?"

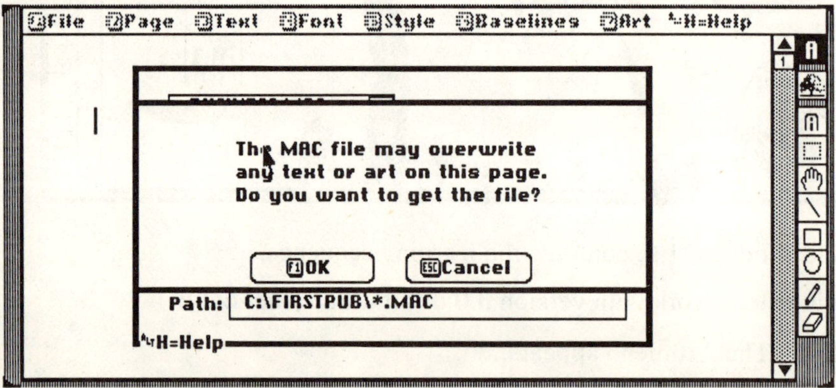

5. Press **F1** and press **F10** twice.

6. Turn to Module 31 to continue the learning sequence.

Module 19
GET PUBLICATION

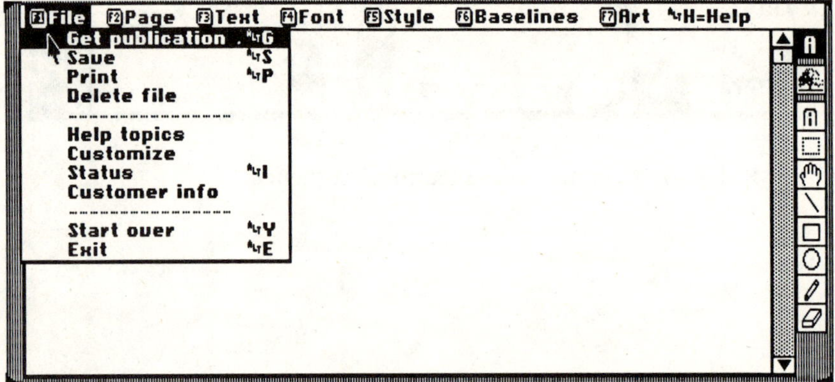

DESCRIPTION

The Get Publication option of the File menu allows you to retrieve previously saved documents. You can also access the Get Publication option using Alt-G. The Get Publication menu shows a listing of publications on the selected drive and path. The path entry on the menu allows you to change the path and drive information. Use this option to retrieve publications only; other options allow you to retrieve other document types.

APPLICATIONS

You use the Get Publication option to retrieve First Publisher documents located in any directory on any drive. After you indicate which file to retrieve, First Publisher opens the file and sets the default parameters to match those in the document. If you select a directory without any First Publisher documents, it display an error message in place of filenames.

TYPICAL OPERATION

This example shows you how to use the Get Publication option to retrieve a First Publisher document. It also shows the messages produced in various situations. Begin this example at the DOS prompt.

1. Type **FP** and press **Enter**. The First Publisher Main menu appears.
2. Press **F1**. The File menu appears.
3. Select the Get Publication option using the **Down Arrow** and pressing **Enter**. The Get Publication dialogue box appears.
4. Select EXAMPLE.PUB using the **Down Arrow** and press **F10**. First Publisher highlights the EXAMPLE.PUB entry.

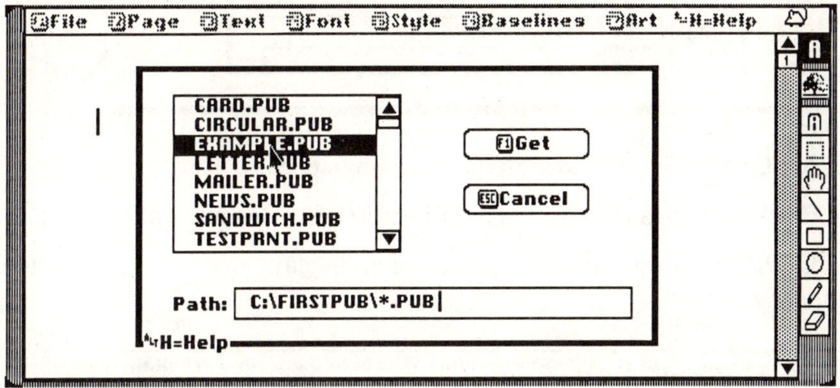

5. Press **F1**. First Publisher displays the message “Getting document” first, then “Now formatting page.”

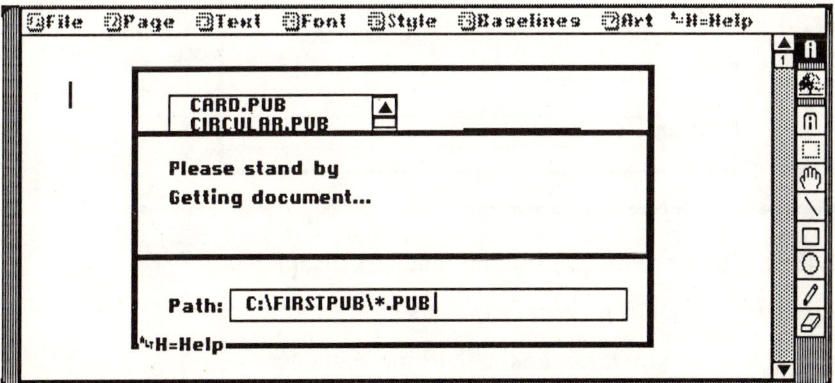

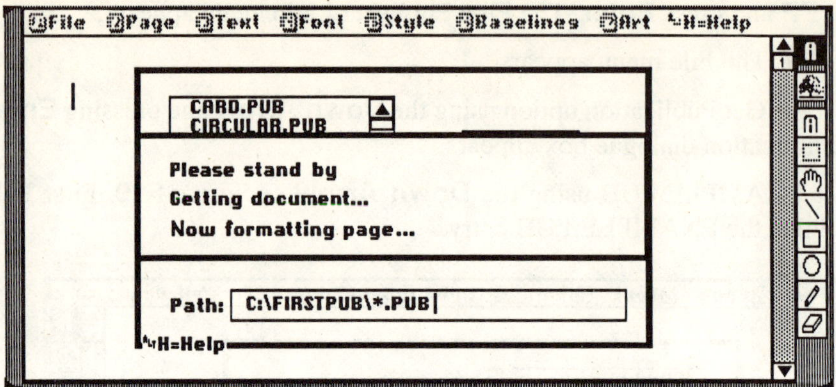

6. Press **Alt-G**. The Get Publication dialogue box appears.
7. Press **Backspace** to remove the old directory and filename entry.
8. Type ***.PUB** and press **Enter**. First Publisher displays an error message in place of the filenames.

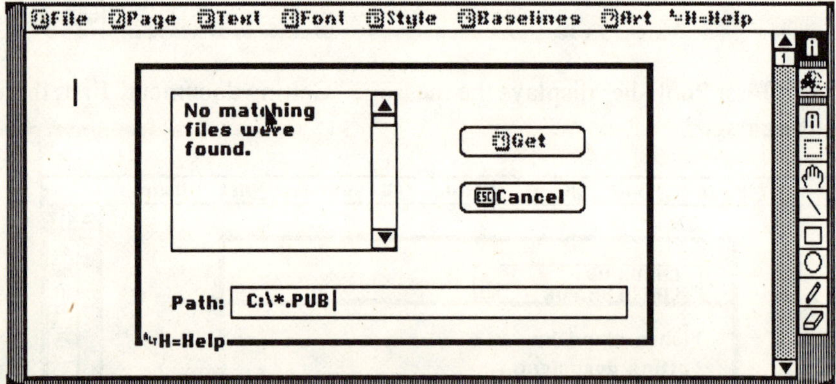

9. Press **Esc**. The Get Publication dialogue box disappears.
10. Press **Alt-E**. The DOS prompt reappears.
11. Turn to Module 37 to continue the learning sequence.

Module 20
GET TEXT

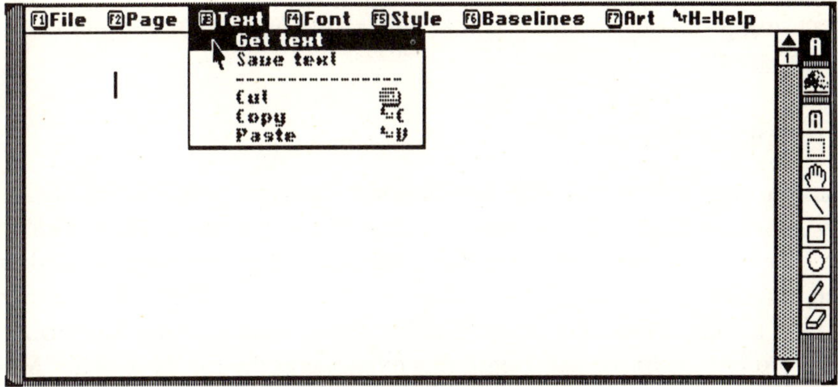

DESCRIPTION

The Get Text option of the Text menu (F3) allows you to convert text from other programs into First Publisher format. This means that you can use your favorite word processing program to create and edit the text, then bring it into First Publisher for final formatting. Performing desktop publishing tasks this way is more efficient than using First Publisher as a word processing program.

Besides several standard word processing programs, First Publisher also allows you to import ASCII text files. Even if your word processor or other application (spreadsheet, database management system, etc.) is not directly supported, most applications allow you to save documents as unformatted text. Since you use First Publisher to format the document, the loss of formatting information is an inconvenience at most.

The Get Text dialogue box contains several entries. These include the search parameters, document path, and document listing. By changing the path, you can find files in the word processing directory of your hard disk. By changing the search parameters, you can reduce the number of files you need to search through looking for a document. The document listing provides an easy-to-use method of telling First Publisher which document to import.

When you try to import a document using a text conversion option that doesn't match the format of the document, First Publisher informs you of the problem by displaying an error message. Rather than import garbage into your publication, First Publisher then returns you to the display without performing the import.

APPLICATIONS

Use the Get Text option to import text from another application program into First Publisher. This allows you to create and edit your document using your favorite word processor or other application. First Publisher not only supports the most commonly used word processing programs, but ASCII text as well, allowing you to import documents from most programs.

TYPICAL OPERATION

In this example you perform two different imports. The first import is the ASCII file you previously saved in Module 32. The example shows how text appears after First Publisher imports it. The second import uses the same file, but attempts to use a word processor conversion instead of the straight ASCII import. The example shows the conversion message, then the error message when First Publisher discovers the file format doesn't match the word processor format. Begin this example at the First Publisher Main menu with nothing loaded. (To clear the screen settings exit First Publisher and reenter.)

1. Press **F3**. The Text menu appears.
2. Select the Get Text option using the **Down Arrow** and pressing **Enter**. The Get Text dialogue box appears.

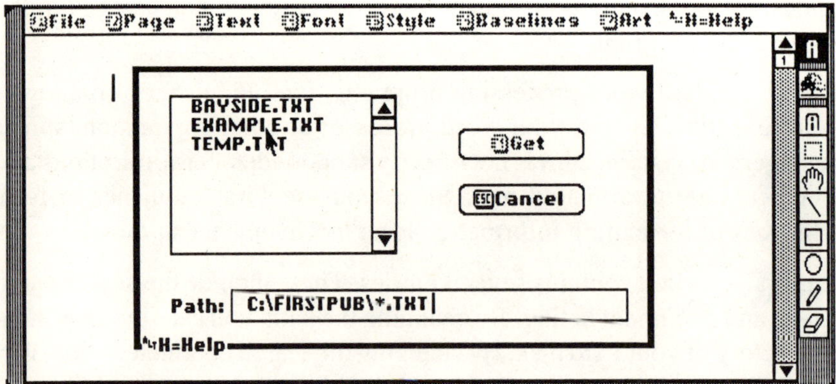

3. Select EXAMPLE.TXT using the **Down Arrow**. Press **F10** then **F1**. The Text Type dialogue box appears.

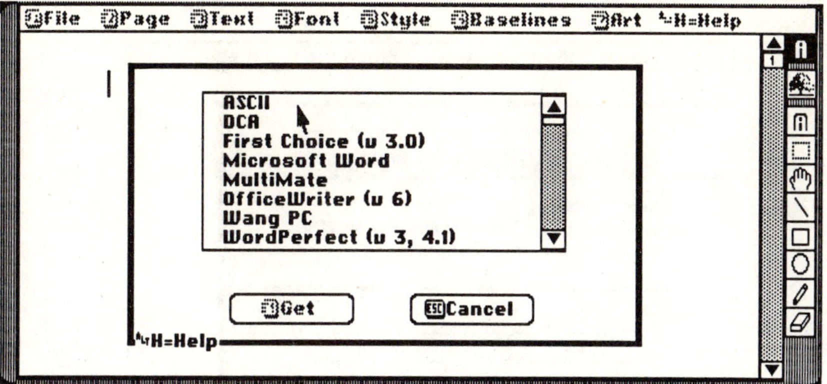

4. Select ASCII using the **Down Arrow**. Press **F10** then **F1**. The Gettysburg Address appears.

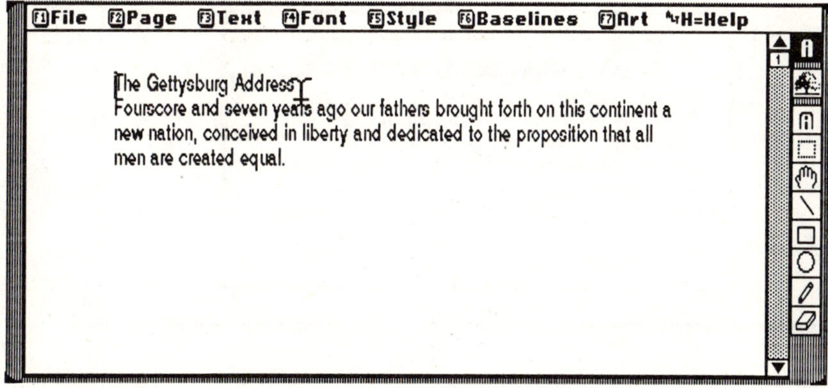

5. Press **F3**. The Text menu appears.
6. Select the Get Text option using the **Down Arrow** and pressing **Enter**. The Get Text dialogue box appears.
7. Select EXAMPLE.TXT using the **Down Arrow**. Press **F10** then **F1**. The Text Type dialogue box appears.

8. Select DCA using the **Down Arrow**. Press **F10** then **F1**. First Publisher displays a converting document message, then an error message. Notice no change occurs on the display (First Publisher does not perform the conversion).

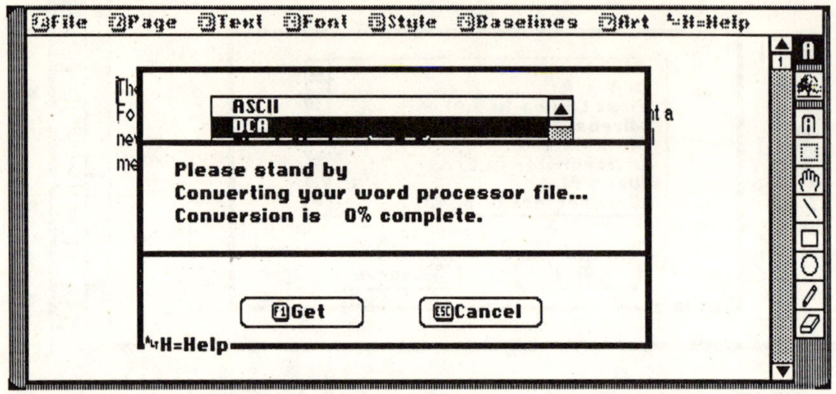

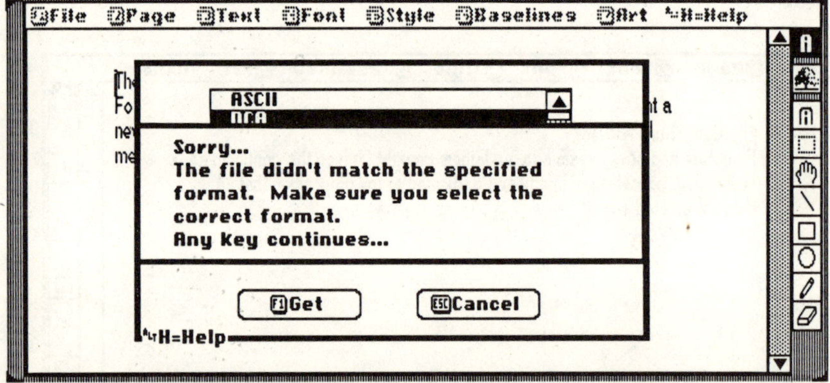

9. Press **Esc** to Cancel.
10. Press **Alt-E** and press **F2** to abandon the changes and return to the DOS prompt.
11. Turn to Module 8 to continue the learning sequence.

Module 21
HELP, HELP TOPICS, CUSTOMER INFO

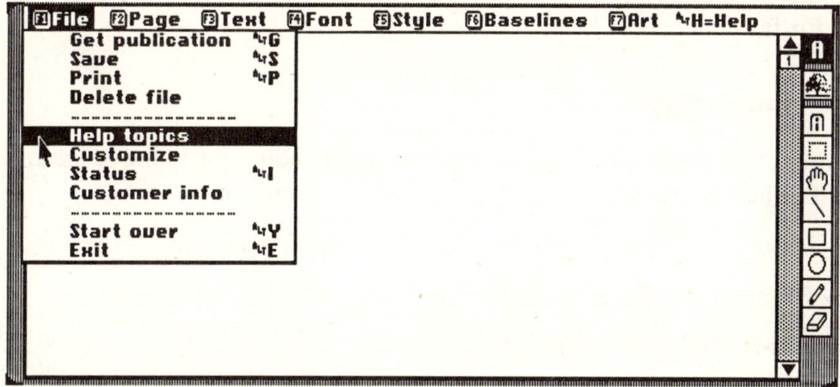

DESCRIPTION

The Help option gives you information about the program without using the manual (in some cases). You access Help using the File menu (F1) or by pressing Alt-H. Help provides a menu so you can select the specific information you're looking for.

You can exit Help at any time by pressing Esc. First Publisher always returns you to the Main menu. With version 2.0 of First Publisher, you cannot invoke help within any menu except the File menu.

With version 3.0 of First Publisher, you can invoke help within any menu, including the File menu. Pressing Alt-H provides context-sensitive help.

(Version 3.0 only) The Help Topics command displays a list of topics for using First Publisher. Choosing a topic displays instructions that tell you what to do next.

(Version 3.0 only) The Customer Info command displays the same information as the Help Topics command. The only difference is that the Customer Information command first displays a message about registering, upgrading, and obtaining product support. Pressing F1 after this message appears will display the same dialogue box as the Help Topics command.

APPLICATIONS

The Help option provides quick reference information on screen if you forget which option performs a particular task, or how to use an option. You can display Help rather than refer to the manual every time you get stuck or want to refresh your memory.

For additional help on different topics, such as printing or setting up your printer, use the Help Topics command. Since the Customer Info command only differs from the Help Topics command by displaying a Customer Information message, use the Help Topics command for faster access to help.

TYPICAL OPERATION

In this example, the Help option displays information about how to move around in First Publisher. Begin this example at the First Publisher Main menu.

The following steps work with version 2.0 of First Publisher only:

1. Type **FP** and press **Enter**. The First Publisher Main menu appears.
2. Press **Alt-H**. The Help menu appears.

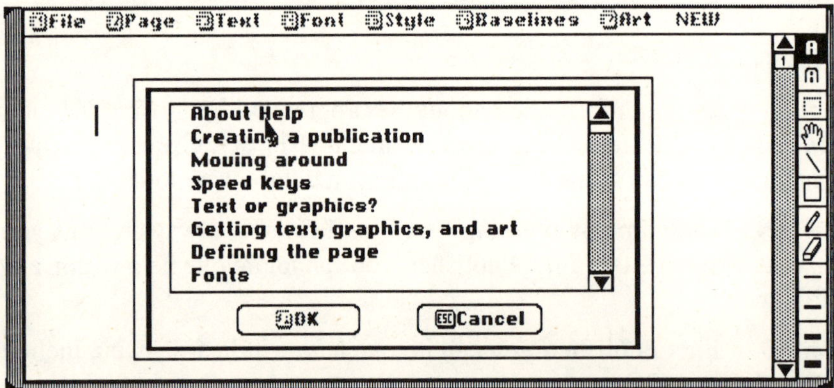

3. Select the Moving Around option using the **Down Arrow**. Press **F10** then **F1**. The Help dialogue box appears.

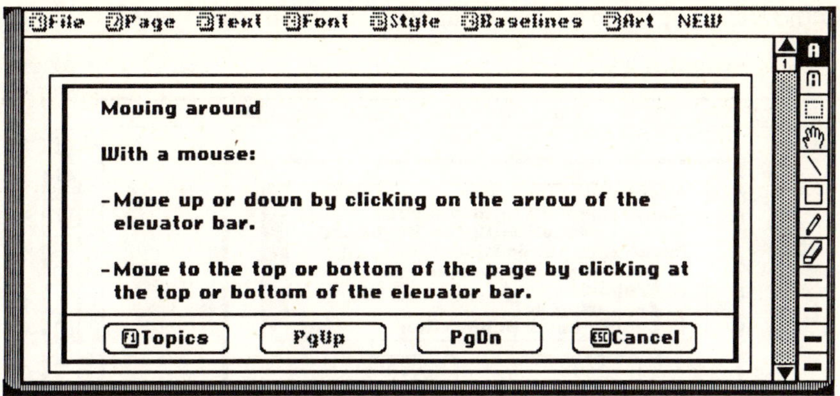

4. Press **PgDn**. Notice the dialogue box advances.

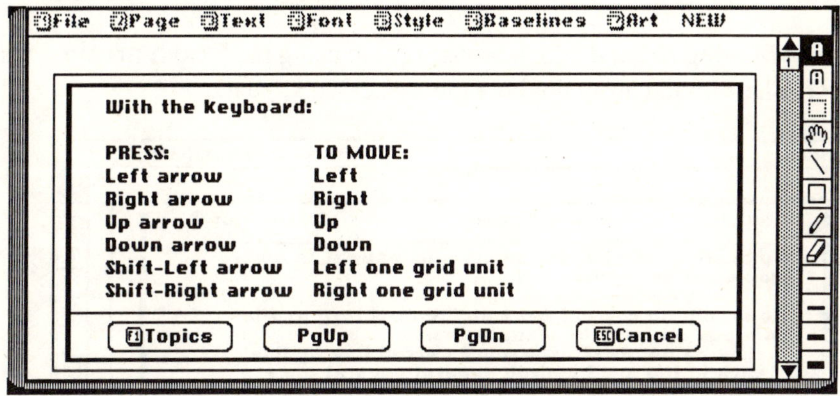

5. Press **F1**. Notice the Help menu reappears.
6. Press **Esc**. Notice the Help menu disappears and the edit area is clear.
7. Press **Alt-E**. The DOS prompt reappears.
8. Turn to Module 30 to continue the learning sequence.

The following steps work with version 3.0 of First Publisher only:

1. Type **FP** and press **Enter**. The First Publisher Main menu appears.
2. Press **F1**. The File menu appears.

3. Select the Help Topics command using the **Down Arrow**. Press **Enter**. The Help Topics dialogue box appears.

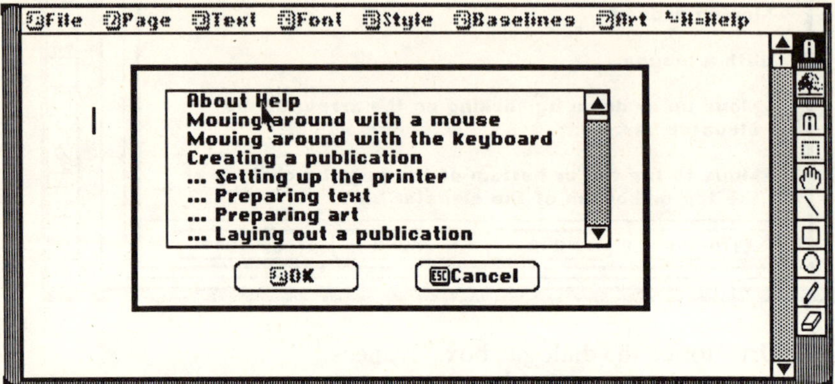

4. Select the Moving Around with a Mouse option using the **Down arrow**. Press **F10** then **F1**. The Moving around with a mouse screen appears.

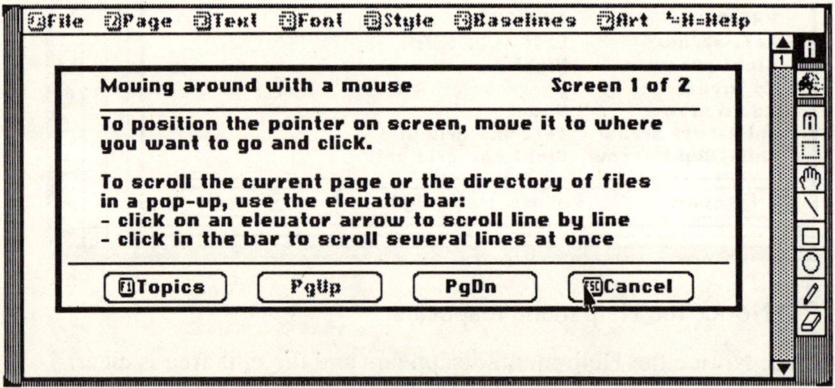

5. Press **PgDn**. Notice that the dialogue box advances.

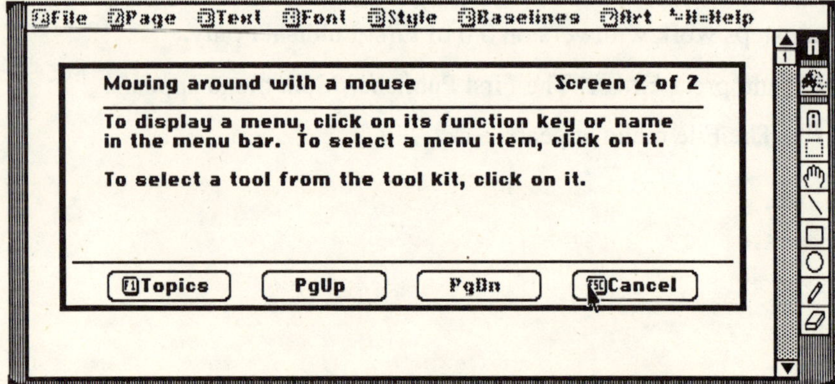

6. Press **F1**. Notice the Help Topics dialogue box reappears.
7. Press **Esc**. Notice the Help Topics dialogue box disappears and the edit area is clear.
8. Press **F1**. The File menu appears.
9. Press **Alt-H**. Notice that a Using the menus screen appears.

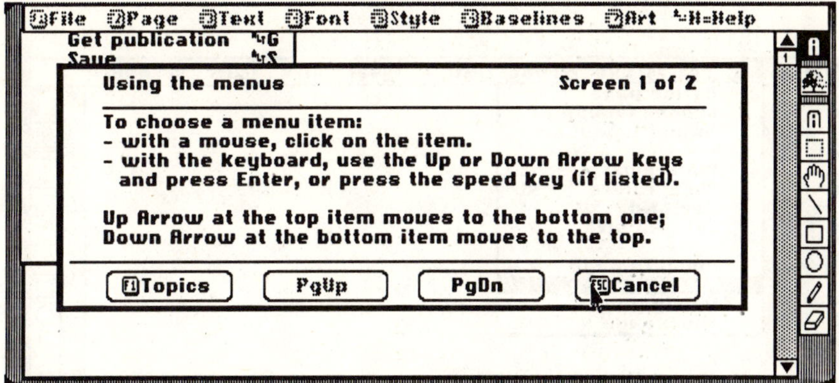

10. Press **Esc**. The Using the menus screen disappears.
11. Select the Customer Info option using the **Down Arrow**. Press **Enter**. A Customer information screen appears.

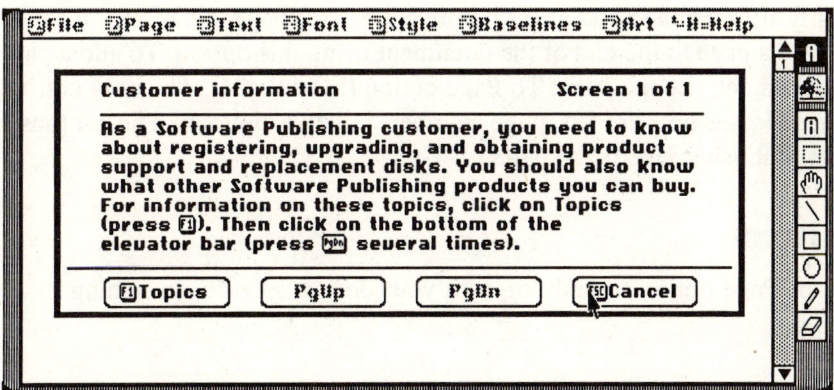

12. Press **F1**. Notice the same Help Topics dialogue box appears as seen in step 3.
13. Press **Esc**. Notice the Help Topics dialogue box disappears.
14. Press **Alt-E**. The DOS prompt reappears.
15. Turn to Module 30 to continue the learning sequence.

Module 22
INSERT PAGE

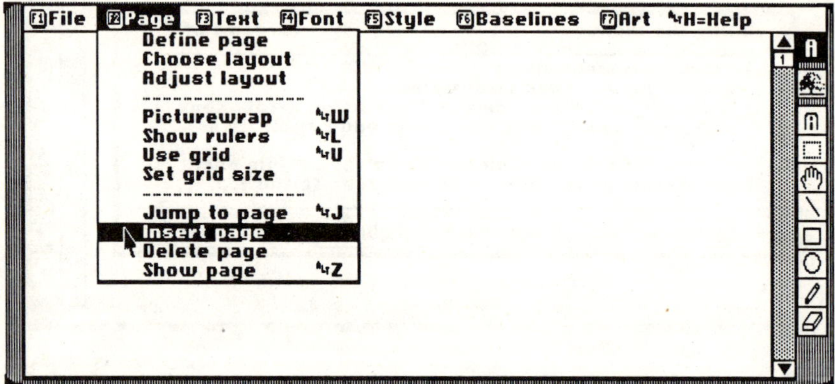

DESCRIPTION

The Insert Page option of the Page menu allows you to add a page to your document. First Publisher only allows you to add pages before a specified page, not after. This means that you cannot add a page to the end of the document using this option. To add a page to the end of the document, use the Jump To Page option (Module 24). The only entries on the Insert Page dialogue box are the page number and two buttons. The buttons control whether First Publisher inserts the page.

APPLICATIONS

Use the Insert Page option to add pages to your document prior to adding new text or graphics.

TYPICAL OPERATION

This example shows you how to use the Insert Page option. Begin this example at the First Publisher Main menu with EXAMPLE.PUB loaded.

1. Press **F2**. The Page menu appears.
2. Select the Insert Page option using the **Down Arrow**. Press **Enter**. The Insert Page dialogue box appears.

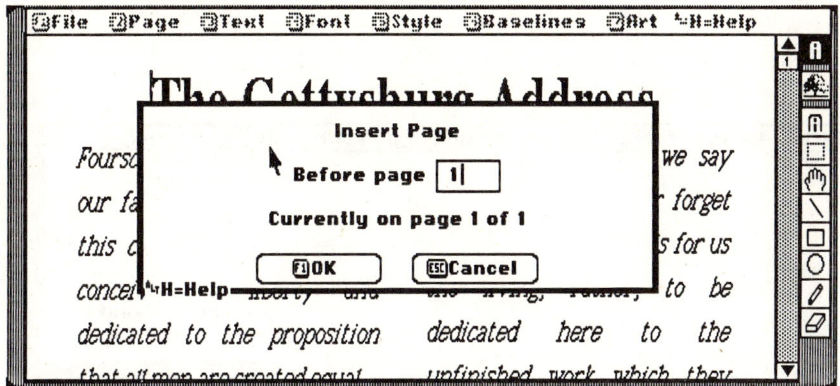

3. Type **2** then press **F1**. First Publisher displays an error message.

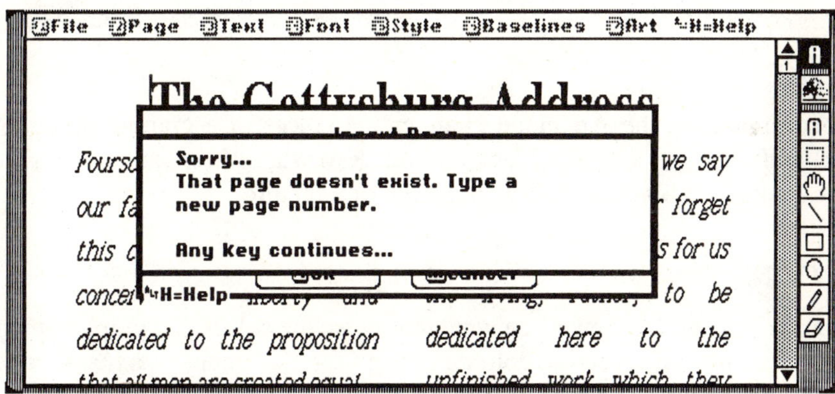

4. Press **Enter**. The error message disappears.
5. Type **1** then press **F1**. A blank page appears.
6. Press **Alt-E** the **F1**. First Publisher asks if you want to overwrite the old copy of EXAMPLE.PUB.
7. Press **F1**. First Publisher displays a saving file message.
8. Turn to Module 24 to continue the learning sequence.

Module 23
INVERT

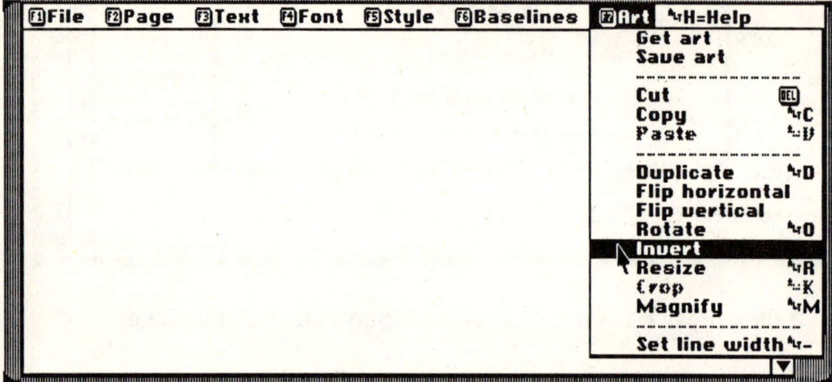

DESCRIPTION

The Invert command on the Art menu changes the colors of a graphic image to their opposite value. It changes white to black and black to white. In most cases, this causes the image to look like a black and white negative of a picture.

APPLICATIONS

Use the Invert command whenever you want to reverse the colors of a graphic image. For example, if you wanted to invert the colors in a logo for placement on a black rather than white background, the Invert command would do it for you quickly and easily.

TYPICAL OPERATION

In this example you learn how to use the Invert command to quickly change the colors in a graphic image. Begin this example at the First Publisher Main menu with EXAMPLE.MAC loaded.

1. Press **Alt-U**. The grid appears.
2. Activate the Selection Tool. Position the graphics arrow above and to the left of the first graphics image using the arrow keys. Press **F10.** Surround the graphic image using the arrow keys. Press **F10**. First Publisher selects the first graphic image.
3. Press **F7**. The Art menu appears.
4. Select the Invert command using the **Down Arrow**. Press **Enter**. First Publisher changes all white dots to black and all black dots to white. Notice the change affects only the specified area.

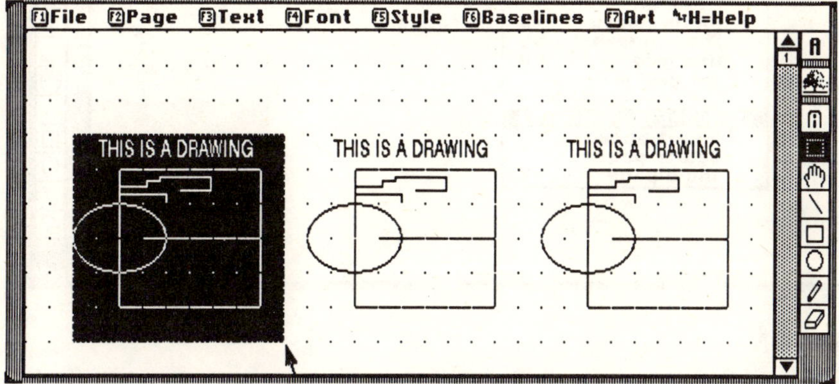

5. Press **Alt-S**, **F4**, type **EXAMPLE** as the filename, then press **F1**. First Publisher asks if you want to overwrite the existing file.
6. Press **F1**. First Publisher displays a saving file message.
7. Turn to Module 15 to continue the learning sequence.

Module 24
JUMP TO PAGE

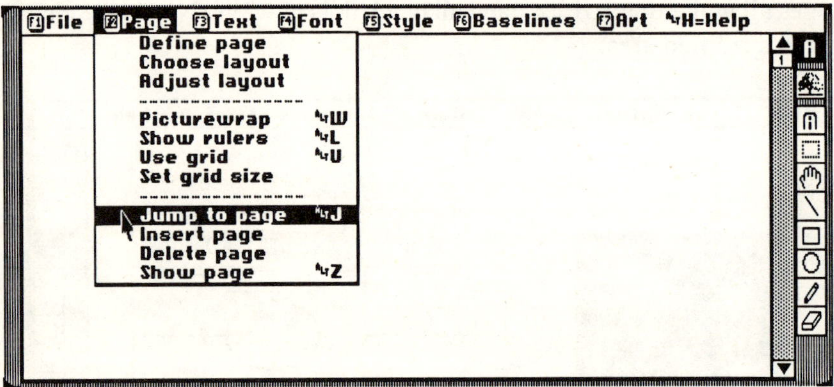

DESCRIPTION

The Jump To Page option on the Page menu provides two functions. The first function allows you to move from one page to another. You can also jump from page to page by pressing Shift-+ (+ on the numeric keypad) to advance one page and Shift- – (– on numeric keypad) to go back one page. The second function adds a new page to the end of a document. To add a page, enter a number larger than the current number of pages. First Publisher automatically adds one page with the next available number (no matter what page number you enter above the maximum). You can access the Jump To Page option using the Page menu or by pressing Alt-J. The Jump To Page dialogue box provides an indication of the current page and the total number of pages. It also contains an entry for the jump to page and two buttons. The buttons control whether or not First Publisher executes the command.

APPLICATIONS

Use the Jump To Page option whenever you need to change page numbers. First Publisher uses a number on the elevator to show the current page.

A second purpose for the Jump To Page option is adding pages to the end of the document. For example, if you import a document too large to fit on a single page, add a blank one to accept the excess. Or, if you decide to add more text to the end of a document, use the Jump To Page option to add a blank page to accept the input.

TYPICAL OPERATION

In this example you use the Jump To Page option to jump from one page to another. You also add a blank page to the end of a document. This example begins at the First Publisher Main menu with EXAMPLE.PUB loaded.

1. Press **F2**. The Page menu appears.
2. Select the Jump To Page option using the **Down Arrow**. Press **Enter**. The Jump To Page dialogue box appears.

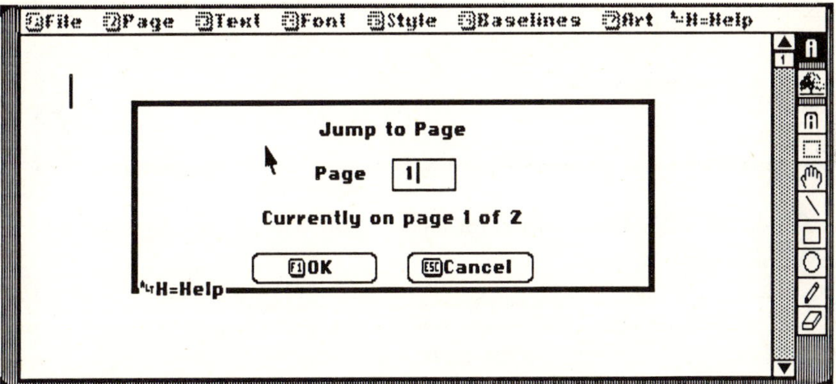

3. Type **2** then press **F1**. The Gettysburg Address appears. Notice the page indicator changes to 2.

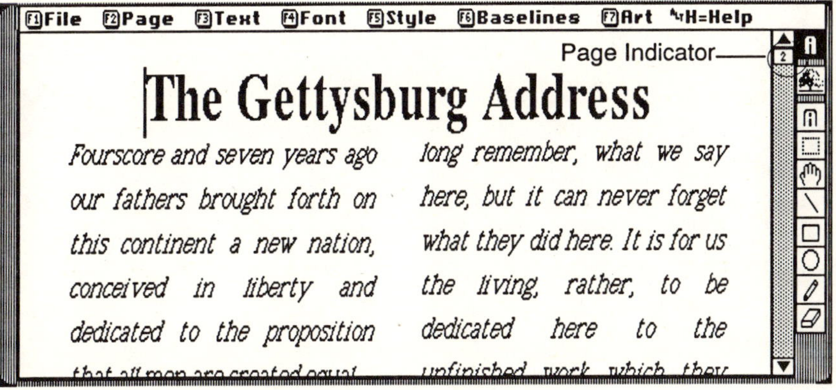

4. Press **Alt-J**. The Jump To Page dialogue box appears.

5. Type **4** then press **F1**. First Publisher inserts a blank page at the end of the document. Notice the page indicator changes to 3.

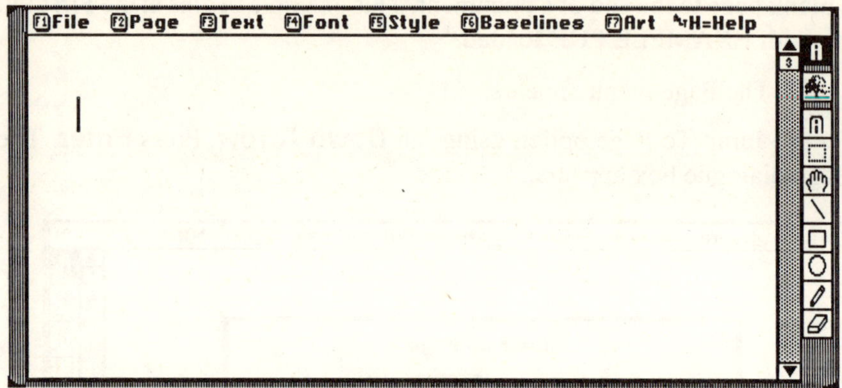

6. Press **Alt-E** then **F1**. First Publisher asks if you want to overwrite the old copy of EXAMPLE.PUB.
7. Press **F1**. First Publisher displays a saving file message.
8. Turn to Module 11 to continue the learning sequence.

Module 25
MAGNIFY, CROP

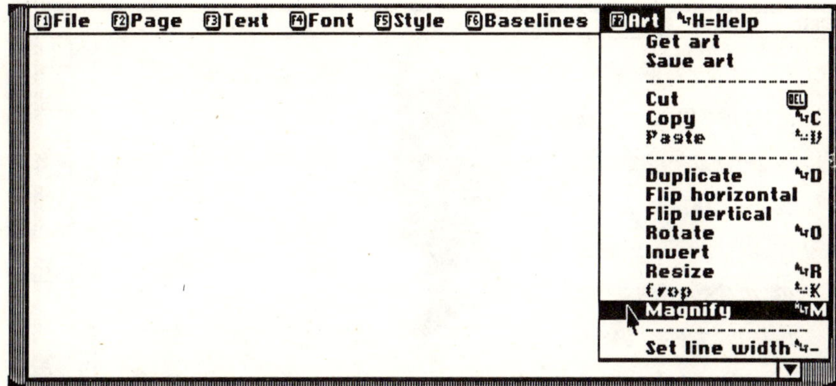

DESCRIPTION

The Magnify command on the Art menu provides an enlarged view of a graphic image. You can access the Magnify command using the Art menu or by pressing Alt-M. First Publisher allows access to the Magnify command only when you select a graphic image for editing using the Selection Tool.

The Crop command on the Art menu lets you shrink or expand the white space surrounding art. As a shortcut, you can press Alt-K to choose the Crop command.

APPLICATIONS

Use the Magnify command whenever you want to perform bit editing of a graphic image. This allows you to modify or enhance a graphic image before printing. See Appendix F for an overview of bit editing techniques.

Use the Crop command whenever you want to adjust the distance text flows around a piece of art.

TYPICAL OPERATION

In this example you learn how to use the Magnify command. Begin this example at the First Publisher Main menu with EXAMPLE.PUB loaded.

1. Press **Alt-U** then **F9** until the Selection Tool is highlighted. The graphics cursor and grid appear. The text turns gray.
2. Position the graphics cursor at the upper left corner of the silhouette of Lincoln using the arrow keys.
3. Press **F10**. Press **Shift-Right Arrow** eight times. Press **Shift-Down Arrow** nine times. Press **F10**. First Publisher selects the silhouette of Lincoln.

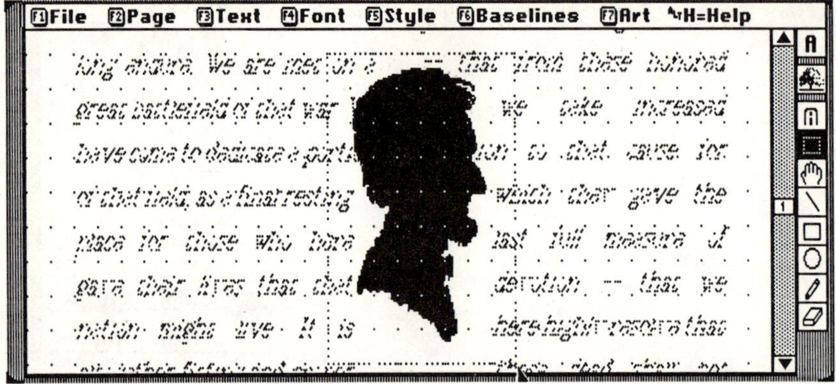

4. Press **F7**. The Art menu appears.
5. Select the Magnify command using the **Down Arrow**. Press **Enter**. The magnifying glass icon appears.

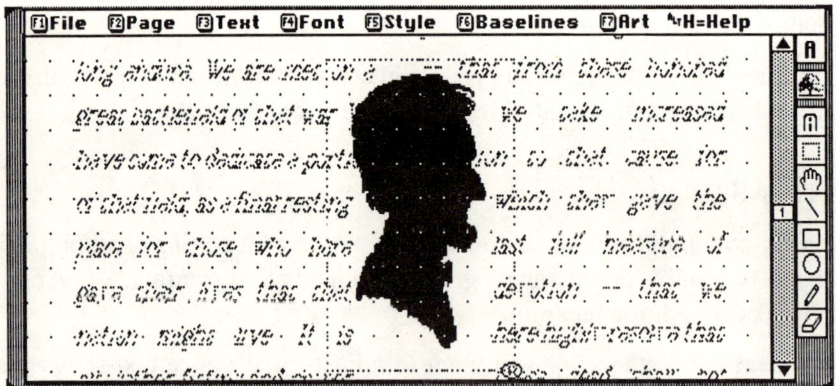

6. Position the magnifying glass at the tip of Lincoln's nose using the arrow keys. Press **F10**. The Pencil Tool appears.

NOTE

Version 2.0 of First Publisher displays the following screen. Press F10 to show an enlarged view of the silhouette of Lincoln as displayed after step 7.

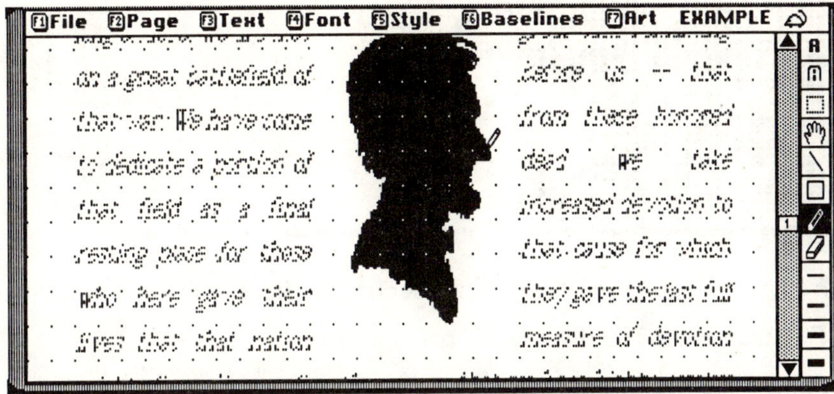

7. An enlarged view of the silhouette of Lincoln appears. Notice the normal display in the upper left corner.

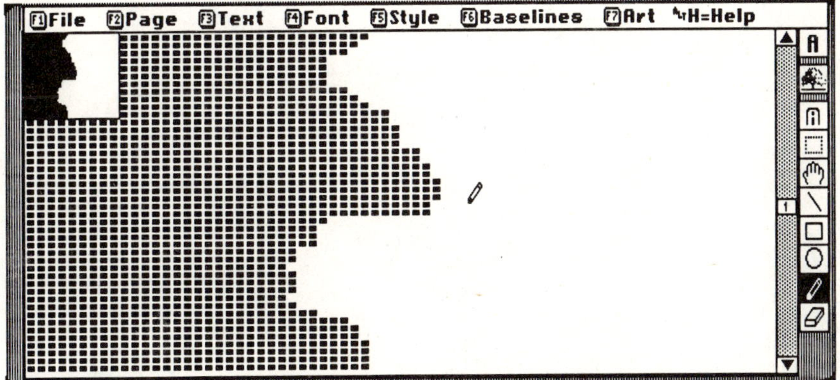

8. Press **F10**. Press the **Right Arrow** four times. First Publisher draws a line. Notice the line also appears in the normal display.

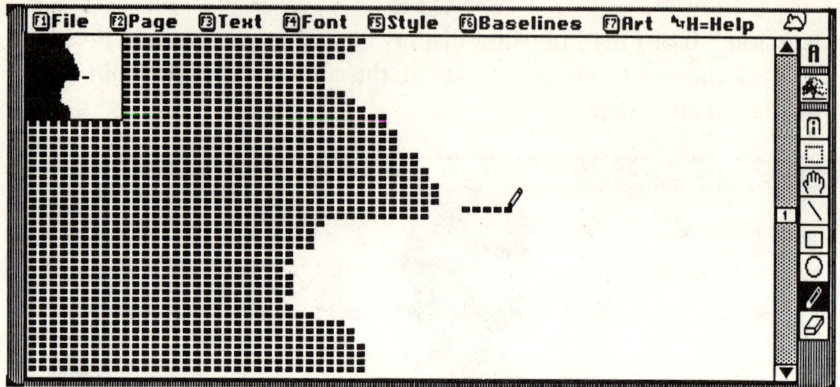

9. Press **F10** twice. Press the **Left Arrow** four times. First Publisher removes the line.
10. Press **F10** then **Esc**. The display returns to normal.
11. Press **Alt-E**. The DOS prompt appears.
12. Congratulations! You have just finished the learning sequence.

Module 26
PICTUREWRAP

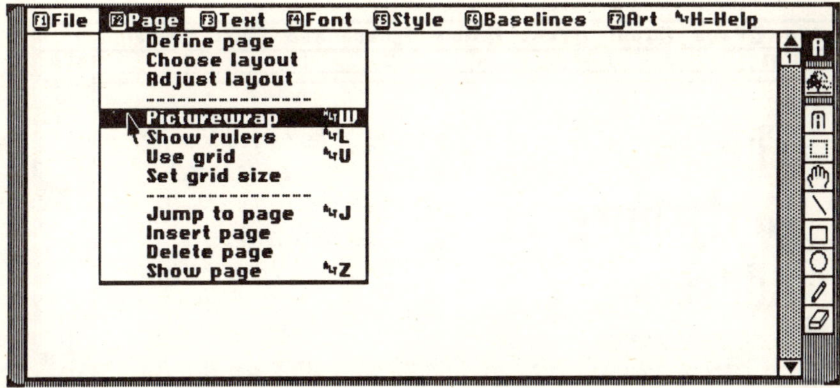

DESCRIPTION

The Picturewrap command on the Page menu tells First Publisher to move the document text so that graphic images do not hide it. Normally, First Publisher places the graphic directly over the document text. Both effects are good on different occasions. For example, if you used a translucent picture, a reader could still see the text below. Some magazines use this effect on their front cover. Normally, text wraps around the graphic for the sake of legibility. You can access the Picturewrap command using the Page menu or by using the Alt-W key combination.

APPLICATIONS

Use the Picturewrap command to tell First Publisher to wrap the document text around the selected graphic image. First Publisher does not automatically flow text around other graphic images on the page when using this command. You can obtain the same effect using the Adjust Single command described in Module 32.

TYPICAL OPERATION

This example shows you the effect of turning Picturewrap on after importing a graphic image. Begin this example at the First Publisher Main menu with EXAMPLE.PUB loaded.

1. Press **Alt-U** then **Alt-L**. The rulers appear.
2. Press **F7**. The Art menu appears.
3. Select the Get Art option by pressing **Down Arrow**. Press **Enter**. The Get Art dialogue box appears.
4. Select LINCOLN.ART by pressing **Down Arrow**. Press **F10** then **F1**. The grid and Hand Tool appear.

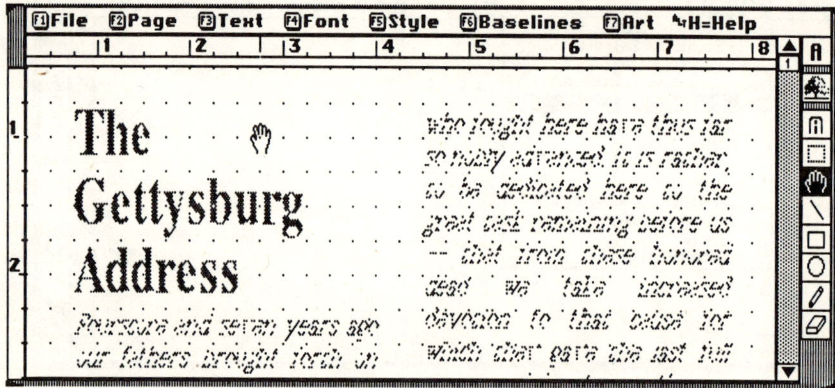

5. Press **F10**. Press the **Left Arrow** until the top position indicator shows 3 ¾". Press the **Down Arrow** until the left position indicator shows 4 ½".

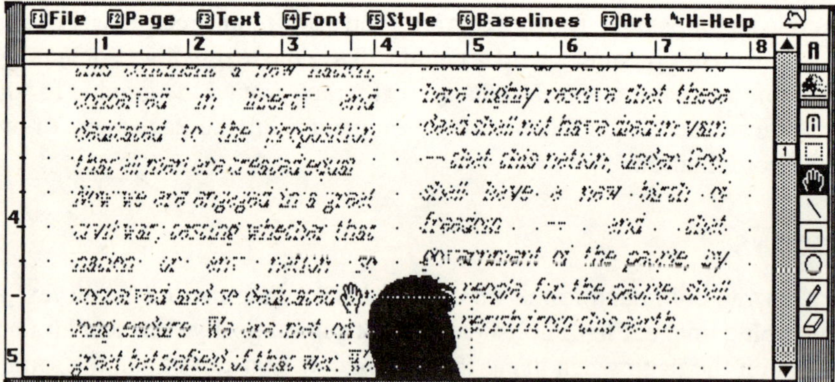

6. Press **F10**. First Publisher places the graphic image over the text. Notice the graphic hides part of the text.
7. Press **Shift-F9**. First Publisher displays the text normally. The grid disappears.
8. Press **F2**. The Page menu appears.

9. Select the Picturewrap command by pressing **Down Arrow**. Press **Enter**. Press **PgDn** twice. First Publisher flows the text around the graphic image.

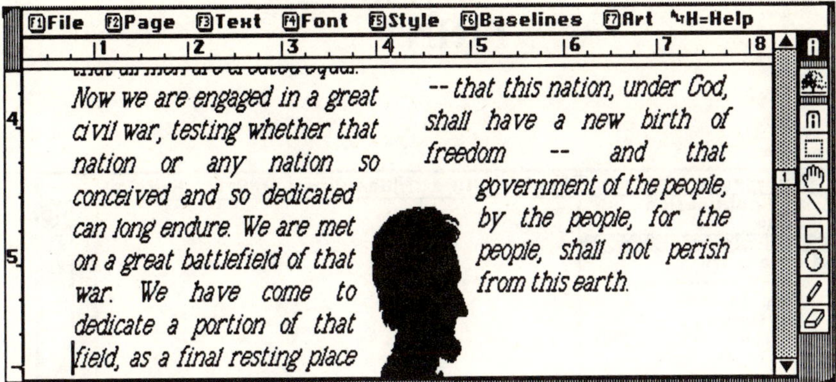

10. Press **Alt-S** then **F1**. First Publisher asks if you want to overwrite the old copy of EXAMPLE.PUB.
11. Press **F1**. First Publisher displays a saving document message.
12. Press **Alt-E** to exit First Publisher.
13. Turn to Module 7 to continue the learning sequence.

Module 27
PRINT

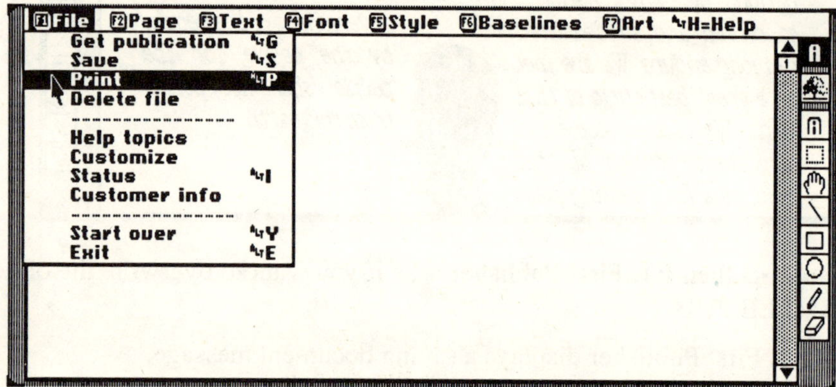

DESCRIPTION

The Print option on the File menu allows you to output your work to a printer attached to any parallel/serial port on your pc. First Publisher also allows you to send the output to a print file instead of a printer. This feature is useful for batch printing or printing when more than one person uses the printer. First Publisher protects you from overwriting a previous print file by warning you if the requested filename exists. You can access the Print dialogue box using the Alt-P key combination instead of using a menu.

First Publisher supports three levels of print output quality. Each level enhances the output, but requires a greater amount of time to print.

Draft quality print uses only the minimum quality output the printer provides. For example, if a dot matrix printer provides both 120 and 240 dot-per-inch graphic quality levels, First Publisher chooses the 120 dot-per-inch level since it requires less time to print. Use the draft quality output to get an idea of how the final document will look before making final format changes.

Standard quality print uses the top quality output the printer provides. Use the standard quality print when average resolution and quality are adequate for the final output document. This quality level provides a neatly formatted document without the long time required to print high-quality output.

Smoothed quality print uses both the top quality output of the printer and smoothing algorithms provided by First Publisher. Use this level of output when appearance is the only consideration and time is not a factor. When using this option, First Publisher removes the jagged lines from text and art, increasing the apparent resolution of the printer.

First Publisher also provides Print dialogue box entries for the desired number of copies, the starting page, and the ending page. Using these options allows you to spend less time at the printer and more time creating.

APPLICATIONS

Use the Print option to send your document to a printer or disk file. First Publisher allows you to specify a print filename or serial or parallel port as an output device. Other options include print quality, starting page, ending page, and number of copies.

TYPICAL OPERATION

In this example you begin by printing the Gettysburg Address to a file, then test to see what happens if you attempt to write to the file a second time. The second part of the example tests the three different print quality levels. You will see that as the quality increases, so does the time required to print the example. Begin this example at the First Publisher Main menu with EXAMPLE.PUB loaded.

1. Press **F1**. The File menu appears.
2. Select the Print option using the **Down Arrow** and pressing **Enter**. The Print dialogue box appears.

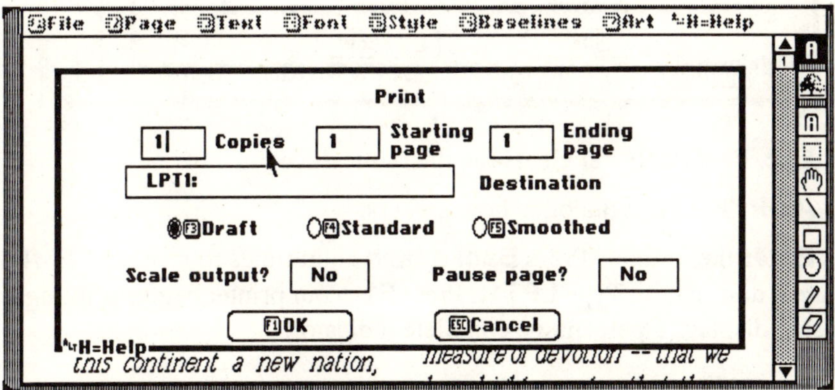

3. Press **Enter** three times. Press **Backspace** five times to remove LPT1: as the destination. Type **TEMP.PRN** and press **F1**. First Publisher displays a percentage complete indicator.

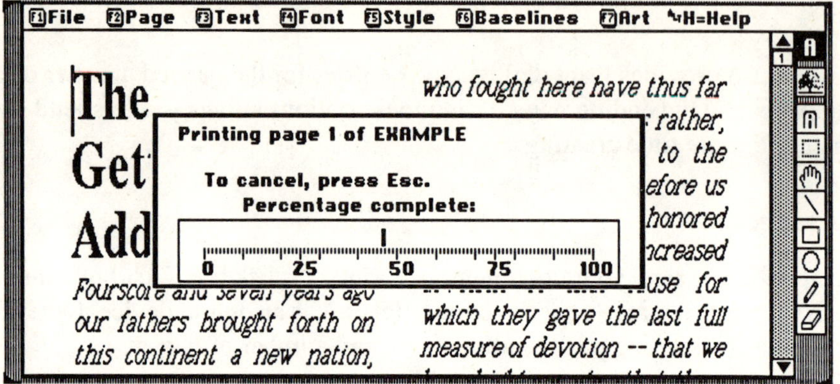

4. Press **Alt-P** then **F1**. First Publisher displays a message asking if you want to replace the old version of TEMP.PRN.

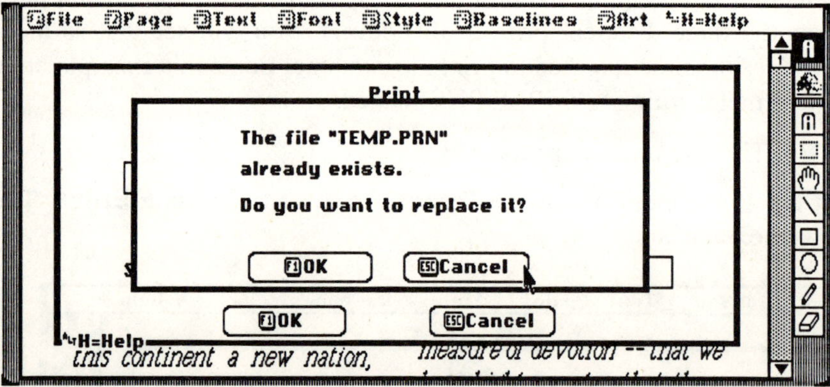

5. Press **Esc**. First Publisher clears the query message.
6. Press **Alt-P**. The Print dialogue box appears.
7. Press **Enter** three times. Press **Backspace** eight times to remove TEMP.PRN as the output destination. Type **LPT1:**. Press **F1**. Your printer begins printing and First Publisher displays a percentage complete indicator.

8. Press **Alt-P, F4,** then **F1**. (Version 3.0 only. Press **F1** when First Publisher displays the Scaled Font Location dialog box.) Your printer begins printing and First Publisher displays a percentage complete indicator. Notice the quality of the output using this setting is much improved and the printout took about twice as long to complete.
9. Press **Alt-P, F5,** then **F1**. (Version 3.0 only. Press **F1** when First Publisher displays the Scaled Font Location dialog box.) Your printer begins printing and First Publisher displays a percentage complete indicator. Notice the quality of the output using this setting is much better than the standard quality and the printout took about three times as long to complete. Also notice that First Publisher smoothed the characters and the print resolution appears higher.
10. Turn to Module 39 to continue the learning sequence.

Module 28
REALIGN TEXT

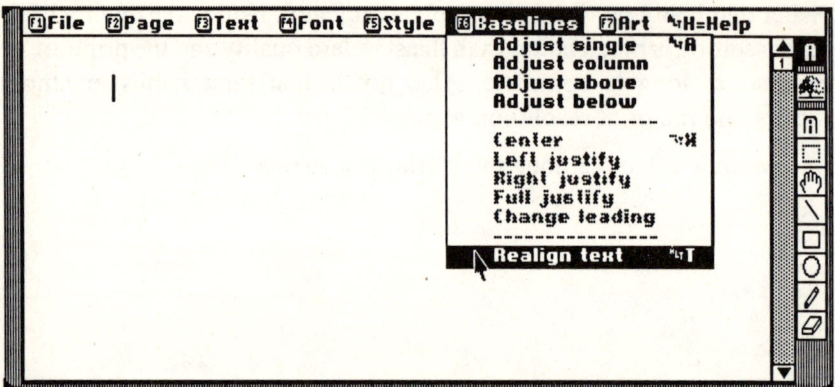

DESCRIPTION

The Realign Text command on the Baselines menu allows the text that disappears during baseline adjustment to reappear. The text appears in the correct position to reflect the changes made to the baseline. You can access this command using the Baselines menu or by pressing the Alt-T key combination.

APPLICATIONS

Use the Realign Text command when using any of the baseline adjustment commands. This allow you to see the effect of an adjustment without leaving the adjustment mode.

TYPICAL OPERATION

In this example you see the effect of using the Realign Text command on misaligned text. Begin this example at the First Publisher Main menu with EXAMPLE.PUB loaded.

1. Press **Alt-A**. First Publisher displays the baseline adjustment lines and graphics cursor.
2. Press **F10**. Select the left horizontal position block using the **Left Arrow**. First Publisher selects the title line.

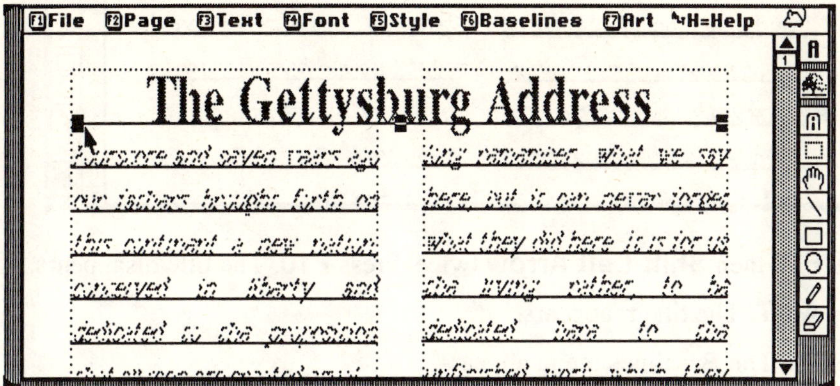

3. Press **Shift-Right Arrow** twice. Press **F10**. The title disappears.

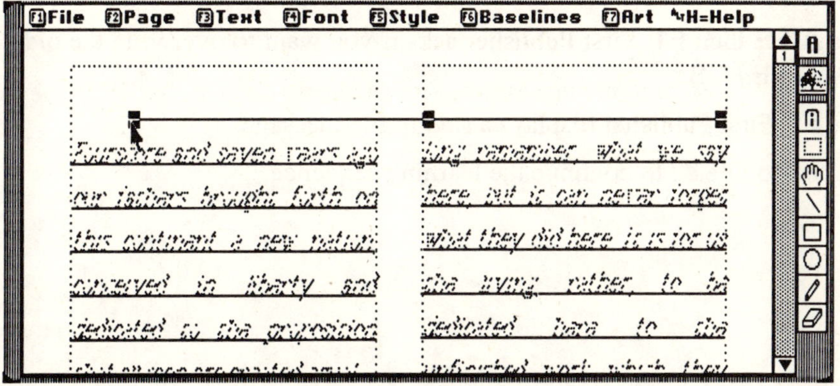

4. Press **F6**. The Baselines menu appears.
5. Select the Realign Text command using the **Down Arrow**. Press **Enter**. The title reappears.

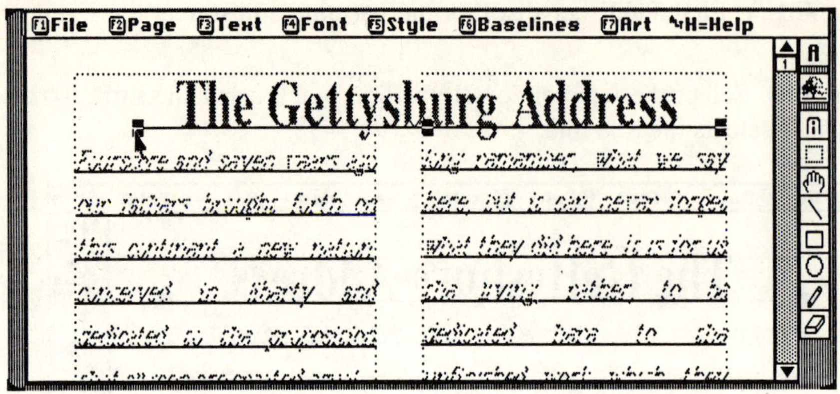

6. Press **F10** then **Shift-Left Arrow** twice. Press **F10**. The title disappears.
7. Press **Alt-T**. The title reappears.
8. Press **F6**. The Baselines menu appears.
9. Select the Adjust Single command using the **Down Arrow** and pressing **Enter**. First Publisher displays the text normally. The adjustment lines and graphics cursor disappear.
10. Press **Alt-E** then **F1**. First Publisher asks if you want to overwrite the old copy of EXAMPLE.PUB.
11. Press **F1**. First Publisher displays a saving file message.
12. Turn to Module 22 to continue the learning sequence.

Module 29
RESIZE

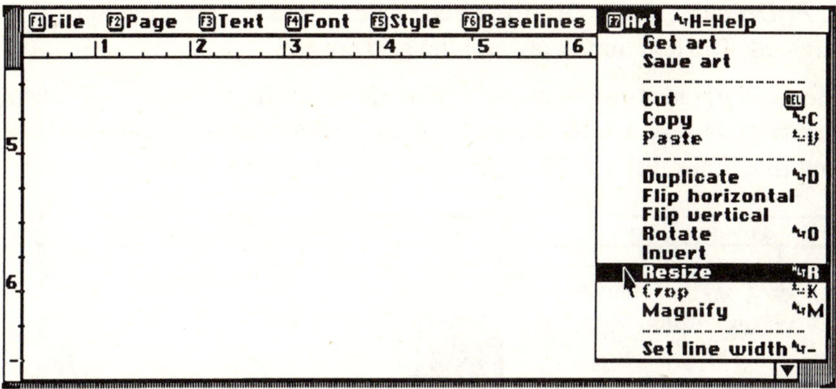

DESCRIPTION

The Resize command on the Art menu allows you to change the dimensions of a graphic image. You can access this command using the Art menu or by pressing Alt-R.

When you use the Resize command, First Publisher places solid squares at each corner of the selected graphic image. Selecting a particular square (by pointing to it and pressing F10) moves that corner of the graphic image.

APPLICATIONS

You use the Resize command to create graphic images that fill a reserved area. This command also allows you to create special effects. For instance, a narrow tall graphic of a city with skyscrapers can appear as an industrial area if you elongate the graphic. Unfortunately, First Publisher uses bit-mapped rather than vector graphics. This severely limits the extent of the work you can perform with the Resize command.

The Resize command also works well with graphic lettering. By typing the text the approximate size you need, you can reduce any distortion caused by stretching or compressing and still achieve some unique effects.

TYPICAL OPERATION

In this example you learn how to use the Resize command on a graphic image. This example shows the effect of the Resize command on graphic images. Look for signs of distortion or overly jagged lines while manipulating the graphic. Begin this example at the First Publisher Main menu with EXAMPLE.PUB loaded.

1. Press **Alt-U, Alt-W,** and **Alt-L**. The ruler appears.
2. Press **PgDn** twice. Press **Down Arrow** twice. Press **F9** until the Selection Tool is highlighted. The text turns gray and the grid appears.
3. Position the graphics cursor above and to the left of the silhouette of Lincoln using the arrow keys. Press **F10**. Press the **Down Arrow** eight times and the **Right Arrow** five times. Press **F10**. First Publisher selects the graphic image.

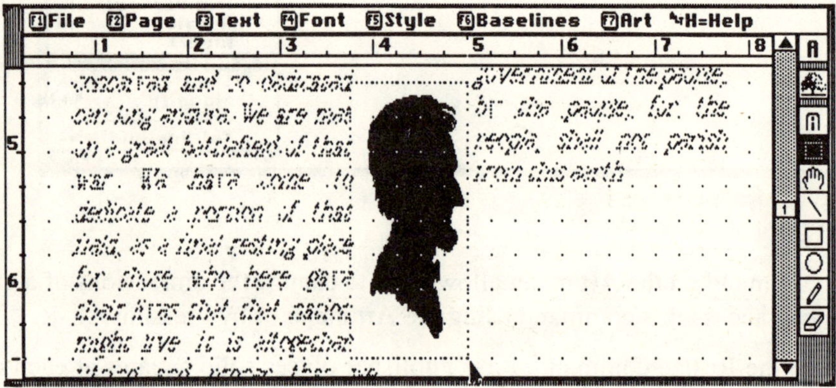

4. Press **F7**. The Art menu appears.
5. Select the Resize command using the **Down Arrow**. Press **Enter**. First Publisher places a block at each corner of the dashed box.

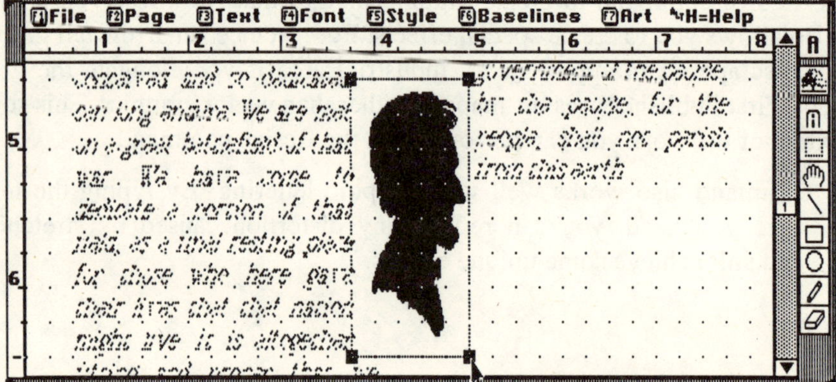

6. Press **F10**. Press **Down Arrow** then **Right Arrow**. First Publisher increases the size of the graphic in the requested direction.
7. Press **F10**. The graphic image increases in size. Notice First Publisher shows the position of the old boundaries.

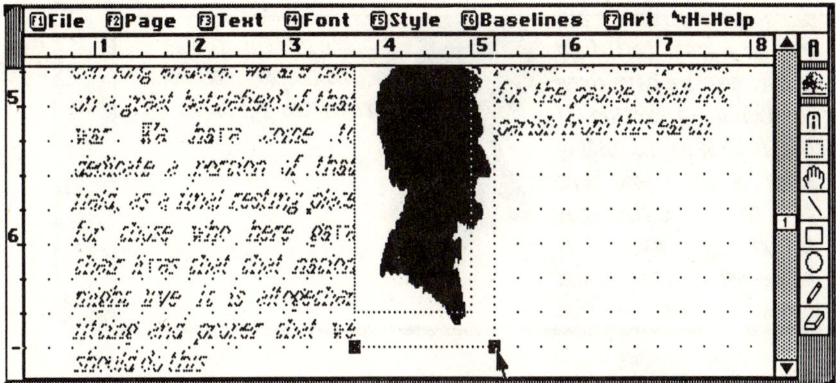

8. Press the **Left Arrow** six times. Press **F10**. Press the **Left Arrow**. Press **F10**. The graphic image increases in size.

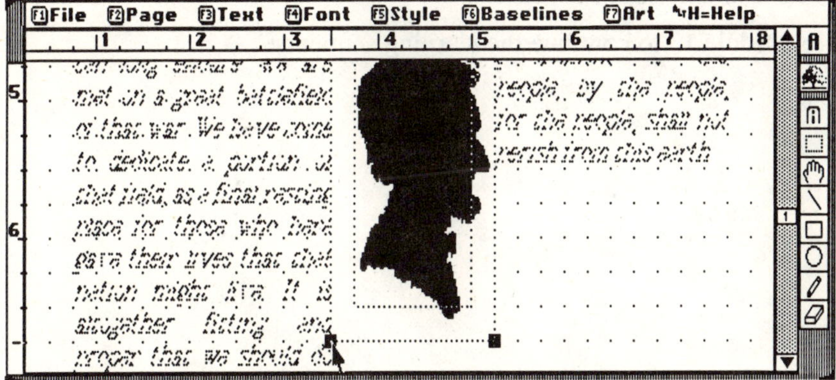

9. Press **Shift-F9**. First Publisher returns the text color to normal. The graphics cursor and grid disappear. Since the Picturewrap command is active, First Publisher automatically flows the text around the increased graphic size.

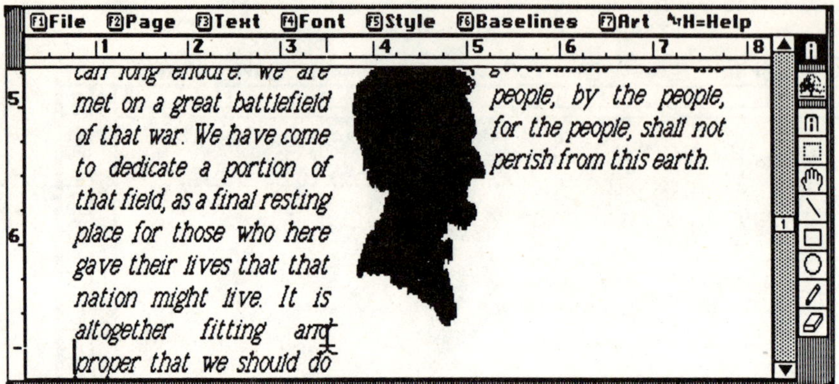

10. Press **Alt-S** then **F1**. First Publisher asks if you want to overwrite the old copy of EXAMPLE.PUB.
11. Press **F1**. First Publisher displays a saving file message.
12. Press **Alt-E** to exit First Publisher.
13. Turn to Module 13 to continue the learning sequence.

Module 30
SAVE

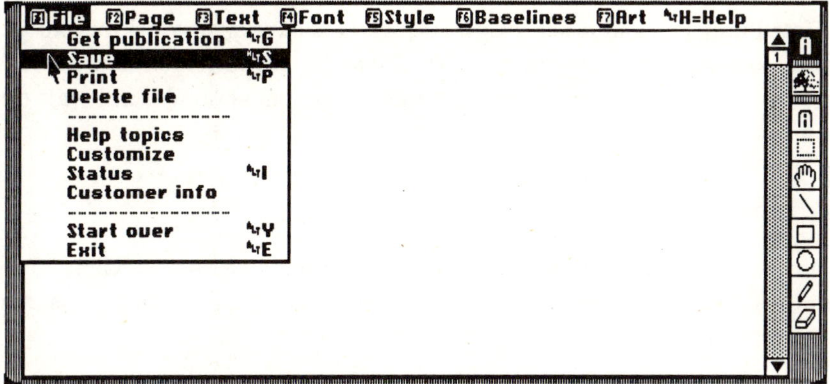

DESCRIPTION

The Save option stores a document on disk so you can retrieve your work at a later date. You access it using the File menu or by pressing Alt-S. By saving your work often, you can reduce data loss caused by power loss and equipment failure. As long as your hard disk continues to work, the data you save during a session is safe. Making backups of your hard disk removes some of the hazards of hard disk failure as well.

The Save option allows you to store files to disk in three different formats. The first format stores entire publications including graphics. It uses the .PUB format. In this format, text in the document stays in text form, while graphics remain in graphics form.

The second format stores files in a graphics format compatible with some paint and word processing formats. Even though the extension on the file is .MAC, it resembles the .PCX format closely enough that you can use it with programs using that format. Using this format, First Publisher converts any text in your document to a graphics format.

The third format is an ASCII text format. Use this format to transfer text between First Publisher and other programs. The file extension used for these files is .TXT.

When you save your file, First Publisher asks you to supply a filename and path (it automatically supplies the filename NEW). The filename is the identifier DOS uses to store the file. DOS allows filenames eight characters or less in length. The path tells DOS where to put the file (directory). DOS always assumes the current directory if you don't supply one.

If the filename you supply already exists in the specified directory, then First Publisher tells you the file exists. You must tell First Publisher whether or not to overwrite the file.

APPLICATIONS

You use the Save option to store your work for later retrieval or for transferring documents between First Publisher and other programs. Always save your work before you make any drastic changes to your document. This allows you to retrieve the previous version when necessary. It is also important to save your document at regular intervals during the editing process.

TYPICAL OPERATION

In this example you save a publication to disk using the text format. Then you save the publication a second time to see the results of overwriting a file. Begin this example at the DOS prompt.

1. Type **FP** and press **Enter**. The First Publisher Main menu appears.
2. Press **Alt-S**. The File Save dialog box appears.

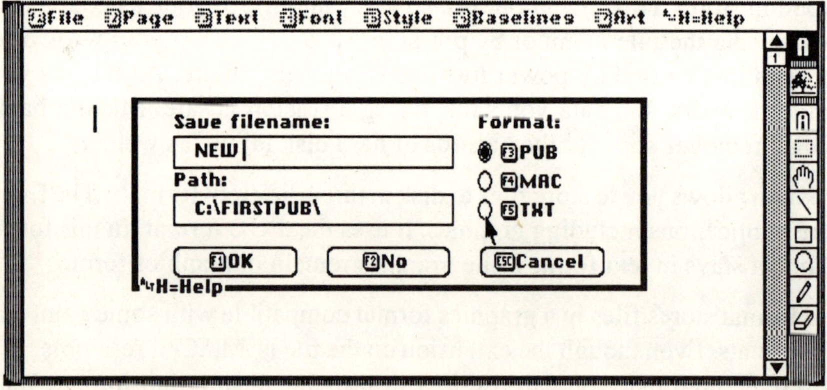

3. Press **F5**. The format type changes to .TXT. Notice the format always defaults to .PUB.

4. Type **TEMP** and press **F1**. A saving file message appears, then the edit screen returns to normal.

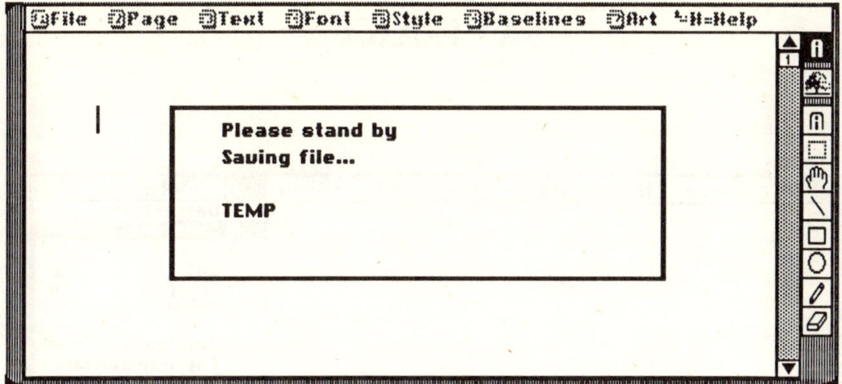

5. Press **Alt-S**. The File Save dialog box appears.
6. Press **F5**. The format type changes to .TXT.
7. Type **TEMP** and press **F1**. First Publisher tells you the file exists and asks if you want to replace it.

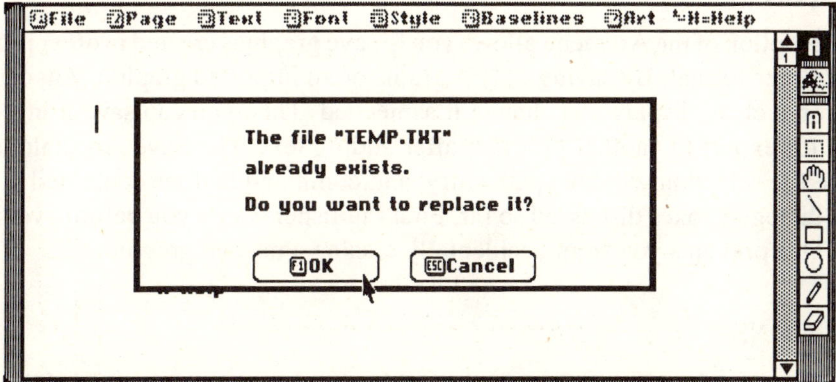

8. Press **F1**. A saving file message appears, then the edit screen returns to normal.
9. Press **Alt-E**. The DOS prompt appears.
10. Turn to Module 9 to continue the learning sequence.

Module 31
SAVE ART

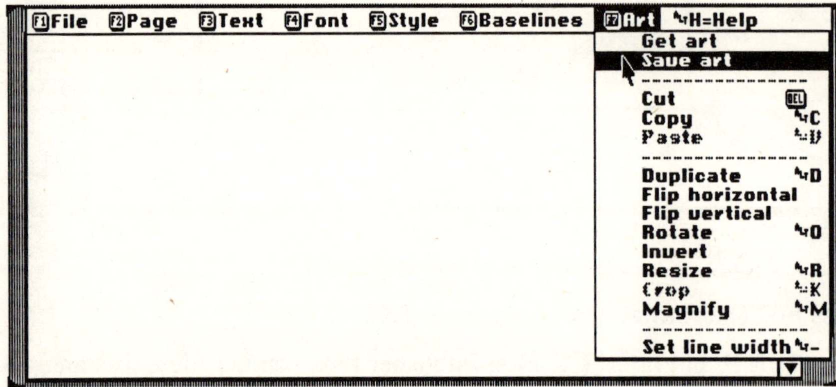

DESCRIPTION

The Save Art option of the Art menu allows you to save graphics created in other programs in First Publisher format. By saving only portions of an imported graphic, you can place the art file on a clean display and change it as needed. Then you can save it in a .MAC file format for export to another program after adding text. The Save Art dialogue box contains the file selection window, path entry, and command buttons contained in all the file related dialogue boxes discussed so far. First Publisher warns you before overwriting an art file. This prevents you from accidentally erasing a needed graphic.

APPLICATIONS

Use the Save Art option to save imported graphics for future use. You can also use this option to save sections of previously altered graphics or text.

TYPICAL OPERATION

In this example you learn how to save a section of an imported graphic using the Selection Tool and the Save Art option. This example also shows the result of trying to overwrite a previously saved file. Begin this example at the First Publisher Main menu with HOLIDAYS.MAC loaded.

The following steps work with version 2.0 of First Publisher only:

1. Press **PgDn** twice.
2. Press **F9** until you have highlighted the Selection Tool in the Side Tool menu.
3. Position the graphics arrow at the upper left corner of the silhouette of Lincoln using the arrow keys. Press **F10**. Surround the entire image with a box using the arrow keys. Press **F10**. First Publisher places a dashed box around the silhouette of Lincoln.

4. Press **F7**. The Art menu appears.
5. Select the Save Art option using the **Down Arrow**. Press **Enter**. The Save Art dialogue box appears.

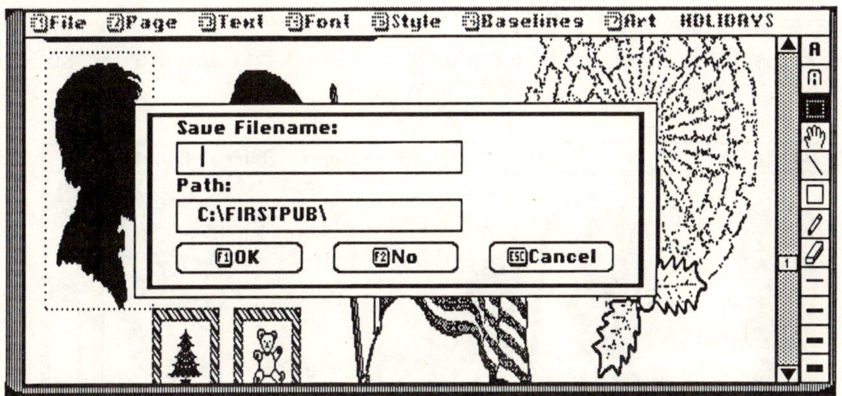

6. Type **LINCOLN** and press **F1**. First Publisher saves the art file.
7. Press **F7**. The Art menu appears.

8. Select the Save Art option using the **Down Arrow**. Press **Enter**. The Save Art dialogue box appears.
9. Type **LINCOLN** and press **F1**. First Publisher tells you the file already exists and asks if you want to replace it.

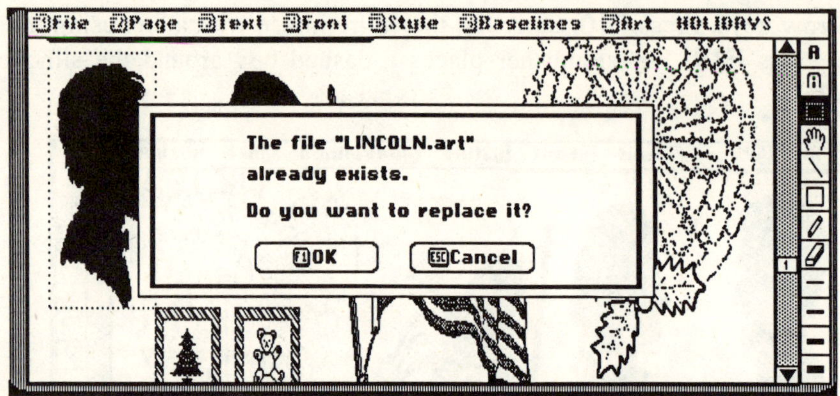

10. Press **Esc**. First Publisher clears the message from the display.
11. Turn to Module 17 to continue the learning sequence.

The following steps work with version 3.0 of First Publisher only:

1. Press **F9** until you have highlighted the Selection Tool in the Side Tool menu.
2. Press **PgDn** twice.
3. Position the graphics arrow at the upper left corner of the silhouette of Lincoln using the arrow keys. Press **F10**. Surround the entire image with a box using the arrow keys. Press **F10**. First Publisher places a dashed box around the silhouette of Lincoln.

4. Press **F7**. The Art menu appears.
5. Select the Save Art option using the **Down Arrow**. Press **Enter**. The Save Art dialogue box appears.

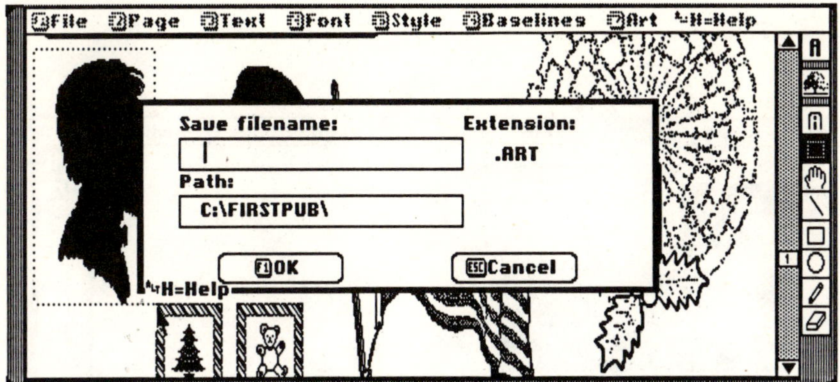

6. Type **LINCOLN** and press **F1**. First Publisher saves the art file.
7. Press **F7**. The Art menu appears.
8. Select the Save Art option using the **Down Arrow**. Press **Enter**. The Save Art dialogue box appears.
9. Type **LINCOLN** and press **F1**. First Publisher tells you the file already exists and asks if you want to replace it.

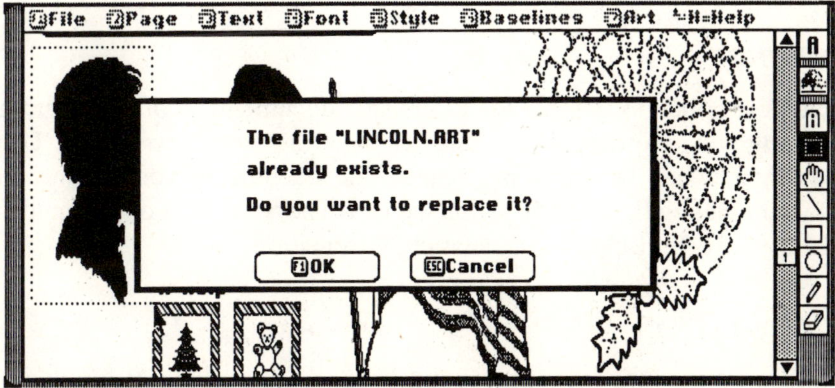

10. Press **Esc**. First Publisher clears the message from the display.
11. Turn to Module 17 to continue the learning sequence.

Module 32
SAVE TEXT

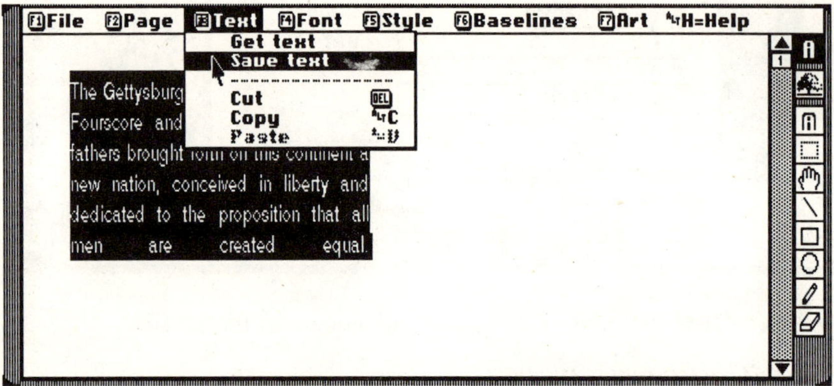

DESCRIPTION

The Save Text option on the Text menu converts text in First Publisher publication format to standard ASCII format. This allows other applications to accept text written in First Publisher.

APPLICATIONS

Use the Save Text option to transfer First Publisher documents to other programs. You do this by highlighting the desired text and selecting the Save Text option. Using this option saves time, when other people require the documents you produce in First Publisher, by eliminating the need to retype the text. The Save Text option converts text to ASCII format only. It discards all formatting information.

TYPICAL OPERATION

This example shows you how to save text using the Save Text option. Begin this example at the DOS prompt.

1. Type **FP** and press **Enter**. The First Publisher Main menu appears.
2. Press **Alt-G**. The Get Publication menu appears.

3. Select EXAMPLE.PUB using the **Down Arrow** and press **F10**. First Publisher highlights the EXAMPLE.PUB entry.
4. Press **F1**. First Publisher loads EXAMPLE.PUB.
5. Type **The Gettysburg Address** and press **Enter**.
6. Type the following:

   Fourscore and seven years ago our fathers brought forth on this continent a new nation, conceived in liberty and dedicated to the proposition that all men are created equal.

7. Press **Ctrl-Home**. The cursor goes to the beginning of the document.
8. Press **F10** then **Ctrl-End**. First Publisher highlights the entire text.

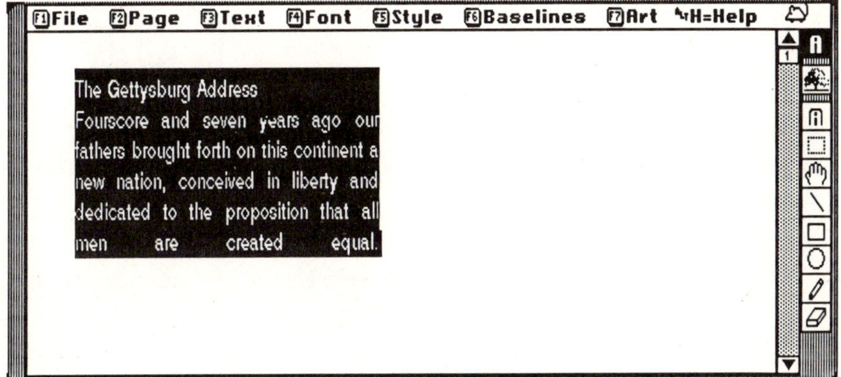

9. Press **F10** then **F3**. The Text menu appears.
10. Select the Save Text option using the **Down Arrow** and pressing **Enter**. The Save Text dialogue box appears.

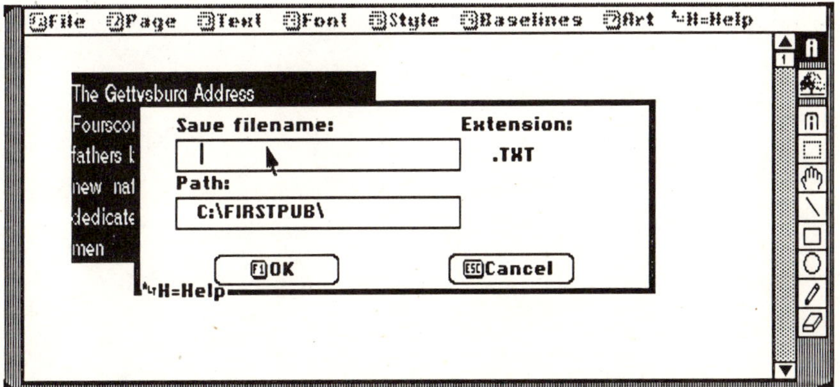

11. Type **EXAMPLE** and press **F1**. First Publisher saves the text as an ASCII file.
12. Press **Alt-E**. The File Save menu appears.
13. Press **F1**. First Publisher asks if you want to replace the original document.
14. Press **F1**. First Publisher saves the document. The DOS prompt appears.
15. Turn to Module 16 to continue the learning sequence.

Module 33
SET GRID SIZE

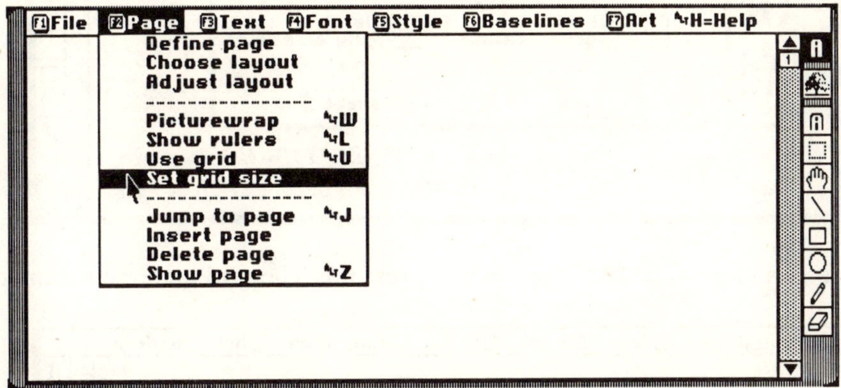

DESCRIPTION

The Set Grid Size option on the Page menu allows you to change the increment between grid points. The Grid Size dialogue box contains two entries. The first entry is the horizontal increment; the second entry is the vertical increment. You can select small increments for precision graphics placement or large increments for quick movement around the display area.

APPLICATIONS

Use the Set Grid Size option to refine cursor movement around the display area and graphics placement on the page.

TYPICAL OPERATION

In this example you change the grid increment to see the effects on cursor movement. Begin this example at the First Publisher Main menu with EXAMPLE. PUB loaded.

1. Press **F9**. The Gettysburg Address text grays.
2. Press **Alt-U**. The grid appears.
3. Press **F2**. The Page menu appears.

4. Select the Set Grid Size option using the **Down Arrow** and pressing **Enter**. The Set Grid Size dialogue box appears.

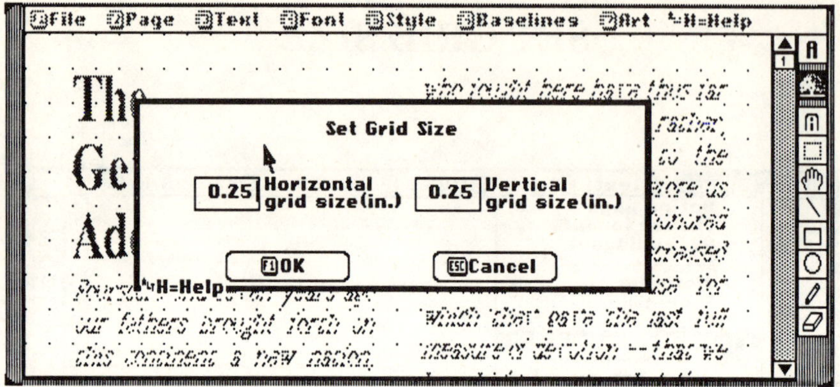

5. Type **.5** and press **Enter**. Type **.5** and press **F1**. The grid increment doubles.

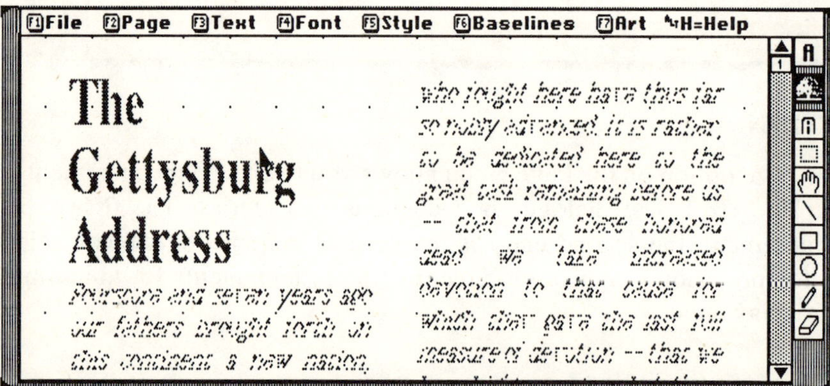

6. Press the arrow keys. Notice the graphics cursor moves in increments equal to the grid increment.
7. Press **F2**. The Page menu appears.
8. Select the Set Grid Size option using the **Down Arrow** and pressing **Enter**. The Set Grid Size dialogue box appears.

9. Type **.125** and press **Enter**. Type **.125** and press **F1**. The grid increment equals one half the original grid increment.

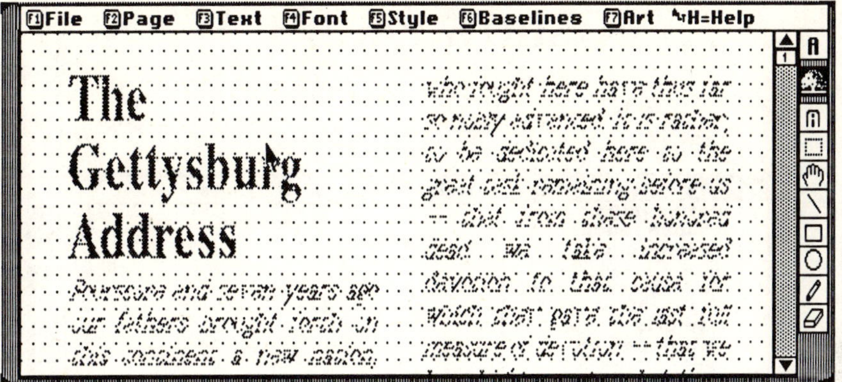

10. Press the arrow keys. Notice the graphics cursor moves in increments equal to the grid increment.
11. Turn to Module 40 to continue the learning sequence.

Module 34
SHOW PAGE

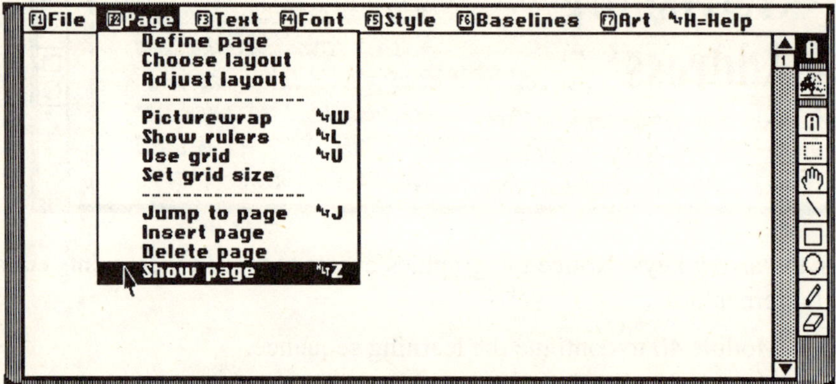

DESCRIPTION

The Show Page command on the Page menu provides you with a reduced view of how the current page will look when printed. Using the Show Page command, you can determine if you need to make any more formatting changes to a page of a document before printing. Besides using the Page menu to access the Show Page command, you can also use the Alt-Z key combination.

Since the resolution of your display is not infinite, First Publisher cannot display some of the text as text (the font becomes too small to display). Instead, it uses a technique known as greeking to display an approximation of letter shape and position. The greeking in fact has the appearance of text reduced too small to read (try reducing text on a copier until it is too small to read).

APPLICATIONS

You use the Show Page command to get an overall view of how a document page will look when printed.

TYPICAL OPERATION

In this example you use the Show Page command to see how the Gettysburg Address document will look when printed. Begin this example at the First Publisher Main menu with EXAMPLE.PUB loaded.

1. Press **F2**. The Page menu appears.
2. Select the Show Page command using the **Down Arrow** and pressing **Enter**. First Publisher displays a reduced view of the document.

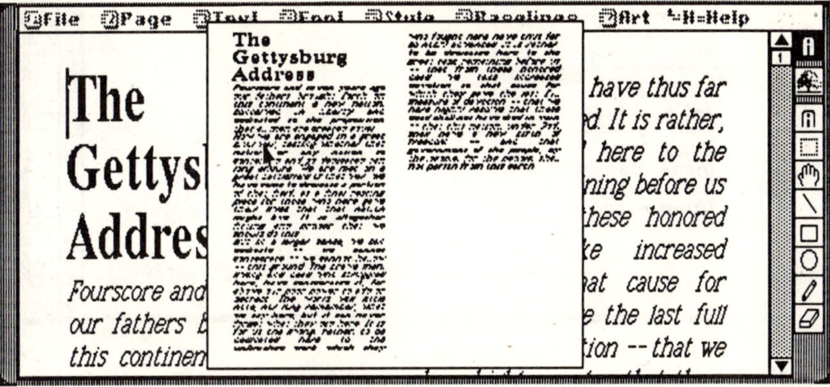

3. Press **Esc**. The Show Page display disappears.
4. Turn to Module 27 to continue the learning sequence.

Module 35
SHOW RULERS

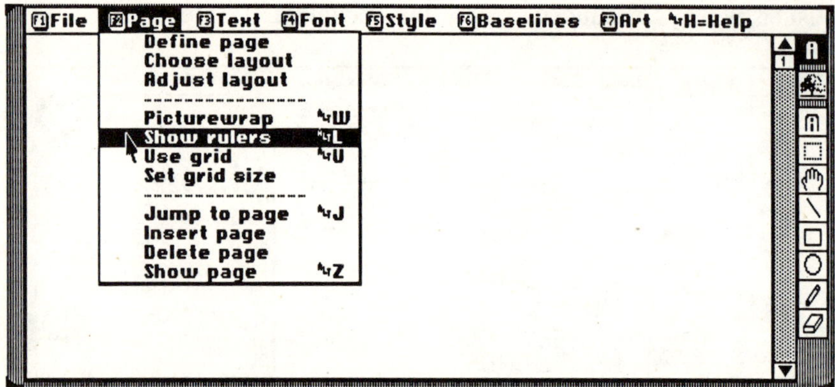

DESCRIPTION

The Show Rulers command of the Page menu displays a ruler along the top and left side of the display area. The rulers always show text or graphics placement on a page in inches. You can also access this command by pressing Alt-L.

APPLICATIONS

You can use the Show Rulers command to accurately place text or graphics on a page. Indicators displayed on both rulers accurately show the present position of the text cursor or graphics tools. This command is exceptionally useful for resizing graphics. The ruler allows you to make the graphic exactly the size you want. The ruler begins at 0.25" on the left, at 8.25" on the right, 0.5" at the top, and 10.5" at the bottom margins since First Publisher does not allow text or graphic placement outside these margins.

TYPICAL OPERATION

In this example you learn how to display the rulers on screen whenever you need them. You use both the control key and menu methods to access the rulers. Begin this example at the DOS prompt.

1. Type **FP** and press **Enter**. The First Publisher Main menu appears.
2. Press **F2**. The Page menu appears.

3. Select the Show Rulers command using the **Down Arrow**.
4. Press **Enter**. The Page menu disappears and a ruler line appears along the top and left side of the edit area.

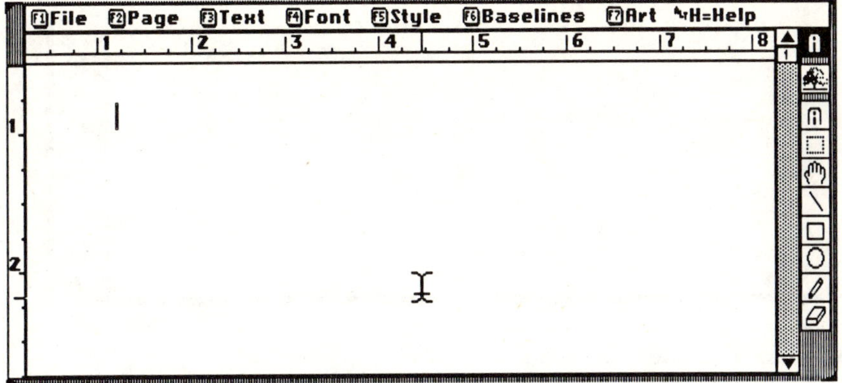

5. Press **F9**. The Tools menu highlights the graphic text tool.
6. Press the **Up Arrow**. The graphics cursor and left position indicator move up.

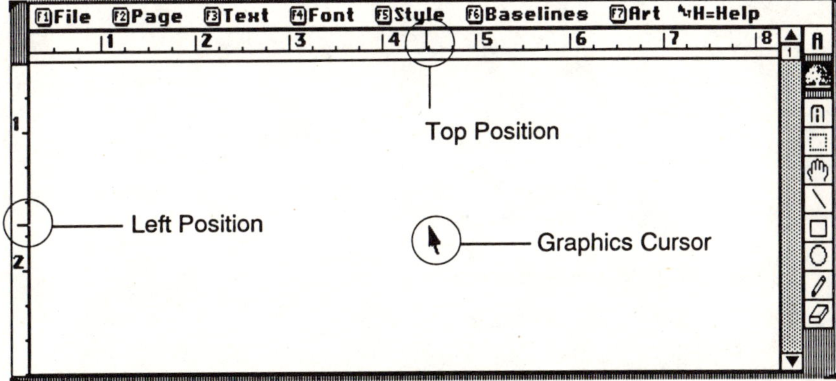

7. Press the **Left Arrow**. The graphics cursor and top position indicator move left.

8. Press **Alt-L**. The ruler disappears.

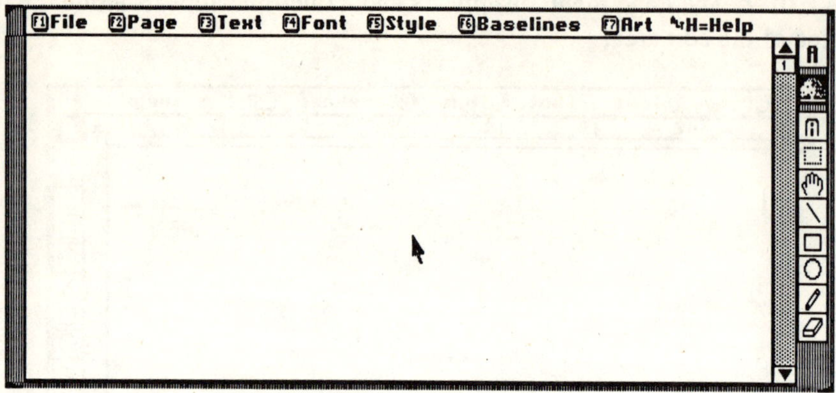

9. Press **Alt-L**. The ruler reappears.
10. Press **Alt-E**. The DOS prompt reappears.
11. Turn to Module 32 to continue the learning sequence.

Module 36
START OVER

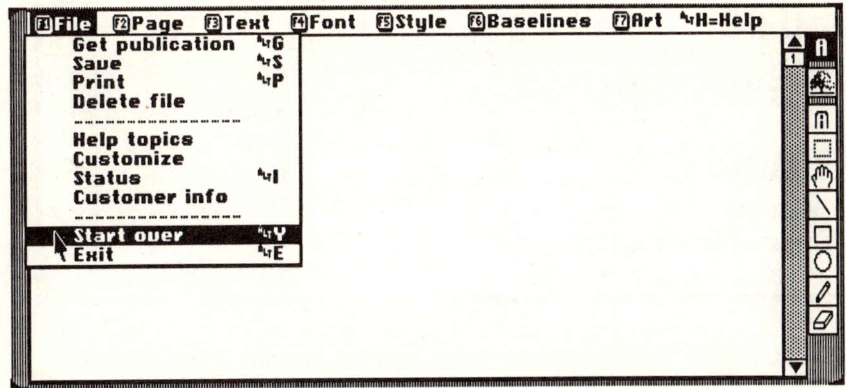

DESCRIPTION

The Start Over command, located on the File menu, allows you to clear all text and graphics from a document without disturbing any of the document settings. Even though First Publisher clears the display, the disk file containing any saved parts of the document remains intact. The only method available to reverse the effect of the Start Over command is to reload the document from disk. Unfortunately, you cannot recover any changes not saved to the disk file.

APPLICATIONS

Use the Start Over command to reverse the effect of radical document modification or to clear the display area when an experiment fails. You erase the effect of any changes made to the document by clearing the display area using the Start Over command. Then you read the disk file containing the original document back into memory. Using the Start Over command when experimenting with various page setups or graphics designs allows you to save the document setup, saving valuable time.

TYPICAL OPERATION

In this example you load a document into memory and examine the settings for two document parameters. Then you use the Start Over command to erase the display area contents and examine the same document parameter settings for change. Begin this example at the First Publisher Main menu with EXAMPLE. PUB loaded.

1. Press **Ctrl-Home** to go to the top of the publication. Press **F4**. First Publisher displays the current font setting.

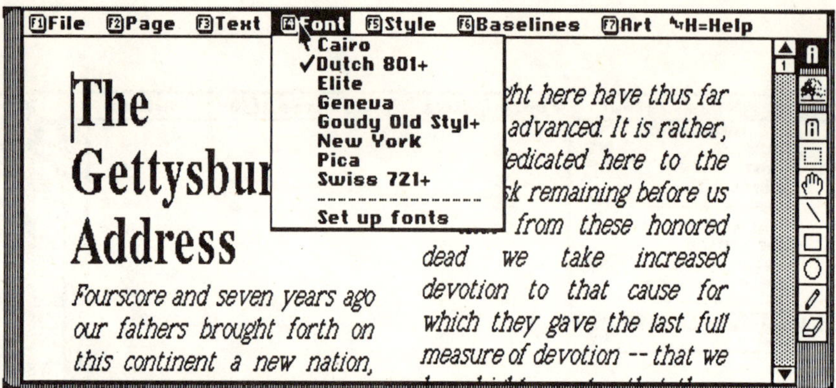

2. Press **Esc** then **F5**. First Publisher displays the current style settings.

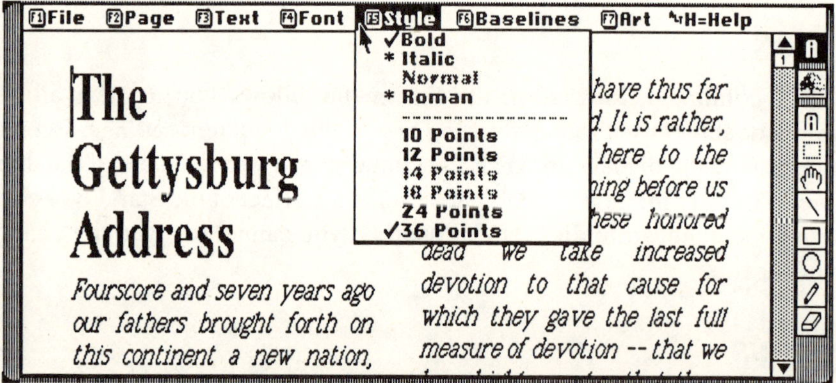

3. Press **Esc** then **F1**. The File menu appears.
4. Select the Start Over command using the **Down Arrow** and pressing **Enter**. First Publisher clears the display.
5. Press **F4**. Notice First Publisher retained the font setting.
6. Press **Esc** then **F5**. Notice First Publisher retained the style settings.
7. Turn to Module 20 to continue the learning sequence.

Module 37
STATUS, CUSTOMIZE

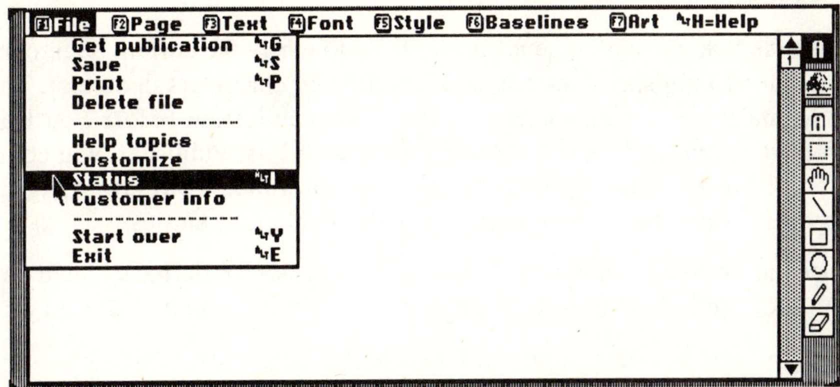

DESCRIPTION

The Status option of the File menu shows version number, filename, printer type and port, font type and size, font leading, the page number, and the number of characters displayed and overflowed. You can also access this option using Alt-I.

The version number assists you when you need to determine if your program is current or requires an upgrade. It also assists service personnel helping you find problems encountered during program use.

You adjust the printer type and port using the printer utility discussed in Appendix I. Make sure you have First Publisher installed for the correct printer type and port when you experience problems during printing.

Select the font type using the Font menu described in Module 16. Adjust the font size and style using the Style menu described in Module 38. The font leading parameter is one of the Define Page menu options discussed in Module 9. You adjust font leading for individual lines using the Change Leading option of the Baselines menu discussed in Module 6.

The number of characters displayed entry shows the number of characters on the present page. The overflowed characters entry is normally 0. When you import text that requires more space than the current document page provides space for, the overflowed characters entry tells you how many characters First Publisher placed in a special buffer. Use the

Insert Page option of the Page menu discussed in Module 22 to allow space for the overflowed characters. You adjust the page number using the PgUp and PgDn keys, or the Jump to Page option described in Module 24.

The Customize option in the File menu lets you define the colors, path defaults, and measurement units (inches or centimeters) for the ruler and margins.

APPLICATIONS

You can use the Status option whenever you need to verify the current document status. For instance, First Publisher does not save overflowed characters upon exit. Therefore, you need to make sure no characters overflow the publication before you leave First Publisher. If your printer does not work correctly with First Publisher, you could check the printer type entry. The status menu also provides information on current page defaults. Using this option saves time spent looking at individual menu entries.

You can use the Customize option to choose different colors, redefine the path directories for .TXT, .ART, and .PUB files, or change the measurement units between inches and centimeters.

TYPICAL OPERATION

In this example you learn how to request the status option from First Publisher. Begin this example at the DOS prompt.

The following steps work for version 2.0 of First Publisher only:

1. Type **FP** and press **Enter**. The First Publisher Main menu appears.
2. Press **F1**. The File menu appears.
3. Select the Status option using the **Down Arrow**. First Publisher highlights the Status option.
4. Press **Enter**. First Publisher displays the publication status.

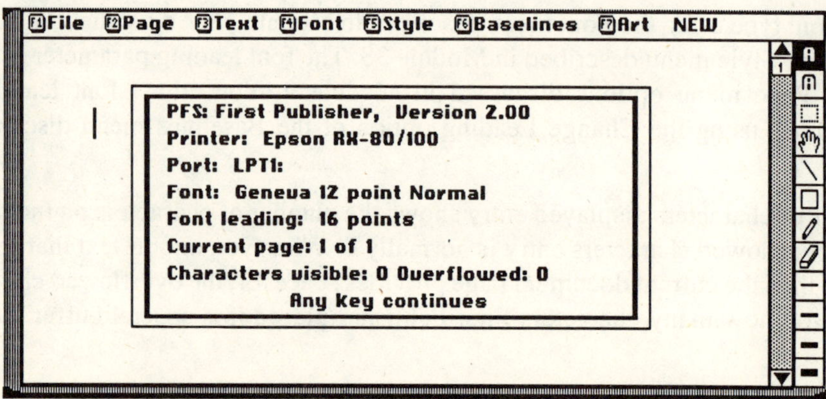

5. Press **Enter**. The Status option disappears.
6. Press **Alt-E**. The DOS prompt reappears.
7. Turn to Module 35 to continue the learning sequence.

The following steps work for version 3.0 of First Publisher only:

1. Type **FP** and press **Enter**. The First Publisher Main menu appears.
2. Press **F1**. The File menu appears.
3. Select the Status option using the **Down Arrow** and press **Enter**, or press **Alt-I**. First Publisher highlights the Status option. First Publisher displays the publication status.

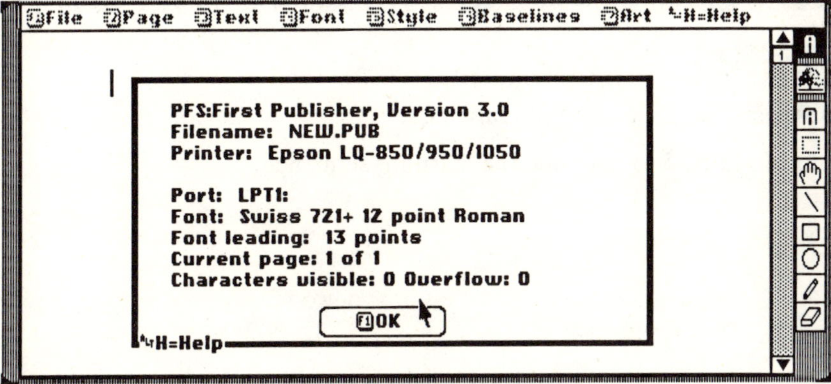

4. Press **F1**. The Status option disappears.
5. Press **F1** to display the File menu. Then select the Customize option by using the **Down Arrow** and pressing **Enter**. First Publisher displays a Customize dialogue box.

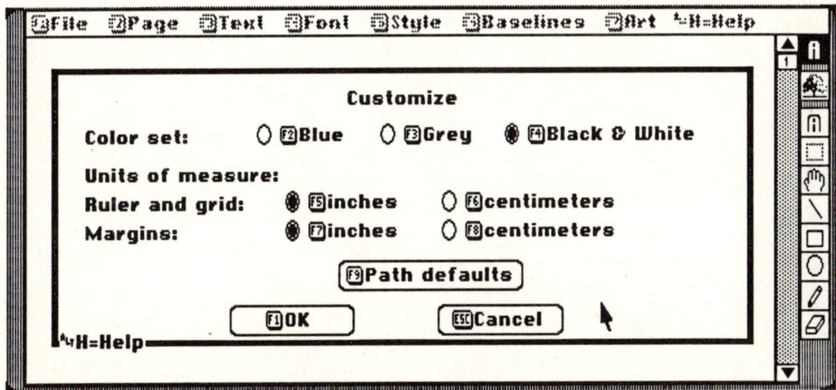

6. Press **F9**. First Publisher displays the default drive and path dialogue box.

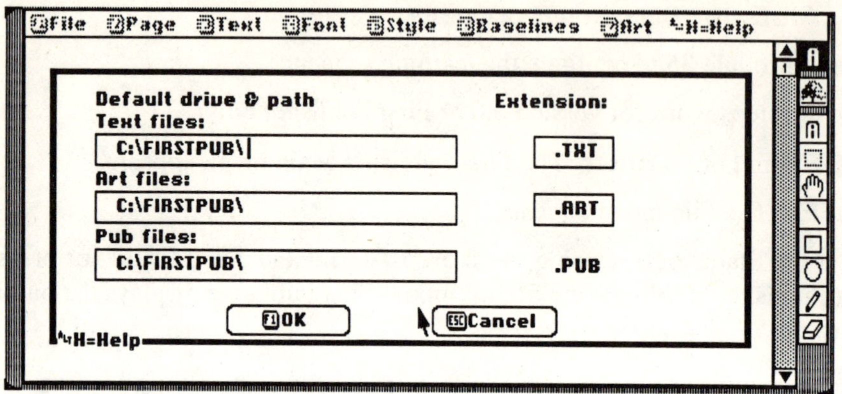

7. Press **Esc** twice.
8. Press **Alt-E**. The DOS prompt reappears.
9. Turn to Module 35 to continue the learning sequence.

Module 38
STYLE MENU

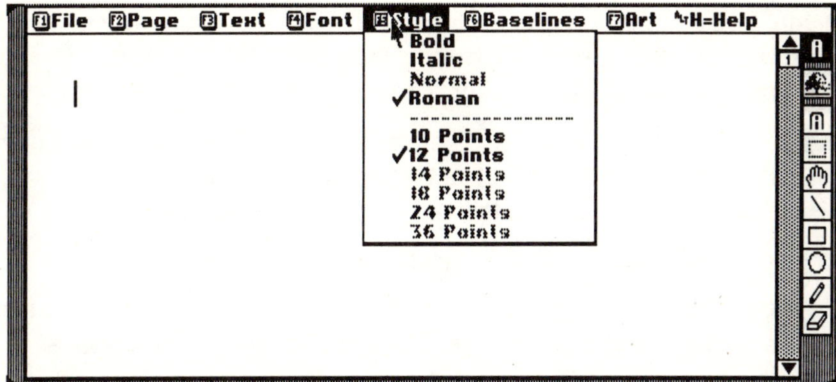

DESCRIPTION

The Style menu (F5) works hand-in-hand with the Font menu (F4). The Font menu changes the typeface, while the Style menu changes the appearance of the type. The Style menu provides two categories of typeface appearance change. The first category is size, the second is characteristic.

The Style menu provides selections for supported font sizes in points. The selected size appears with a check mark beside it. When using the standard MASTER.FNT file, First Publisher defaults to a font size of 12 points.

There are four different font characteristics normally supplied with font packages. The first characteristic is normal, the font is not thickened or slanted. The second characteristic is italic, the font is slanted but no thicker than the normal font. The third characteristic is bold, the font is thicker than normal but not slanted. The fourth characteristic is bold italic, the font is both thicker than a normal font and slanted. Most fonts slant to the right; although, a few slant to the left (none supplied with First Publisher). When using the standard MASTER.FNT file, First Publisher defaults to the normal font characteristic.

APPLICATIONS

Use the Style menu to add flavor to your desktop publishing by enhancing the appearance of the fonts you use. The use of italic or bold type in various places draws the reader's attention to that word or phrase. The use of different font sizes also tends to draw the reader's attention first to the large type, then to progressively smaller type sizes. Remember that adding too many enhancements, like too many fonts, detracts from rather than enhances document appearance.

TYPICAL OPERATION

In this example you learn how to change the appearance of two different typefaces using the Style menu. Begin this example at the First Publisher Main menu with nothing loaded. (Exit First Publisher by pressing Alt-E then typing F1 (if necessary). Reenter First Publisher by typing FP and pressing Enter. This clears the previous settings.)

1. Press **F5**. The Style menu appears. Notice First Publisher places check marks next to Normal (Roman for version 3.0) and 12 Points. These are the default values First Publisher uses for new documents (when the default font supports these values).
2. Press **Esc** then **Alt-G**. The Get Publication menu appears.
3. Select EXAMPLE.PUB using the **Down Arrow**. Press **F10** then **F1**. First Publisher displays a getting document message. The Gettysburg Address appears.
4. Press **F10** then **End**. First Publisher highlights the title.

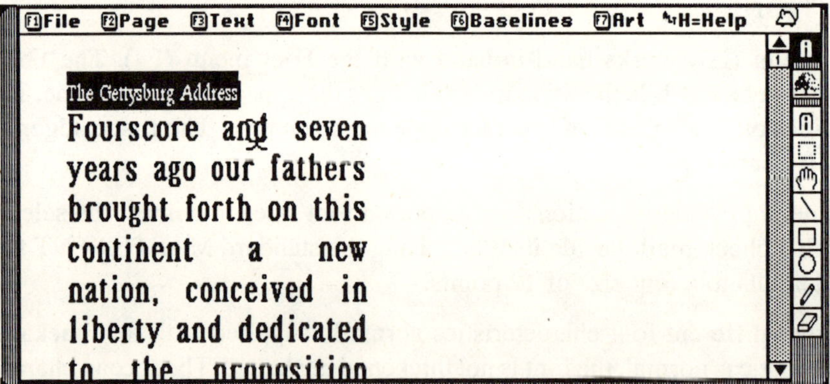

5. Press **F10** then **F5**. The Style menu appears.
6. Version 3.0 only. Highlight Bold using the **Down Arrow**. Press **Enter**. Press **F5**. The Style menu appears.

7. Select 36 Points using the **Down Arrow** and pressing **Enter**. Notice the title typeface size changes.

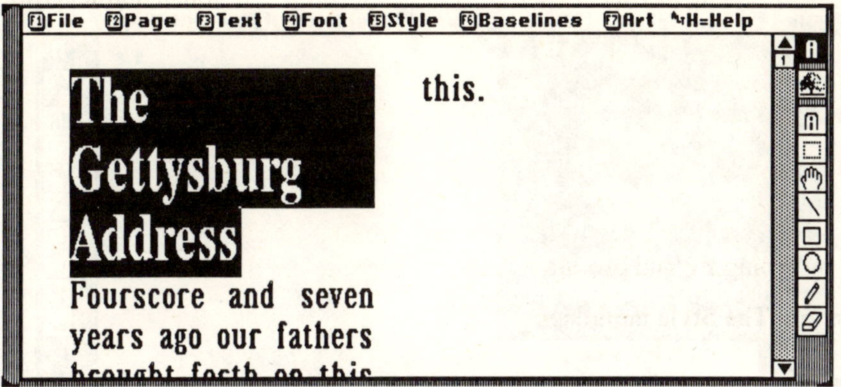

8. Press **F10** twice then **Down Arrow** once. Press **Home, F10,** then **Ctrl-End**. First Publisher highlights the text.

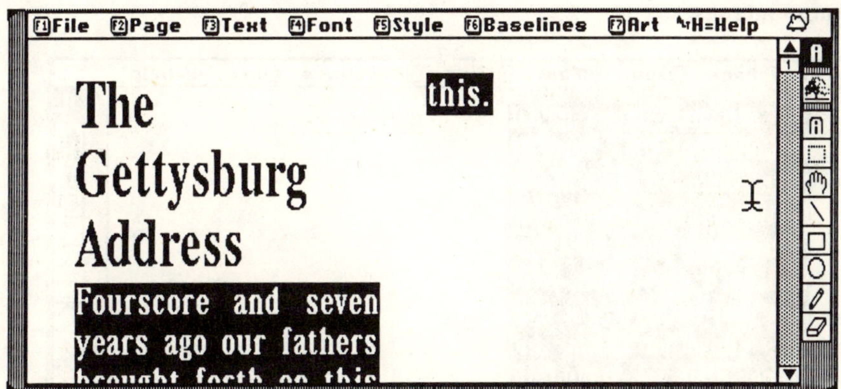

9. Press **F10** then **F5**. The Style menu appears.
10. Version 3.0 only. Highlight Normal using the **Down Arrow**. Press **Enter**. Press **F5**. The Style menu appears.

11. Select 14 Points using the **Down Arrow** and pressing **Enter**. Notice the text size changes.

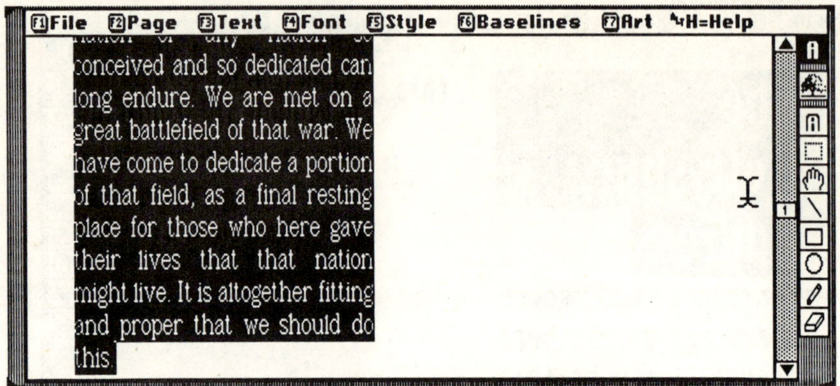

12. Press **F5**. The Style menu appears.
13. Select Bold using the **Down Arrow** and pressing **Enter**. Notice the text letter thickness increases.

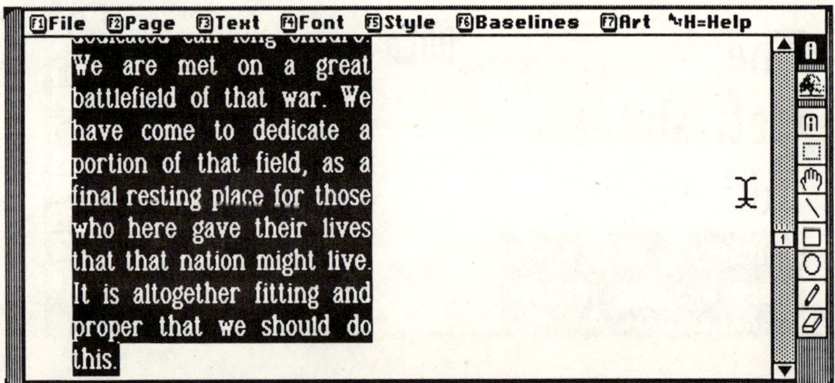

14. Press **F5**. The Style menu appears.
15. Select Italic using the **Down Arrow** and pressing **Enter**. Notice the letter thickness decreases and the letters slant right.

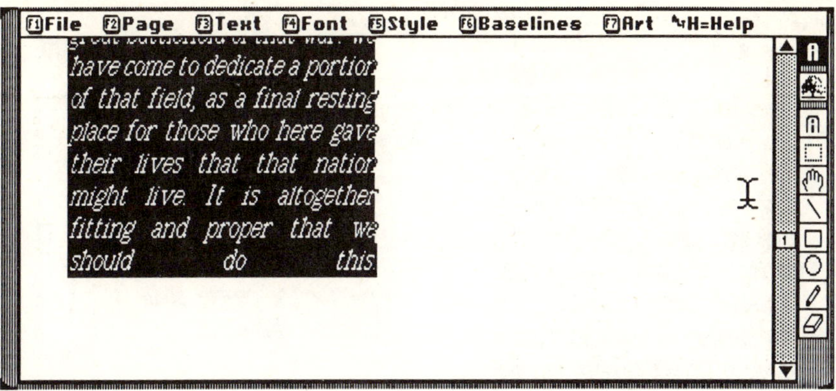

16. Press **F10** twice. First Publisher removes the text highlight.
17. Press **Enter** then type the following text:

    But in a larger sense, we can dedicate — we cannot consecrate — we cannot hallow — this ground. The brave men, living and dead who struggled here, have consecrated it, far above our poor power to add or detract. The world will little note, nor long remember, what we say here, but it can never forget what they did here. It is for us the living, rather, to be dedicated here to the unfinished work which they who fought here have thus far so nobly advanced. It is rather, to be dedicated here to the great task remaining before us — that from these honored dead we take increased devotion to that cause for which they gave the last full measure of devotion — that we here highly resolve that these dead shall not have died in vain — that this nation, under God, shall have a new birth of freedom — and that government of the people, by the people, for the people, shall not perish from this earth.

18. Press **Enter** then **F5**. Notice First Publisher used the previously selected, rather than the default style values for the new text.

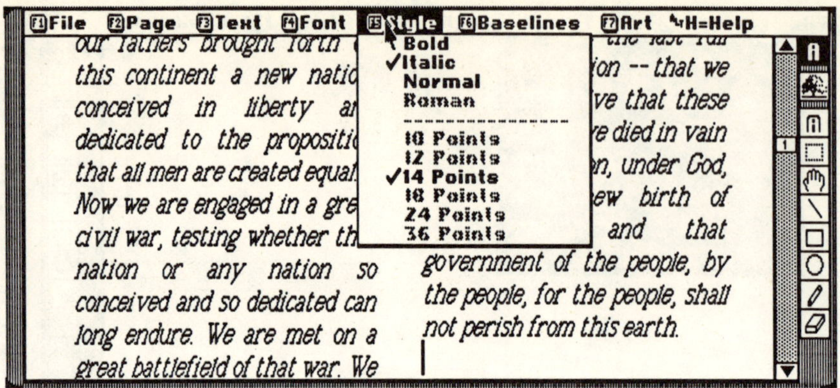

19. Press **Esc** then **Alt-S**. The Save Publication dialogue box appears.
20. Press **F1**. First Publisher asks if it should replace the old version of EXAMPLE.PUB.
21. Press **F1**. First Publisher displays a saving file message.
22. Proceed to Module 36 to continue the learning sequence.

Module 39
USE GRID

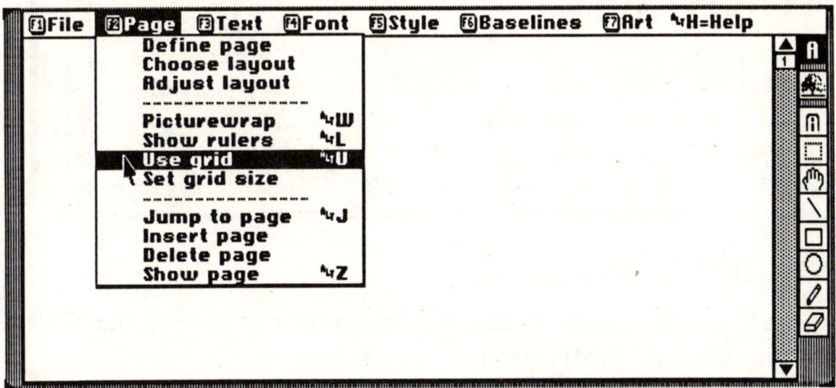

DESCRIPTION

The Use Grid command on the Page menu displays evenly spaced nonprinting dots you can use to align graphics with text. The dots only appear when using any of the graphics tools located on the Side Tools menu. The dots disappear when you select the Text Tool. The graphics cursor normally moves the space specified by the grid interval each time you press the direction keys. You can also toggle the grid using the Alt-U key combination.

APPLICATIONS

You use the Use Grid command to turn the grid on or off whenever you want to accurately place graphic images on the screen. The grid is also useful when using the drawing primitives supplied by First Publisher on the Side Tools menu.

TYPICAL OPERATION

In this example you test the Use Grid command in various situations. This example also shows the two methods for turning the grid on or off. Begin this example at the First Publisher Main menu with EXAMPLE.PUB loaded.

1. Press **F9** (twice for version 3.0). The text on the display turns gray and the graphics cursor appears.

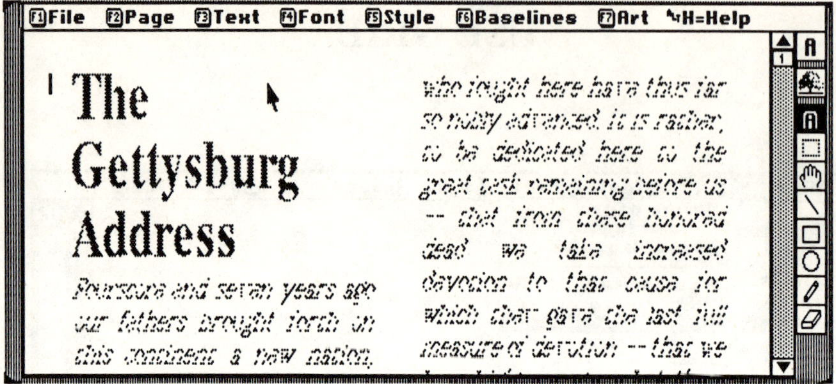

2. Press **F2**. The Page menu appears.
3. Select the Use Grid command using the **Down Arrow** and pressing **Enter**. Evenly spaced gray dots (the grid) appear on the display.

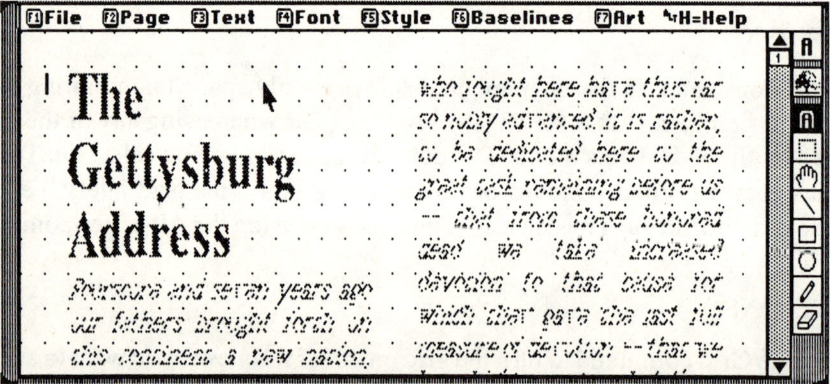

4. Press the arrow keys. Notice the graphics cursor moves in increments exactly matching the grid interval.
5. Press **F9** until the Text Tool is highlighted in the Side Tools menu. Notice the grid remains displayed for all graphics Side Tools menu selections, but disappears when using the Text Tool.

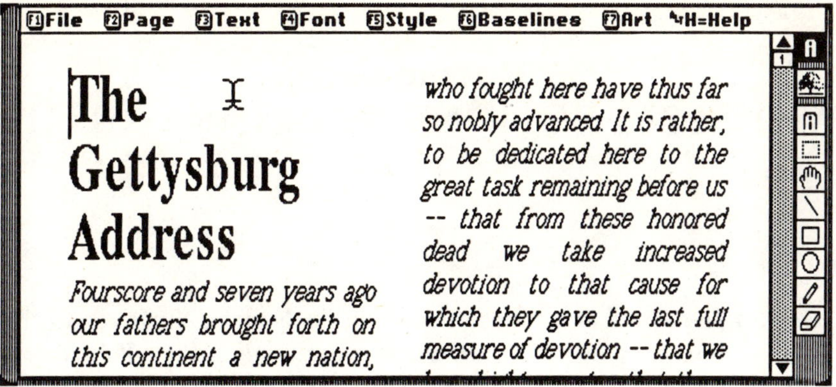

6. Press **F9**. The grid reappears.
7. Press **Alt-U** to turn the grid off. The grid disappears.
8. Press **Alt-E** to exit First Publisher.
9. Turn to Module 33 to continue the learning sequence.

Module 40
WIDTH SELECTIONS, SET LINE WIDTH

DESCRIPTION

(Version 2.0 only) The Width Selections of the Side Tools menu allow you to change the thickness of lines, boxes, or free-form drawings created using First Publisher drawing primitives. These Width Selections automatically highlight when you select one of the drawing tools or the Eraser Tool. To change the thickness of the line, press Alt-F9. First Publisher highlights the next size. The highlighted size is the active size for the active drawing tool. First Publisher supplies four line thicknesses: 1, 2, 3, and 4 points.

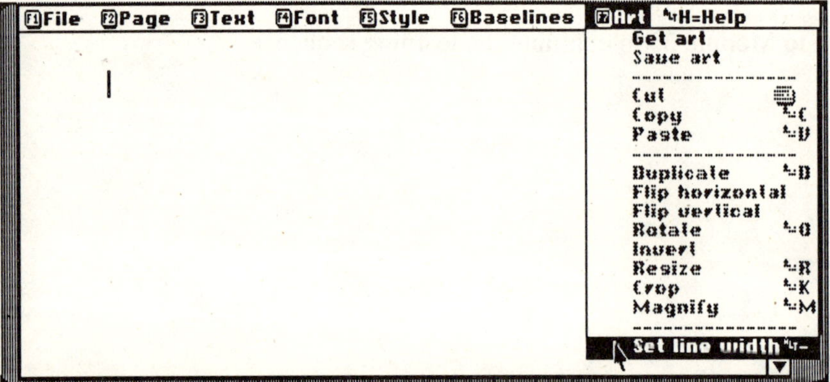

(Version 3.0 only) The Set Line Width option appears on the Art menu. This command lets you change the thickness of lines, boxes, or free-form drawings created using First Publisher drawing primitives.

APPLICATIONS

You use the Width Selections or the Set Line Width option to change the line thickness of the active drawing primitive. By changing the line width, you can produce very attractive graphics using only the three graphics primitives provided.

TYPICAL OPERATION

In this example, you see the effect of changing the line width while drawing lines. Begin this example at the First Publisher Main menu with nothing loaded. (To clear the display exit and reenter First Publisher.)

The following steps work with version 2.0 of First Publisher only:

1. Press **F9** four times. First Publisher highlights the Straight Line tools and 1 Pt Width on the Side Tools menu.

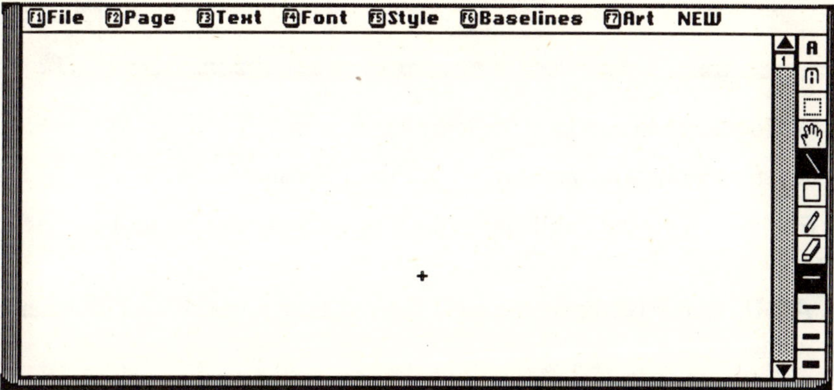

2. Press **Alt-U** then **F10**. Press the **Left Arrow** four times. First Publisher draws a 1-point line.
3. Press **F10, Down Arrow, Alt-F9,** then **F10**. Press the **Right Arrow** four times. First Publisher draws a 2-point line.
4. Press **F10, Down Arrow, Alt-F9,** then **F10**. Press the **Left Arrow** four times. First Publisher draws a 3-point line.
5. Press **F10, Down Arrow, Alt-F9,** then **F10**. Press the **Right Arrow** four times. First Publisher draws a 4-point line.
6. Press **F10**. Notice the difference in the four line weights.

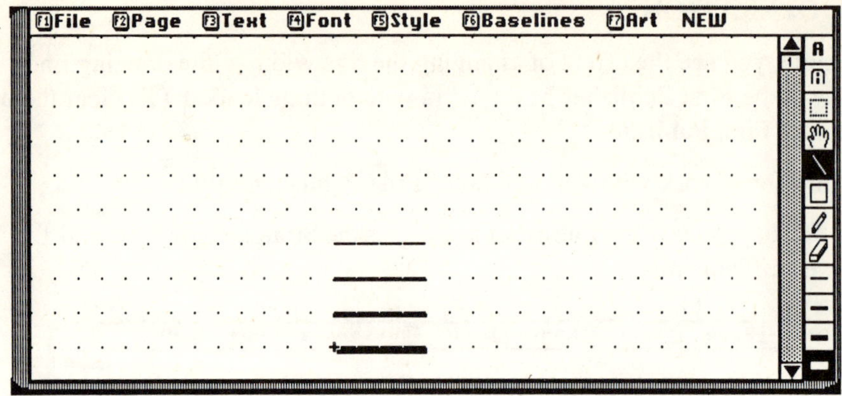

7. Turn to Module 12 to continue the learning sequence.

The following steps work with version 3.0 of First Publisher only:

1. Press **F9** five times. First Publisher highlights the Straight Line tool on the Side tools menu.
2. Press **Alt-U**, then **F10**. Press the **Left Arrow** four times. First Publisher draws a 1-point line.
3. Press **F10** and **Down Arrow**.
4. Press **Alt-** to display the Set Line Width dialogue box.

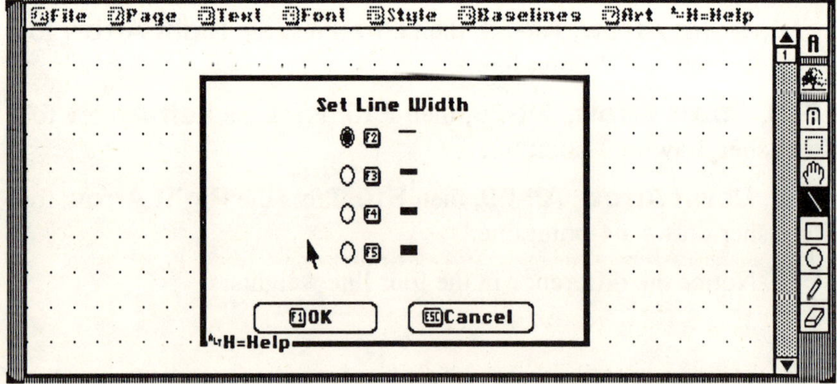

5. Press **F3** then **F1**.
6. Press **F10** and then press the **Right Arrow** four times.
7. Press **F10**. First Publisher draws a 2-point line.
8. Press **Down Arrow**.
9. Press **Alt-** to display the Set Line Width dialogue box.
10. Press **F4** then **F1**.
11. Press **F10** and then press the **Left Arrow** four times.
12. Press **F10**. First Publisher draws a 3-point line.
13. Press **Down Arrow**.
14. Press **Alt-** to display the Set Line Width dialogue box.
15. Press **F5** then **F1**.
16. Press **F10** and then press the **Right Arrow** four times.
17. Press **F10**. First Publisher draws a 4-point line. Notice the difference in the four line weights.

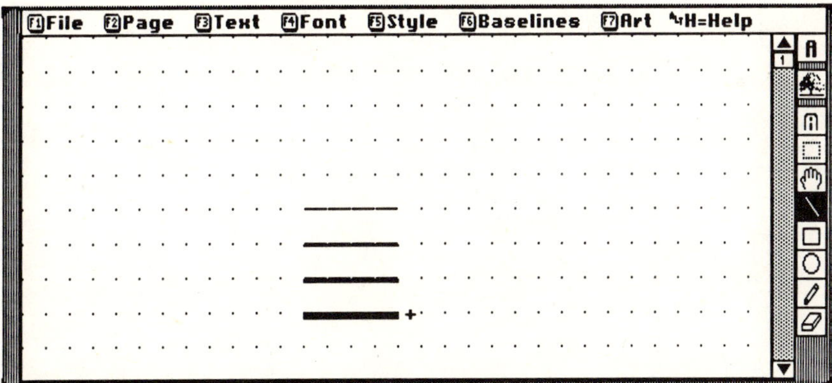

18. Press **Alt-E** and **F2** to exit without saving.
19. Turn to Module 12 to continue the learning sequence.

Appendix A
TERMS AND DEFINITIONS

ASCII	(American Standard Code for Information Interchange) First Publisher uses this code to store the text part of the document. The formatting information is stored as control codes interspersed with the text.
Baseline	An imaginary line on which the bottom of most letters rests. Letters like "g," "j," "p," "q," and "y" hang below the baseline. In First Publisher, you change the baseline using the Baselines menu.
Box Drawing Tool	The Box Drawing Tool allows you to draw squares and rectangles. The selected drawing width determines the thickness of the box outline. The Side Tools menu represents the Box Drawing Tool as the square icon.
Column	A vertical division of a page. You can divide pages into columns using the Define Page option of the Page Menu.
Column Rule	A vertical line that separates columns of text. You can make column rules by selecting the Pencil or Straight Line Tool from the Side Tools menu.
Crop	To cut off portions of a picture to omit unwanted detail. You can crop a picture by choosing the Eraser Tool from the Side Tools menu and resizing the picture block.
Cut	To delete text or graphics from a page. You can cut text by choosing the Cut command from the Text menu. You can cut graphics by choosing the Cut command from the Art menu
Cut and Paste	To move text or graphics from one page to another page or document. You can cut text or graphics by choosing the Cut command from the Text menu (for text) or Art menu (for graphics). Then move the pointer to the desired position. Paste the text or graphic by choosing the Paste command from the Text menu or Art menu.
Eraser Tool	The Eraser Tool removes unwanted graphics from the document. The Side Tools menu represents it as the cube icon.
Font	A set of characters (letters and numbers) with a consistent look and size. First Publisher has five standard fonts called Geneva, Elite,

	New York, Helvetica, and Pica. It also has nine extra fonts called Athens, Cairo, Chicago, London, Los Angeles, Monaco, Seattle, Toronto, and Venice included in the EXTRA.FNT file. Use the font menu to select these fonts.
Graphic Object	A drawing you create using First Publisher. The drawing can be free-form, a line, a rectangle, or combination of all three. You create a graphic object using the Line, Box, and Pencil Tools located on the Side Tools menu and the Magnify command located on the Art Menu.
Graphics Text Tool	The Graphics Text Tool is the second A on the Side Tools menu. It selects graphics mode text (see text tool) for use with drawings inserted in your document.
Grid	A nonprinting pattern of rectangles that help you place text, pictures, or graphic objects on a page. You select a grid by choosing the Use Grid command from the Page menu. You change grid size by choosing the Set Grid Size option from the Page menu.
Gutter	The space between two columns of text. You define the gutter width using the Define Page option of the Page menu.
Hand Tool	The icon in the Side Tools represented as a hand. The Hand Tool lets you move selected graphics within a window.
Hanging Indent	A paragraph where the second and following lines of text appear to the right of the first line. This entire paragraph is an example of a hanging indent. You can create a paragraph with hanging indents by choosing the Adjust Column command from the Baselines Menu.
Justification	The alignment of text with respect to the right and left edge of the page. First Publisher provides four methods of aligning text. Left justification aligns text with the left side of the page (right side uneven). Right justification aligns text with the right side of the page (left side uneven). Center justification aligns text with the middle of the page (both right and left side uneven). Finally, full justification aligns text with both the right and left of the page. You adjust text alignment using the Define Page option of the Page menu.
Leading	The amount of space between two lines of text (pronounced ledding). First Publisher provides two methods of adjusting the leading between lines. The first method adjusts the leading globally by using the Define Page option of the Page menu. The other method adjusts leading for the selected lines only by using the Change Leading option of the Baselines menu.

Margin	The white space surrounding text and graphics. You can define the margins of a page using the Define Page option of the Page menu.
Pencil Tool	This tool allows you to draw free-form images in your document. The pencil icon on the Side Tools menu represents it. The Width selections on the Side Tools menu control the line thickness obtained with the pencil tool.
Pica	A publishing unit of measurement for size and distances of text and graphics on a page. One pica equals twelve points (see Point) or $\frac{1}{6}$th of an inch.
Point	A publishing unit of measurement often used to show the size of type. Twelve points equal one pica (see Pica) or $\frac{1}{72}$nd of an inch.
Running Heads	A masthead that appears on every page of a document. In most books this masthead contains the chapter number and name, and the page number. In some cases, the right-hand pages contain the book name and page number. The left-hand pages contain the chapter title and page number.
Selection Tool	The Selection Tool is the dashed rectangle on the Side Tools menu. It allows you to select a graphic for editing, cutting, copying or pasting.
Side Tools	A set of graphics and text manipulation icons located below the menu bar.
Straight Line Tool	A graphics tool represented as an angled line on the Side Tools menu. It allows you to draw lines at any angle in your document. The Width selections on the Side Tools menu control line thickness.
Text Block	A defined (highlighted) area of your document containing only text. In First Publisher you can cut, paste, and copy text blocks.
Text Tool	The Text Tool is the first A on the Side Tools menu. It selects character mode text (see graphics text tool) for standard print.
Text Run-around	The flow of text around graphics you insert in your document. To flow text around graphic objects, you can choose the Picturewrap command from the Page menu.
Width Selections	These selections change the width of all other tools on the Side Tools menu. They come in four sizes (1 point through 4 points).

Appendix B
DESKTOP PUBLISHING GUIDELINES

INTRODUCTION

A desktop publishing program like First Publisher provides many complex and robust features. You can change the style, font, and size of text as well as pasting graphics or digitized photographs directly into a document. However, like all programs, you should follow certain guidelines when using First Publisher.

Guideline #1: Use white space
Determine the width and height of the page margins, headers, and footers. Most pages leave at least an inch-wide margin around the edges of the page. Use plenty of white space around headings to make them stand out from the rest of the page. Pages crammed packed with text almost dare the reader to look at it, let alone understand it.

Guideline #2: Use grids to line up your pages
Grids keep text columns and graphics lined up with equal spacing in between. A grid creates a consistent alignment of margins, headers, footers, and columns for every page. Without a grid, you have to align every column and graphic object manually, increasing the possibility of misalignment.

Guideline #3: Use graphics to supplement and clarify
Desktop publishing programs, such as First Publisher, let you paste graphics into text documents. However, use graphics sparingly and only when necessary. Remember, the purpose of a document is to inform, clarify, and educate. If graphics can help, then use them. Otherwise, leave them out.

Guideline #4: Use the minimum number of fonts on a page
Most pages, such as those found in newspapers and magazines, mix two or three fonts on a single page. Too many fonts on a single page can be distracting. Also, choose fonts that look good together. Two wildly different fonts can be difficult to read.

Guideline #5: Use the right size type for your text
Letters that look too small will be hard to read. Letters that look too large can waste page space. For headlines, use large type. For most text, use a smaller type size. The most common text type size is about 12 points.

Guideline #6: Use line spacing

The distance between each line should be large enough to prevent the lines from crowding one another. By leaving plenty of room between each line, you make all the lines easier to read. The most common spacing between single spaced lines is $\frac{1}{2}$ the point size of the text font. (Example: if the text font is 12 points, the line spacing is 6 points.)

Guideline #7: Use short line lengths

It's no accident that newspapers and magazines print articles in two or three columns per page. Short lines look more inviting to read than long lines, even if both fit in the same page space.

Guideline #8: Use lines to divide your pages

Even with the proper column and line spacing, a page might still look crowded. In these cases, use straight thin lines to divide columns from one another. Enclose graphics in boxes to separate them from the surrounding text. Your page will then look neater and more organized. The average line size is 1 point ($\frac{1}{72}$ inch). Make the lines as long as the text. Use lines to enclose graphics.

Guideline #9: Be consistent!

Look at your favorite newspaper and magazine to see how each page uses the same layout. It has two or three columns per page and graphics in certain parts of the page. Inconsistency destroys the sense of order and structure of a page. A reader sensing this disorganization will likely turn the page or throw it away altogether.

Guideline #10: Identify the purpose of each page

The purpose of a desktop publishing program is to enhance the appearance of a document. You can do that by adding graphics, using different fonts, styles, and sizes, and organizing your page into columns and grids. Each element of a page must make the page inviting to read. Define a theme for each page. Then make every item on the page reflect that theme. Eliminate any page element that does not do this.

Guideline #11: Use role models

Look at your favorite newspapers and magazines to see how they designed their pages. Copy their styles and use them yourself, enhancing or altering them slightly for your particular needs. The more you practice designing pages, the more skilled you will become. A desktop publishing program, such as First Publisher, cuts out the tedium of designing pages, freeing you to focus on the creative aspect of page designing. By following the above guidelines, you can start producing documents that you can be proud of using your computer and First Publisher.

Appendix C
USING GRAPHICS WITHIN A DOCUMENT

INTRODUCTION

Graphics and text go hand-in-hand. There are many different types of graphics used in documents. Some graphics are computer generated (spreadsheet graphs, paint program art, etc.), while other graphics are scanned into the computer from photographs or other sources using a scanner. Whatever graphic source you use, the following rules will help you determine the best mix of graphics and text.

DEFINITIONS

Bit-Mapped Graphics - A drawing composed of bits. This type of drawing requires more storage space and is less flexible than vector graphics. However, it requires less time to load, manipulate, and print than vector graphics. Also called raster graphics.

Bitonal - See Line Drawing.

Blow-Up - A drawing or photograph that is enlarged to show greater detail.

Continuous-Tone Images - Images that use a large variety of shades. An example of a continuous-tone image is a photograph.

Cropping - Removing uninteresting or unimportant parts of photograph or drawing. This usually allows more text or a blown-up version of the photograph or drawing on the page.

Dithering - Most laser printers produce only one color. Dithering forms dots of various sizcs to approximate different halftones.

Dots Per Inch - The dots produced by a printer, scanner, or graphics display per linear inch. Many laser printers produce 300 dots per inch. Dot matrix printers usually produce from 120 to 180 dots per inch. Scanners produce from 80 to 300 dot-per-inch images.

Gray Scale - The range of gray values produced by a printer, scanner, or graphics display.

Halftones - The process of converting continuous-tone images into a pattern of dots. A screen with a fixed number of dots per inch approximates the gray scale for that drawing section. The number of dots produced by a screen are actually measured using the lines of dots produced by the screen per inch. Screen line-per-inch values range from 65 to 120 lines per inch. The printer approximates the halftones using dithering.

Isometric Drawing - One type of three-dimensional drawing. It is a line drawing representing the way the actual object would appear to the human eye. The parts closer to the viewer appear larger, while the parts farther away are smaller. It shows three connected sides of the object.

Line Drawing - A drawing without halftones or any type of other shading. An example of a line drawing is the blueprints drawn by drafters. Also called bitonal.

Orthographic Drawing - A two-dimensional drawing. It shows only one side of an object.

Pixel - One dot on a display or scanner. The number of bits per pixel determines the number of colors read or displayed by the device. If, for example, a monitor has 4 bits per pixel, then it is capable of displaying 16 colors.

Raster Graphics - See Bit-Mapped Graphics

Resolution - The number of dots or pixels displayed or read per linear inch by displays, printers, and scanners. Resolution is an important factor in the final appearance of text or graphics. The higher the resolution, the less jagged a graphic appears. Even when using vector graphics, the final result appears at the selected resolution of the printer or display (scanners do not produce vector graphics).

Vector Graphics - Images stored using vector graphics use mathematical representations for various parts of a drawing. There are equations that represent circles, arcs, squares, rectangles, and lines. The memory required by vector graphics is significantly less than bit-mapped graphics. Because they are smaller, computers transmit and load vector graphics faster than bit-mapped graphics. You can easily scale vector graphics with no loss in resolution (mathematic equations have no resolution). No matter how much you magnify the image, it is always displayed at the maximum resolution of the printer or display. Bit-mapped graphics display and print faster than vector graphics because the computer does not perform the intermediate step of converting them to raster graphic images.

GENERAL GUIDLINES

1. Use graphics that emphasize the accompanying text. Graphics that do not emphasize the text lead the reader's attention away from your message to the graphic image. A graphic that does emphasize the text explains what words can't. Effective graphics sometimes reduce or eradicate the need for text.

2. Use significant graphics. Graphics which contain irrelevant elements detract from the overall graphic effect.

3. Be sure your graphics are clear. Forcing the reader to decipher poorly written text is one way to lose reader interest. Forcing the reader to look at poor graphic images is the other. Never use blurred or indistinguishable graphics.

4. Use graphics of the correct size. Graphic images that are too large for the reader to look at in one glance are usually too large. If a graphic is too small, the reader may not even look at it. A good rule of thumb is to look at the graphic at arms length. If you can see the whole graphic and still see all the details, it is probably the right size.

5. Use lines to separate the graphic from the text. Using a light line to separate small graphics from the surrounding text gives the reader an area to look at. Do not use lines when the graphic extends the entire width or length of the page. Of course, there are exceptions to every rule.

Appendix D
USING FONTS WITHIN A DOCUMENT

INTRODUCTION

PFS: First Publisher provides many useful typefaces and font sizes. To use them effectively requires many years of schooling and experience to study their effect on the reader. However, by following a few simple rules and learning some typesetting terms you can produce effective results.

DEFINITIONS

Alignment: This is the way text lines up with the margin. Another name for alignment is justification. There are four recognized alignment types: right justified (left side ragged, right side aligned), left justified (left side aligned, right side ragged), center justified (text aligns with the middle of the page) and justified (both right and left sides aligned).

Ascender: The portion of a lowercase letter that goes above the X-height.

Baseline: The lower limit of a line of text. It does not include the descender portion of lowercase letters (g and j for instance). Most measurements of letter height (except point size) use the baseline as a point of reference.

Centered Text: See alignment.

CPI: This is an abbreviation for characters per inch. It provides a measure of how many monospaced characters will fit in one linear inch.

Descender: The portion of a lowercase letter that extends below the baseline.

Elite: A unit of measure for monospaced fonts equal to 12 CPI.

Em: A unit of measure for printer's type. It specifies a character about as wide as it is high. Printers use em because the letter M is about as wide as it is high.

En: A unit of measure for printer's type. It specifies a character about half as wide as it is high. Printers use en because the letter N is about half as wide as it is high.

Flush: Refers to text that aligns with either the left or right margin.

Folio: The current page number. It often appears with the chapter title or some other text.

Font: A complete set of letters, numbers, and symbols of a specific point size and typeface. A complete font description tells the point size, typeface, and any special font characteristics (for example: Times Italic 14 point).

Footer: One or more lines of text appearing at the bottom of every page of a document. The page number often appears as a footer.

Greeking: The method a desktop publishing program uses to display text position when text is too small to read due to zooming. Greeking usually consists of small boxes and squares used to approximate the text appearance.

Header: One or more lines of text appearing at the top of every or alternate pages of a document. The chapter or book title often appear as the header. Some books use the chapter title on alternate pages with the book title.

Hyphenation: The determination of where a word breaks between lines of text. The hyphen (-) character separates the beginning of the word from the ending. First Publisher uses hyphenation to make individual lines of text more appealing by reducing the space between letters and words.

Hyphenation Zone: The area between the end of text and the right margin where a word breaks naturally. If a word is too long to fit on the line, First Publisher checks to see if the word contains a hyphen point within the hyphenation zone.

Inside Margin: The edge next to the binding in a book. It is the right margin on left-hand (even-numbered) pages and the left margin on right-hand pages. The inside margin is usually wider than the outside margin to accommodate binding.

Justified Text: See alignment.

Kerning: The space between two letters. Proportionately spaced letters have equal spaces between each letter. Monospaced letters center each character within a specific space. The space is equal for all letters; therefore, the space between each letter is different.

Leading: The space between the baseline of one line of text and the next line. Normally, this space is equal to the point size of the letter plus ⅙th more. For example, when using 12 point type, you would use 14 point leading. This allows 2 points of space between lines.

Line Spacing: See leading.

Monospacing: A typeface in which each character uses exactly the same amount of space. Typewriters use monospaced fonts to alleviate mechanical problems introduced by proportionally spaced fonts.

Oblique: A skewed or slanted typeface like italic.

Orphans: The top line of a paragraph is an orphan when a page break separates it from the rest of the paragraph. This detracts from page appearance (especially on multicolumn text).

Outside Margin: The left margin of a left-hand page or the right margin of a right-hand page. The outside margin is usually less than the inside margin by the amount taken by binding.

Pica: A unit of measure equal to 1/6 inch or 12 points. It also refers to monospaced fonts with 10 CPI spacing.

Pitch: The space each character of a monospaced font requires. The three most common sizes are 10, 12, and 15 characters per inch.

Point: The smallest unit of typographic measurement. There are 12 points to a pica and 72 points to an inch.

Proportional Spacing: A typeface which allows each character to occupy only the space it needs. The space between each character is equal. Proportional spacing closely approximates the way most people write. It is also easier to read than monospaced fonts.

Roman: An unslanted typeface.

Rules or Ruled Lines: Lines drawn on a page to separate columns of text or graphics from text. These lines can be any size, style, or thickness.

Sans Serif: A typeface that does not contain any lines crossing the letter ends. Examples of sans serif letters include Helvetica and Swiss.

Screen: A screen used to produce different shades of gray on art. You produce a screen by placing black dots on a white background. The screen darkness varies as a percentage of white to black. A 100 percent screen is solid black and a 10 percent screen is light gray.

Script: A typeface which looks like handwriting or calligraphy. Some examples of script include Zapf Chancery and Park Avenue.

Serifs: Short lines crossing the ends of the main cross-members of a character. Examples of letters that use serifs include Times Roman, Bookman, and New Century Schoolbook. Publishers use these fonts in book text because they are easier to read than sans serif fonts in small sizes.

Twips: A unit of measure related to dot matrix printers. One twip equals 1/1440th of an inch or 1/20th of a point.

Typeface: The formation of a group of letters. It includes the size, shape, orientation, thickness, and general appearance of the letter.

X-Height: The height of the lowercase letter x in a specified typeface.

GENERAL GUIDELINES

1. *Don't use more than two typefaces on a page.* When you use too many different typefaces, the fonts draw the reader to the lettering rather than the material itself. This detracts from the general appearance of the writing. It does help to use a sans serif typeface for the chapter title and headings and a serif typeface for the text.
2. *Do use type size, thickness, and obliqueness to enhance page appearance.* When you want to emphasize a particular point within the text, use italic type. When you want to emphasize the chapter title, heading, and subheadings, use bold type. Use a larger type size for the title and heading.
3. *Do use a serif typeface for text.* The serifs on Times Roman guide the reader's eyes from one letter to the next. A serif typeface is usually easier to read in small type sizes because the bowls (the circular portions of letter) do not close as easily. Most text is very readable between 8 and 12 points in size.
4. *Do regulate letter kerning.* If character spacing is too close together, they become hard to read. In addition, they bleed together when copied. If character spacing is too far apart, words loose their cohesiveness and become hard to read.
5. *Do use bold, sans serif letters for titles and headings.* When you present a page of text to the reader, you want the reader drawn into the page. Use bold titles between 16 and 24 points to draw the reader's attention to the headings within the text. Using sans serif type makes the heading look less fussy. Then use bold headings one or two point sizes larger than the text to draw the reader into the text.
6. *Do regulate letter leading.* Use spacing between lines of text to add or detract from its importance. If line spacing is too close together, it becomes unreadable and messy looking. If line spacing is too far apart, the paragraph loses cohesiveness. You also waste page space. Within limits, line spacing can add feeling to the page presentation.

Appendix E
USING PFS:FIRST PUBLISHER WITH A MOUSE

INTRODUCTION

Even though you can use First Publisher with the keyboard, it is easier to use with a mouse. This appendix shows you how to use a mouse with First Publisher. The end of this appendix explains problems you might encounter using a mouse.

USING YOUR MOUSE

1. Make sure you buy a mouse that works on the pc and is compatible with First Publisher. Any Microsoft™, Logitech™, Mouse Systems™, or compatible mouse will work with First Publisher.
2. Install your mouse using the manufacturer's directions. Make sure you install any special drivers that you need to make First Publisher work.
3. Turn on your computer and load First Publisher. You should see a mouse icon that looks like a watch. This icon tells you to wait. Next, the icon will change to look like an "I" with curly ends. This is the Text Tool (character mode) icon.
4. Point to one of the menus with the mouse icon. When First Publisher acknowledges that you are pointing to the menu, the mouse icon will change to an arrow. Press the right mouse key, the menu will pull down.
5. Move the mouse icon out of the menu, the menu will disappear.
6. Point to the Graphics Text Tool (second A on the Side Tools menu) or Selection Tool (dashed rectangle) and press the right mouse button. Now move the mouse icon back into the main text area. Notice the mouse icon changes to an arrow.
7. Select the Hand Tool and move the mouse into the main text area. Notice the mouse icon changes to a hand.
8. When you select the Straight Line Tool, Box Drawing Tool, or Pencil Tool, the First Publisher activates the Width selections. To select a specific width, point to it using the mouse icon and press the right mouse button. Notice the width icon lights. The mouse icon for the Straight Line Tool and Box Drawing Tool is a plus sign. The mouse icon for the Pencil Tool is a pencil.

9. Point to the Eraser Tool with the mouse icon and press the right mouse button. Move the mouse into the main text area. Notice the mouse icon changes to a square. When you use the eraser, it erases the entire area the square covers.

By using the steps above, you can see that using the mouse in First Publisher is as easy as pointing.

MOUSE FAULT ISOLATION

There are several problems that can occur during installation of your mouse and after you begin to use it. When your mouse fails to work, the manufacturer's manual is always the final authority on how to fix it. The procedure below will help you find problems not always covered in the manual.

1. Check your mouse for physical damage. A damaged mouse will probably not work.
2. Check your mouse driver. Make sure you have installed it correctly.
3. Some mouse programs require you to indicate the mouse serial port connection. Make sure you install the mouse in the correct port.
4. Make sure the ball on the bottom of your mouse is clean.

CAUTION

Perform the next step with the power switch set to off and the power cord disconnected. Failure to observe this precaution may result in electrical shock.

5. Check the connection between your mouse and the serial port (for a serial mouse) or open the computer and make sure the mouse card is properly seated (for a bus mouse).

Appendix F
HOW TO BIT-EDIT GRAPHICS

EDITING GUIDELINES

When you import graphics into First Publisher, they will almost always require editing after you resize them to fit the page. This means that you require some help from the Magnify command on the Art menu. Module 24 tells you how to use the Magnify command, but you also need some pointers in using the command. The listing below tells you some things to watch for when using the Magnify command.

1. There are four ways to make sure your graphics are as clear as possible (especially when using a dot matrix printer). First, use as many horizontal and vertical lines as possible. When you need to use diagonals, try to make the diagonal lines as close to 45 degrees as possible. When using circles, try to use ellipses (flattened circles) as often as possible. When bit-editing the lines, make sure all lines connect (if possible).
2. Avoid sharp jumps between line sections. Try to smooth line transitions whenever possible.
3. When editing letters, make all letters of equal typeface and size the same.
4. Never over-edit graphics. Smooth the graphic without distorting or changing its shape.

GRAPHICS EDITING EXAMPLE

The graphics editing example below will help you understand the editing guidelines above. You begin this example at the First Publisher Main menu.

1. Press **Alt-L** then **Alt-U**. The editing ruler appears.
2. Press **F7**. The Art menu appears.
3. Press the **Down Arrow** to select the Get Art option, then press **Enter**. A list of art files appears.

4. Point to the previously saved OPENHOUS.ART file (see Module 18) by pressing the **Down Arrow**. Press **F10** then **F1**. Press **F10** again, the graphic appears.

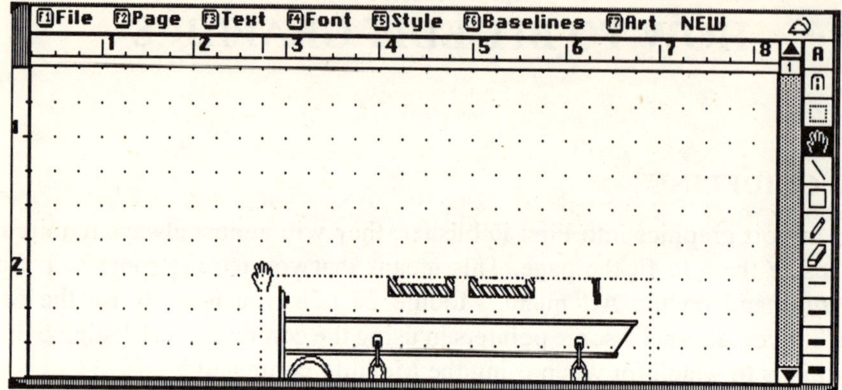

5. Move the graphic into an easy-to-edit position using the arrow keys. Press **F10**. The graphic stops moving.
6. Select the art Resize option by pressing **Alt-R**. The resizing squares appear at each corner of the graphic.
7. Move the cursor to the upper left corner of the graphic. Press **F10**. The resize blocks disappear.
8. Resize the graphic using the **Right/Left Arrows**. Press **F10**. The graphic fills the entire resize area.
9. Press **Alt-R**. The Hand Tool reappears.
10. Move the Hand Tool to the "e" in the word "house." Press **Alt-M**. The magnifying glass icon appears.
11. Press **F10** twice. The fat-bit editing display appears.

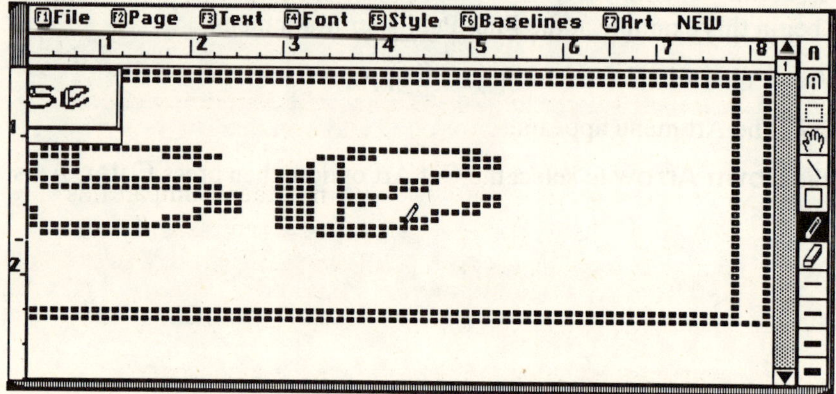

NOTE

The fat-bit display works by allowing you to turn individual pixels on or off. Pressing the F10 key once raises (turns off) the pencil from the screen. Pressing F10 a second time lowers (turns on) the pencil to the screen. The pencil alternates between turning pixels on and turning pixels off when you lower it.

12. Use the fat-bit editing display to modify the letter as shown below.

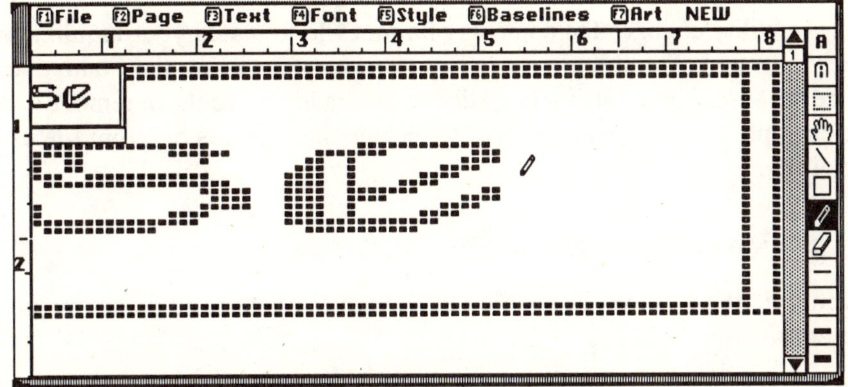

13. Press **ALT-M** to return to the normal editing display.

NOTE

Notice the "e" in the word "house" appears smoother. Compare this "e" with the "e" in the word "open." Printing a sample will show the new degree of smoothness with no distortion.

14. Press **F7, Down Arrow** twice, then **Enter** to select the Save Art option.
15. Type **OPEN2** and press **F1**. First Publisher saves the modified art.

Appendix G
USING THE FONTMOVE UTILITY

INTRODUCTION

The Fontmove utility changes the contents of a font file to match your requirements for a particular document. The three most common reasons for using the Fontmove utility are to reduce RAM requirements for large documents, add new fonts, or remove unneeded fonts. The example below shows you how to change the contents of a font file using the Fontmove utility.

MOVING STANDARD FONTS

Standard fonts are the fonts used specifically by First Publisher and do not include fonts used by laser printers.

1. Type **FONTMOVE** at the DOS prompt and press **Enter**. The Fontmove utility Main menu appears.

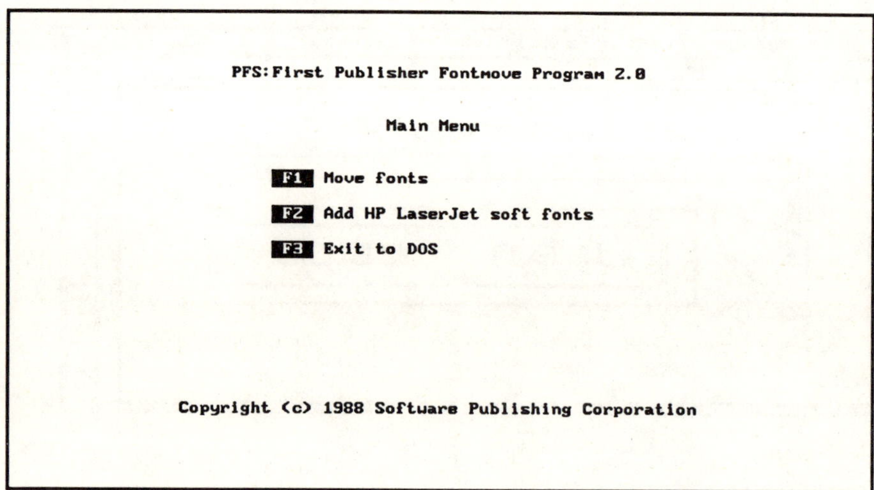

2. Press **F1**. The Move Fonts menu appears.

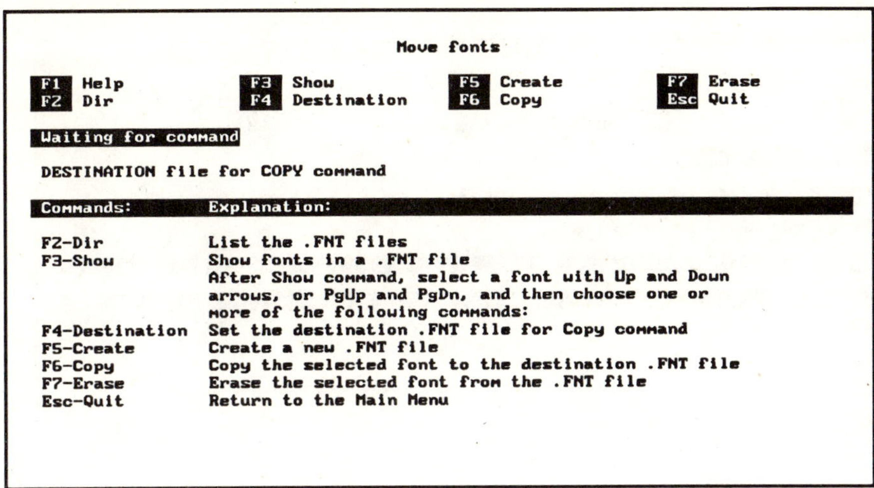

3. Press **F5**. Font move asks which file to create.
4. Type **TEMP** and press **Enter**. Font move indicates TEMP.FNT is the destination file.
5. Press **F3**. Font move asks which file to show.
6. Type **EXTRA.FNT** and press **Enter**. Font move shows which fonts the font file contains.

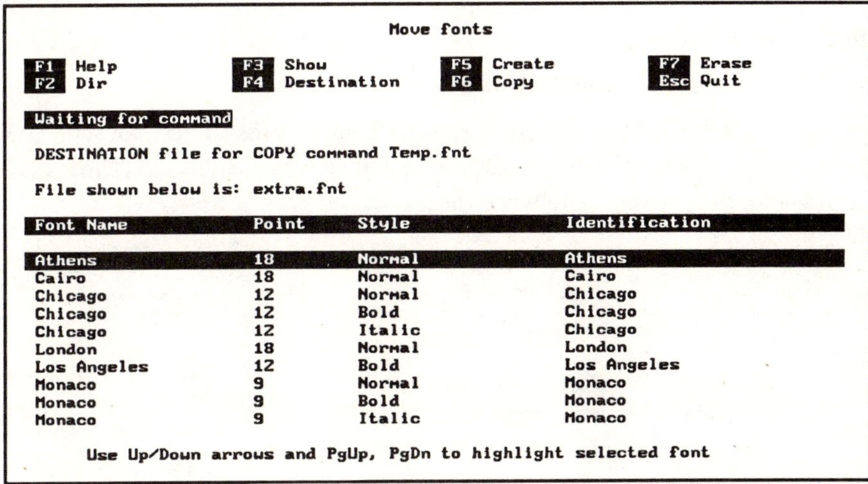

7. Select the LONDON font using the **Down Arrow**. Press **F6**. Font move copies the font to TEMP.FNT.

8. Press **F3**. Type **TEMP.FNT** and press **Enter**. The Fontmove display shows the LONDON font.

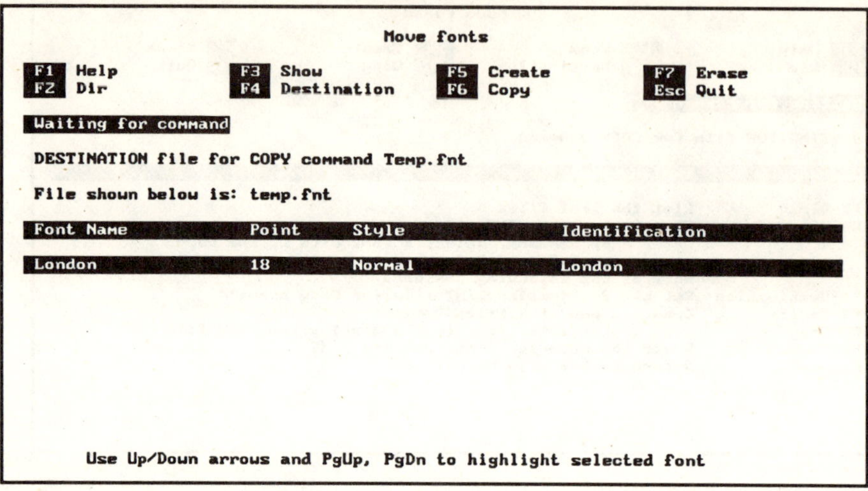

MOVING LASER FONTS

NOTE

This section assumes you have access to laser soft fonts. Bitstream's Fontware program designed the fonts used in the example. The font used is 10-point Dutch Roman.

1. Type **FONTMOVE** at the DOS prompt and press **Enter**. The Fontmove utility Main menu appears.
2. Press **F2**. The Add HP LaserJet Soft Fonts menu appears.
3. Type **AI0100RH.HPF**. Press **Tab** then type **TEMP**. Press **Tab** then type **DUTCH**. Press **Tab** then type **C:\FIRSTPUB**. Press **Enter**. The display first shows a reading font message, then several file write messages.

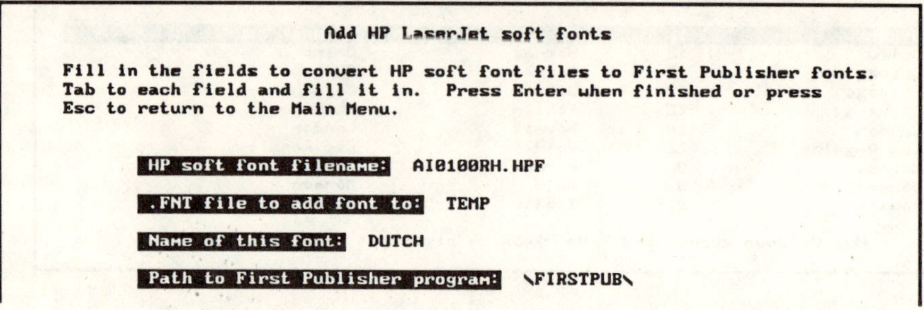

4. Press **Esc**. The Fontmove utility Main menu appears.
5. Press **F3** to return to DOS.

Appendix H
USING THE SNAPSHOT AND SNAP2ART UTILITIES

The Snapshot and Snap2art utilities work hand-in-hand. Snapshot allows you to take pictures of program screens. It stores these screens in memory. Snap2art then develops the picture and places it in a file on disk. The example below shows you how to use both utilities. You begin this example at the DOS prompt.

1. Type **SNAPSHOT** at the DOS prompt and press **Enter**. The display shown below appears.

```
C:\FIRSTPUB>SNAPSHOT
Snapshot program version 1.3
Copyright 1987, 1988 Software Publishing Corporation
Press [Shift-PrtSc] to take a snapshot.
Use SNAP2ART program to create .Art file from snapshot.
C:\FIRSTPUB>
```

NOTE

Even though it appears that nothing really happened in the previous step, DOS loaded Snapshot into memory until the next time you reboot your computer.

2. Press **Shift-PrtSc**. The screen flashes and the computer beeps.

NOTE

Since Snapshot is always in memory, it can monitor your keystrokes. Everytime you press Shift-PrtSc, Snapshot saves the current display in memory. The only time this won't happen is when the application you're using does not allow Snapshot to monitor the keyboard.

3. Type **SNAP2ART** at the DOS prompt and press **Enter**. The Snap2art menu appears.

```
C:\FIRSTPUB>SNAPSHOT
Snapshot program version 1.3
Copyright 1987, 1988 Software Publishing Corporation
Press [Shift-PrtSc] to take a snapshot.
Use SNAP2ART program to create .Art file from snapshot.
C:\FIRSTPUB>

Snap2Art version 1.3, Copyright 1987, 1988 Software Publishing Corporation
        T    use arrow keys to adjust top left corner of box
        B    use arrow keys to adjust bottom right corner of box
        R    remove this help screen
        Q    exit without saving
        E    exit and save the image as file snap.art
```

NOTE

Snap2art knows where to find the display that Snapshot stored in memory. It converts this picture into a disk file that you can use with First Publisher.

4. Modify the display as desired by pressing **T** and using the arrow keys to move the upper left corner, or pressing **B** and using the arrow keys to move the lower right corner.

NOTE

Snap2Art will save a screen portion, not the entire screen.

5. Type **E**. The DOS prompt reappears.
6. Type **FP** and press **Enter**. The First Publisher menu appears.
7. Press **F7** and select the Get Art option. Press **Enter**. The Art Selection menu appears.
8. Select SNAP.ART using the **Down Arrow**. Press **F10** then **F1**. The art selection menu disappears and the hand icon appears in the display area.

9. Position the screen shot using the arrow keys. Press **F10** twice. Notice First Publisher places the screen shot in the display area.

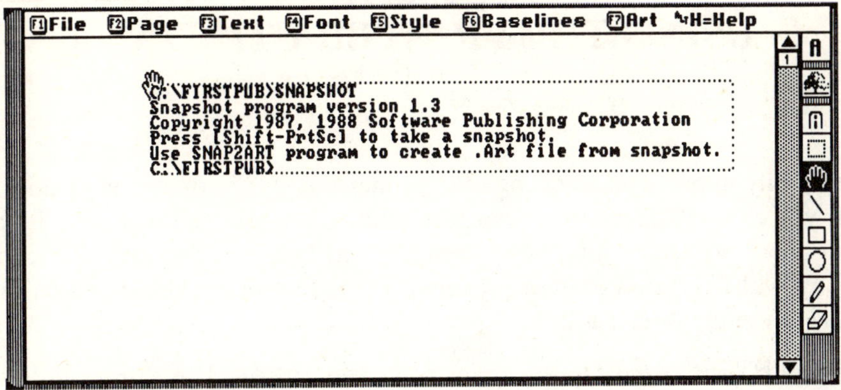

10. Press **Alt-S**. First Publisher shows the Save dialogue box.

11. Type **TEMP2** and press **F1**. First Publisher saves the captured screen shot as a document.

Appendix I
USING THE PRINTER UTILITY

The Printer utility allows you to change the printer you use to output your documents. The printer you choose affects the output resolution of the printed document. It does not affect the fonts or art used within your document. In fact, you can even use converted laser soft fonts with dot matrix printers (the quality greatly suffers). Use the exercise below to learn how to use the Printer utility.

1. Type **PRINTER** at the DOS prompt and press **Enter**. The Printer utility menu appears.

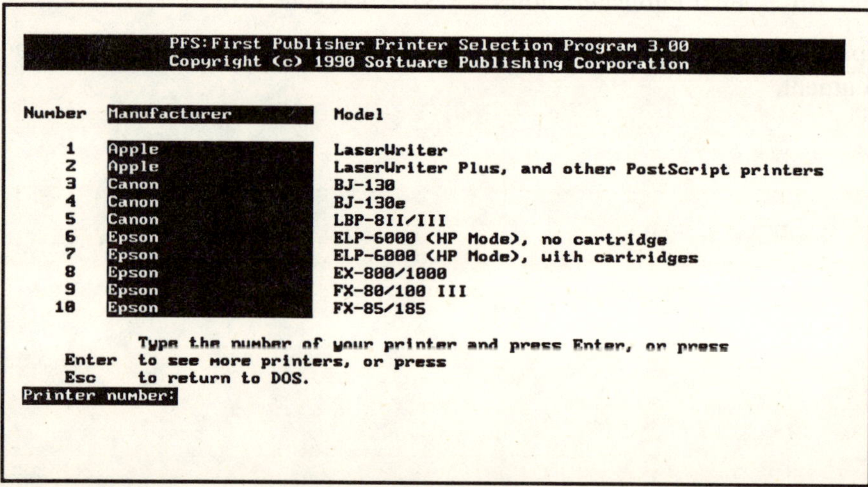

2. Select a printer by entering a printer number and pressing **Enter**. Pressing Enter by itself displays more printer models. The Printer utility asks which port the printer connects to.

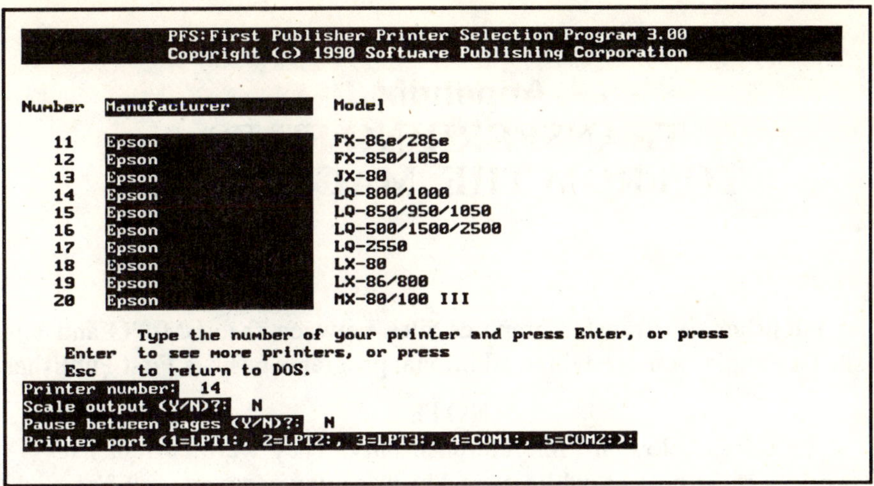

3. Version 3.0 only. Type **Y** if you are using a dot matrix or laser printer. Type **N** if you are using a daisy wheel printer or do not want to decrease print speed using scaled output. Press **Enter**. Type **N** if you are using a dot matrix or laser printer. Type **Y** if you are using a dot matrix printer with a single sheet feeder or a daisy wheel printer. Press **Enter**.

4. Type the number corresponding to the correct printer port and press **Enter**. The DOS prompt reappears.

Appendix J
TRANSFERRING FILES TO/FROM THE MACINTOSH

PFS: First Publisher can transfer graphics files between the IBM PC and an Apple Macintosh. To do this, you need three additional programs besides First Publisher.

NOTE

The prices below are for reference only. They were current list prices at the time of publication. The price you pay may vary from these

IBM PC

1. PFS: First Publisher, $129.00
2. LapLink-Mac, $139.95

Macintosh

1. MacPaint, $125.00 (or a compatible painting program like Ashton-Tate's FullPaint, $99.00).
2. ResEdit (available from Apple Computers)

LapLink-Mac contains a serial cable an a program that transfers files at 57,000 baud between an IBM PC and a Macintosh. Follow the LapLink-Mac manual for installing LapLink-Mac on your IBM PC and Apple Macintosh.

THE FIRST STEP

Before you can transfer files between the two computers, you need to convert your graphics into MacPaint format.

On the IBM PC, draw your pictures using First Publisher, or use a program like Harvard Graphics or AutoCAD. If you draw a picture with another program, First Publisher can capture the screen image and store the file in the .MAC format, which is a MacPaint file.

On the Macintosh, use the mouse to copy a graphics image from whatever program you may be using, and paste it into MacPaint. Now save the file and run LapLink-Mac.

MACINTOSH TO IBM PC

Transfer a graphics file from the Macintosh to the IBM PC with LapLink-Mac. Exit out of LapLink-Mac, load First Publisher, and choose the Get Graphics command.

A dialogue box appears. Choose the file you just transferred from the Macintosh, and First Publisher obediently displays it on the screen. At this point you can save the image as a First Publisher file.

IBM PC TO MACINTOSH

Transfer the graphics file from the IBM PC to the Macintosh with LapLink-Mac. Exit out of LapLink-Mac and look for your file in the Macintosh desktop. If you are displaying your files as icons, your IBM graphics file will look like a plain document icon.

Now load the ResEdit program. Find the file you just transferred and highlight it with the mouse. Choose Get Info from the File Menu (or press Command-I).

A dialogue box appears. Look for the boxes named TYPE and CREATOR. Change the word in the TYPE box to PNTG. Now change the word in the CREATOR box.

For MacPaint owners, change the CREATOR box text to MPNT. For FullPaint owners, change this to PANT. Now exit out of ResEdit.

Look for your file on the Macintosh desktop. This file should now appear as a MacPaint icon.

IBM PC TO MACINTOSH TYPICAL OPERATION

This typical operation assumes you are using First Publisher and LapLink-Mac on an IBM PC, and ResEdit and MacPaint on a Macintosh. The following steps show how to transfer a First Publisher graphic file to the Macintosh.

1. Make sure that you have properly connected the LapLink-Mac cable to both the Macintosh and the IBM PC serial ports.
2. On the Macintosh, double-click on the LapLink-Mac icon to load LapLink-Mac.

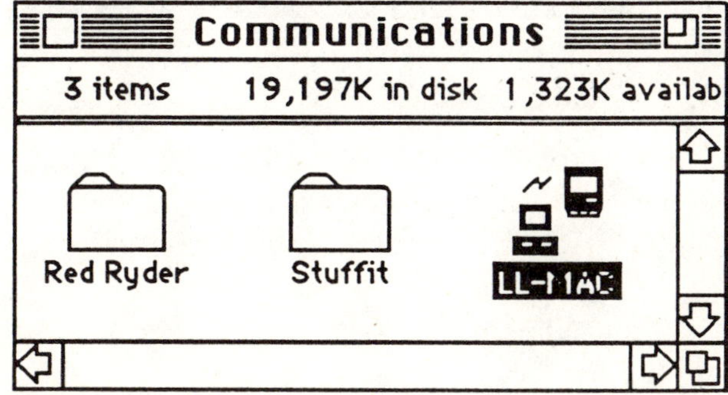

3. On the IBM PC, type **LLMAC** and press **Enter** to load LapLink-Mac.
4. Highlight the LEISURE.MAC file. You may have to change directories using the Log command in LapLink-Mac to see the LEISURE.MAC file on the IBM PC.

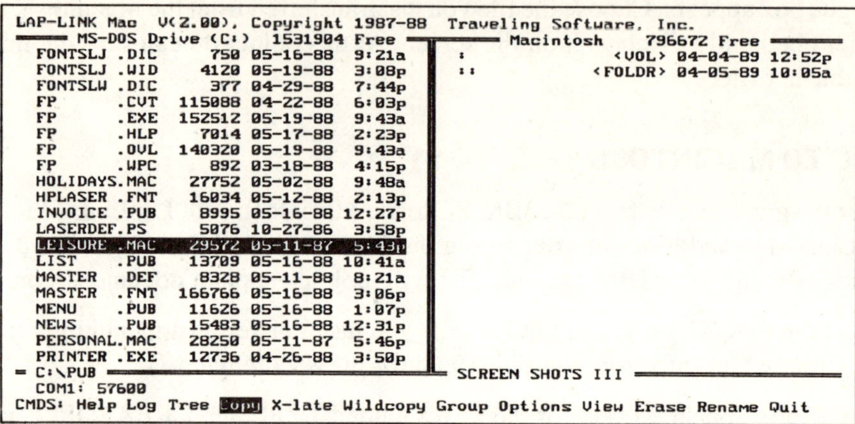

5. Type **C** to choose the Copy command and press **Enter**. LapLink-Mac begins transferring the file to the Macintosh. Notice that LapLink-Mac displays how many blocks of information it has sent.

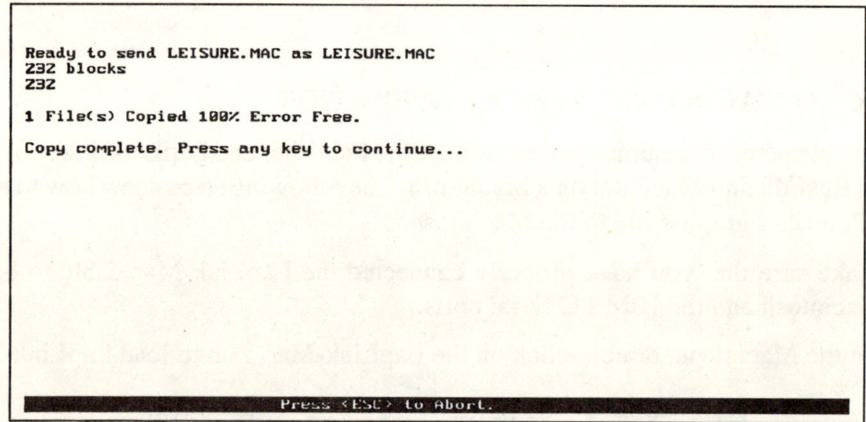

6. Press any key on the IBM PC keyboard to continue. Notice that LEISURE. MAC now appears on the Macintosh side of the LapLink-Mac screen.

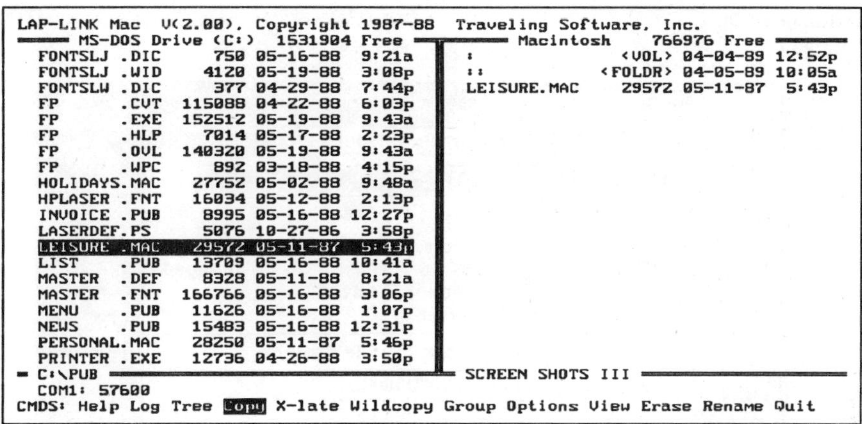

7. Type **Q** then **Y** to quit LapLink-Mac on the IBM PC.
8. Click on the **File** menu and choose **Quit** on the Macintosh to quit from LapLink-Mac, or press **Command-Q**.
9. On the Macintosh, double-click on the **ResEdit** icon to load ResEdit. ResEdit displays the files on your disk in overlapping windows.

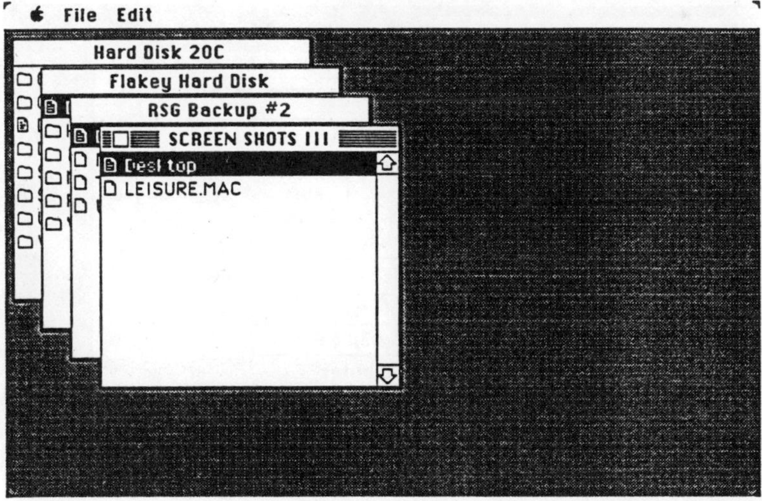

10. Highlight the LEISURE.MAC file.
11. Click on the File menu and choose Get Info, or press **Command-I**. ResEdit displays a dialogue box.

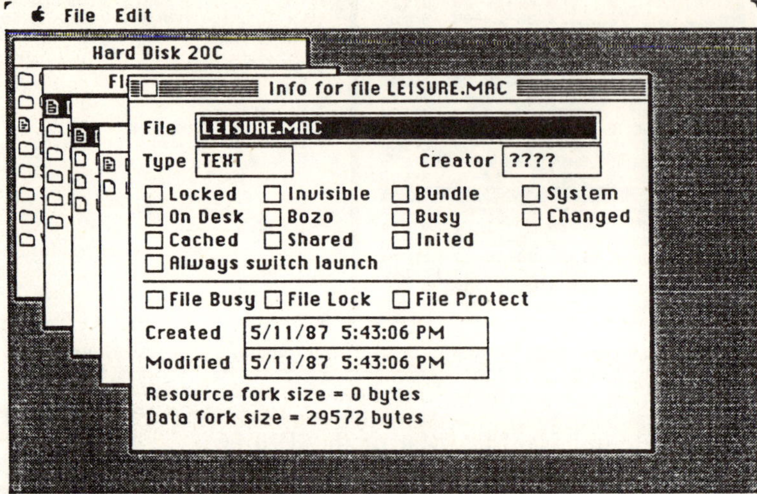

12. Type **PNTG** in the type box.
13. Type **MPNT** in the creator box.

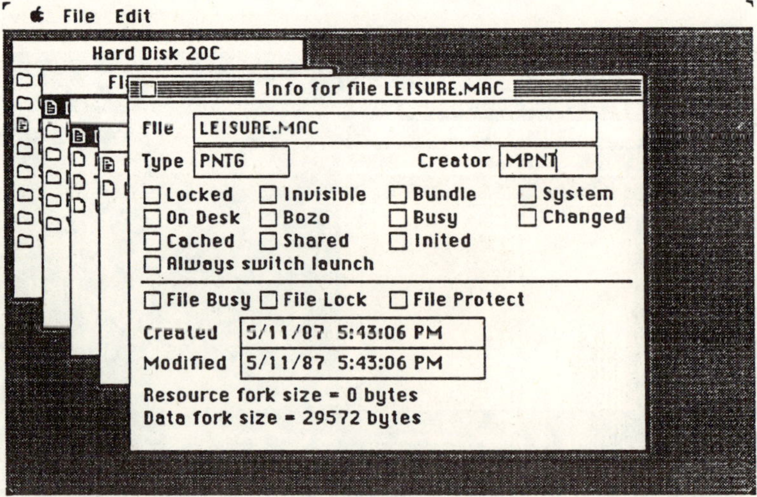

14. Click on the File menu and choose Close, or press **Command-W**. ResEdit displays a dialogue box asking if you want to save the file.

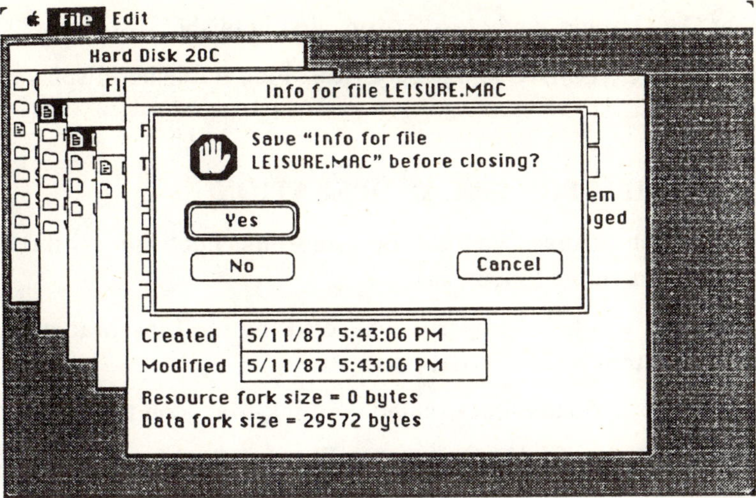

15. Click Yes or press **Enter**.
16. Click on the File menu and choose Quit, or press **Command-Q**.
17. Double-Click on the MacPaint icon to load MacPaint.
18. Click on the File menu and choose Open, or press **Command-O**.
19. Double-Click on the LEISURE.MAC file, or highlight the LEISURE.MAC file and click Open. MacPaint displays the image on the Macintosh.

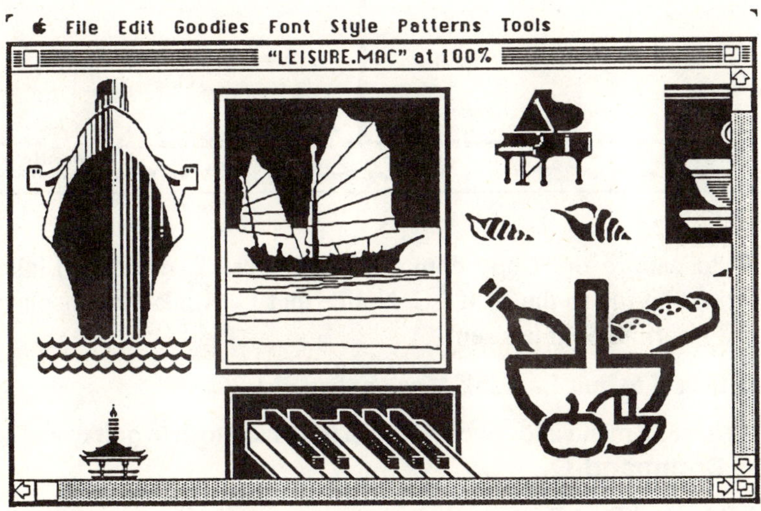

20. On the IBM PC keyboard, type **FP** to load First Publisher.
21. Press **F1** to choose a file.
22. Highlight Get Graphics and press **Enter**. First Publisher displays a list of files.
23. Highlight LEISURE.MAC and press **Enter**. First Publisher displays the image on screen.

MACINTOSH TO IBM PC TYPICAL OPERATION

This typical operation assumes you will be using First Publisher on the IBM PC, and ResEdit and FullPaint on the Macintosh.

1. Make sure that you have properly connected the LapLink-Mac cable to both the Macintosh and the IBM PC serial ports.
2. On the Macintosh, double-click on the LapLink-Mac icon to load Lap Link-Mac.
3. On the IBM PC, type **LLMAC** and press **Enter** to load LapLink-Mac.
4. Highlight the Alphie's Bar file. You may have to change directories in LapLink-Mac to see the Alphie's Bar file on the IBM PC.

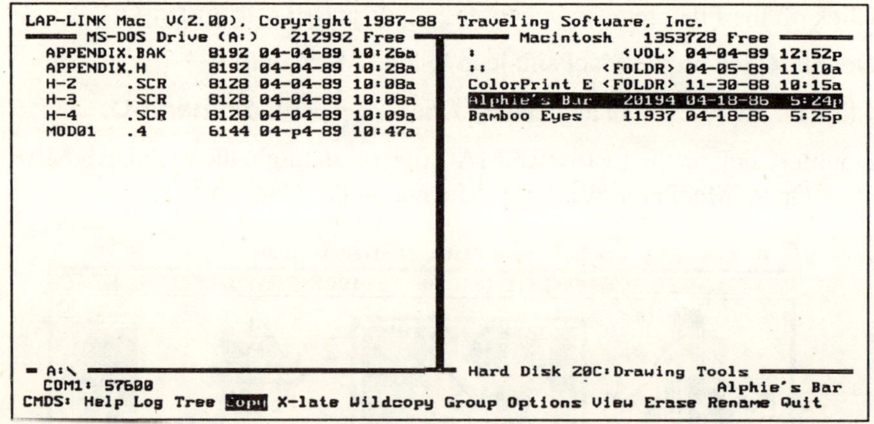

5. Type **C** to choose the Copy command and press **Enter**. LapLink-Mac begins transferring the file to the IBM PC. Notice that LapLink-Mac displays how many blocks of information it has sent.
6. Type **Q** then **Y** to quit LapLink-Mac on the IBM PC.
7. Click on the File menu and choose Quit on the Macintosh to quit from LapLink-Mac, or press **Command-Q**.
8. Type **FP** to load First Publisher.

9. Press **F1** to choose a file.
10. Highlight Get Graphics and press **Enter**. First Publisher displays a list of files.
11. Highlight LEISURE.MAC and press **Enter**. First Publisher displays the image on screen.
12. On the Macintosh, double-click on the Alphie's Bar icon. FullPaint displays the image on screen.

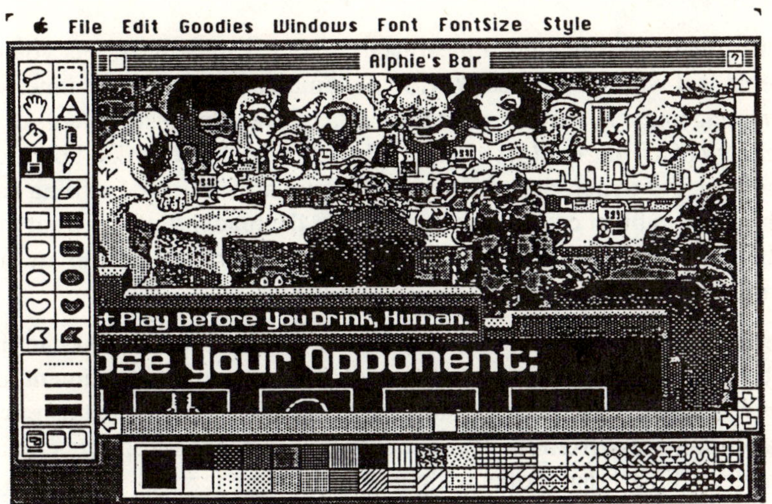

Appendix K
USING CLIP ART

INTRODUCTION

Clip art can greatly enhance the appearance of your document. It lets you express ideas and concepts that words fail to convey. For example, explaining the inner workings of a database management system can test the skills of even the best writer. So, many writers use the analogy of a filing cabinet to explain how the database works. To make the analogy seem more real, the writer will often provide a clip art version of a filing cabinet. Often, parts of the filing cabinet contain labels that help the reader identify what the writer talks about in the accompanying text. This is a complementary use of clip art in a document. The clip art complements the text provided by the writer.

There are many ways that you can use clip art. In some cases you can use clip art to decorate the corners or sides of the document. This makes the document look attractive and draws the reader's attention to the text. Unfortunately, it is just as easy to draw the reader's attention away from the text by using gaudy or inappropriate clip art. You must carefully select clip art that works with, not against, the text.

Another consideration when using clip art is the setting of your text. You need to ask yourself what the audience would like to see. For example, providing a decorative border on a technical document is inappropriate. A person reading a technical document probably wants to see schematics or other explanatory diagrams.

With all these rules in mind, you can select a piece of clip art that helps the reader visualize what you want to say. The following pages show you the clip art provided with First Publisher. In addition, they show the contents of two clip art packages that you may purchase separately from Software Publishing Corporation.

Standard Clip Art

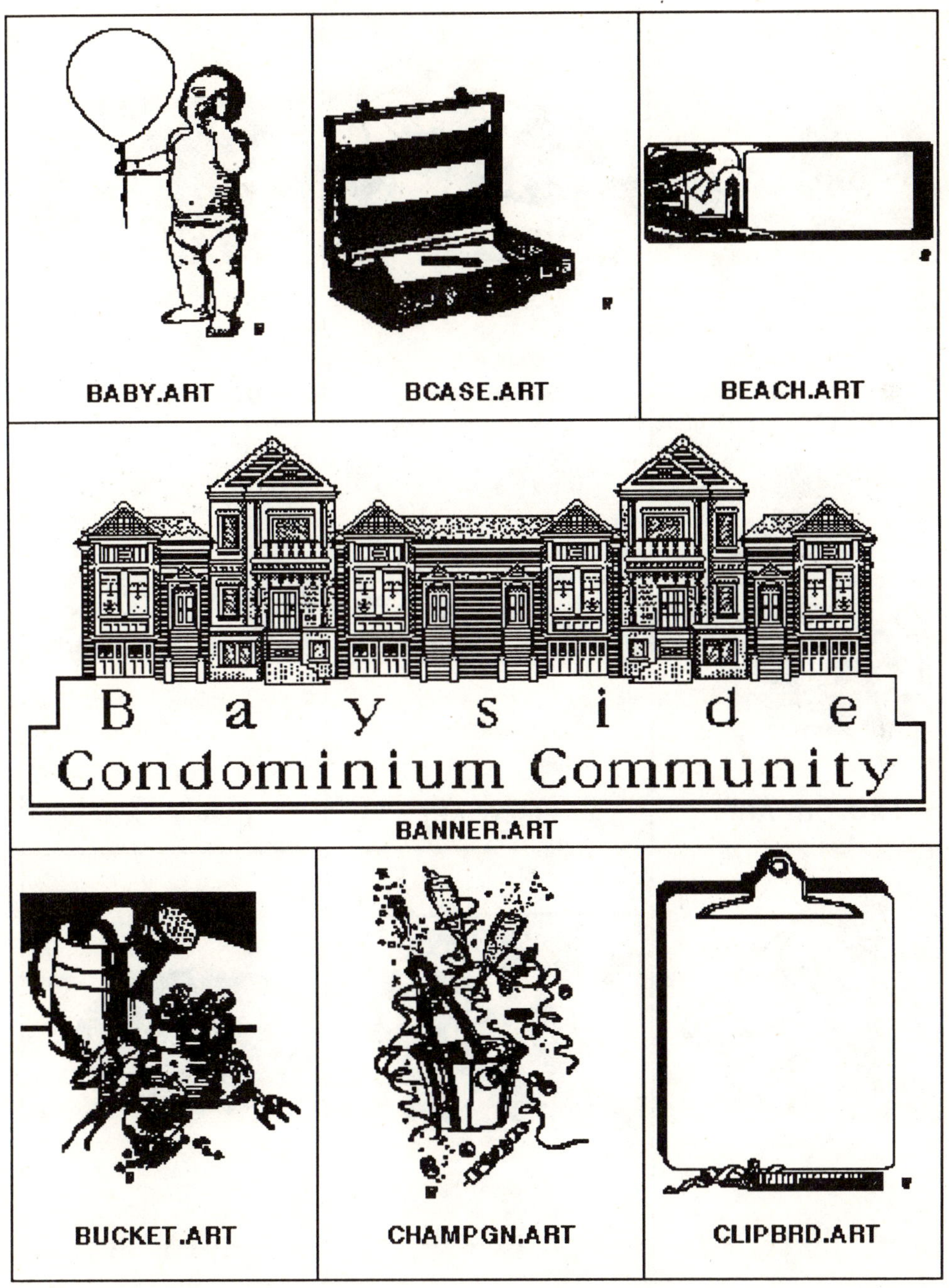

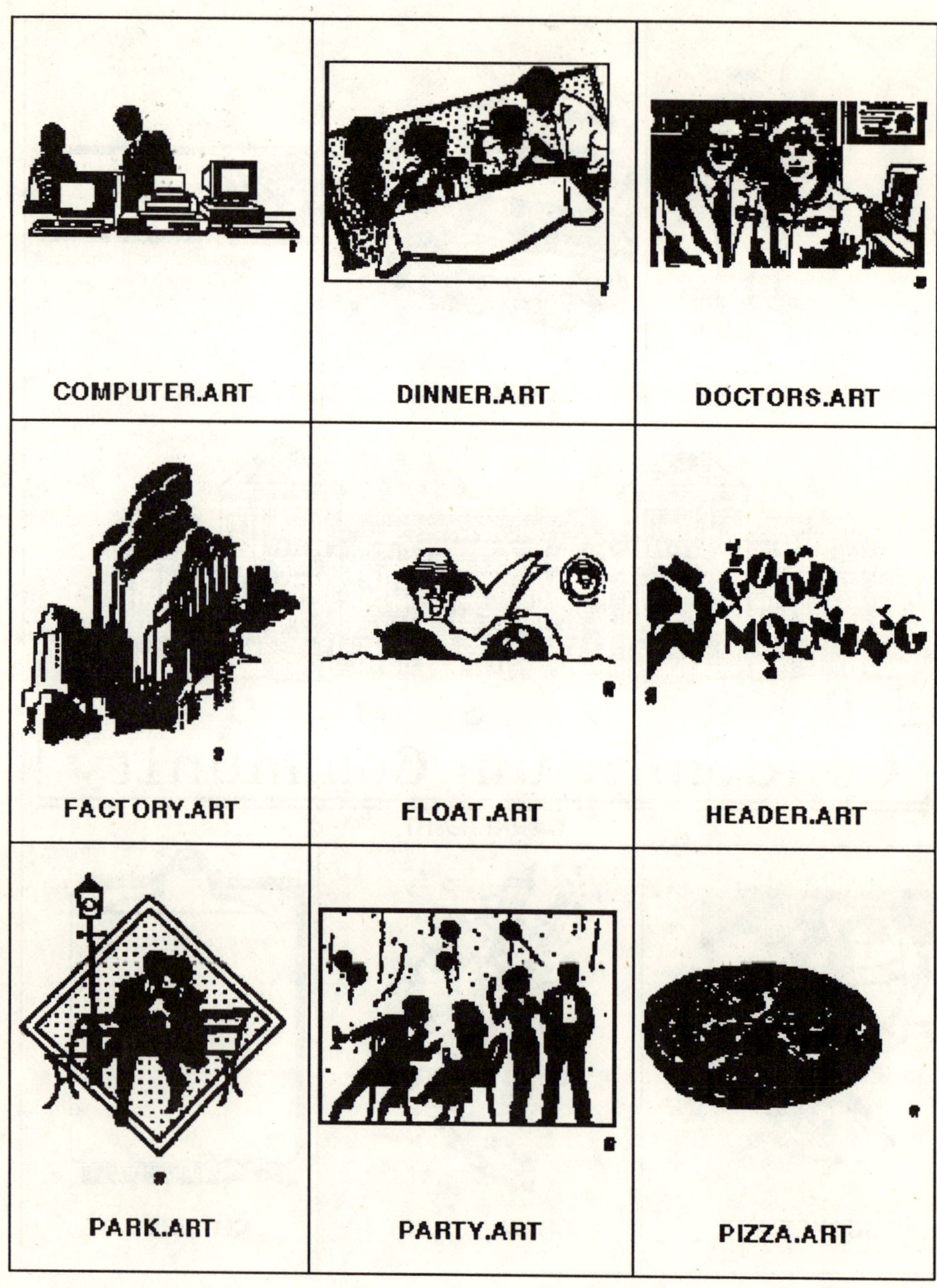

COMPUTER.ART	DINNER.ART	DOCTORS.ART
FACTORY.ART	FLOAT.ART	HEADER.ART
PARK.ART	PARTY.ART	PIZZA.ART

RESTAURT.ART
SLVRWRE.ART
SOCCER.ART
SPORTS.ART
TENNIS.ART

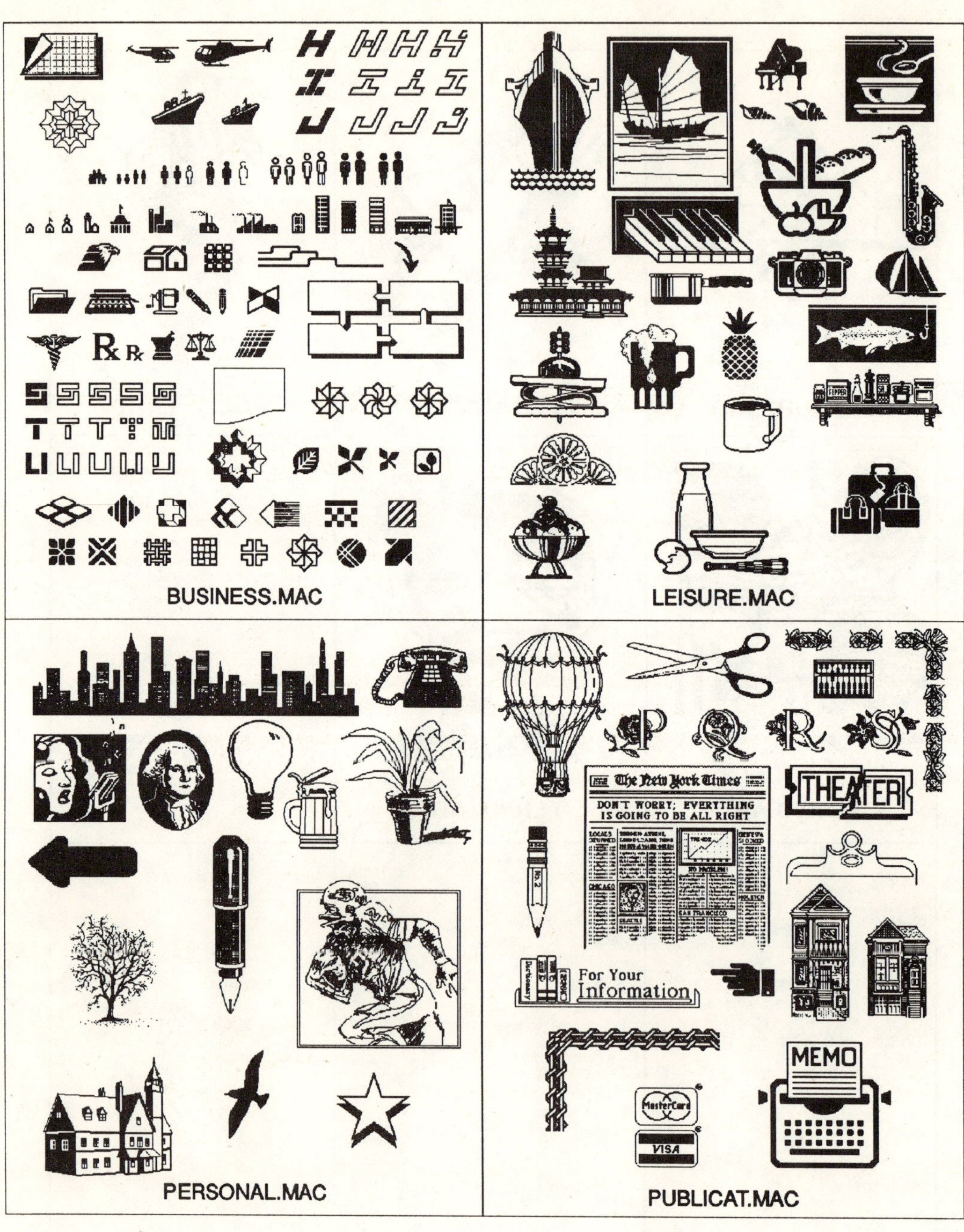
BUSINESS.MAC
LEISURE.MAC
PERSONAL.MAC
The New York Times
DON'T WORRY; EVERYTHING
IS GOING TO BE ALL RIGHT
THEATER
For Your
Information
MEMO
MasterCard
VISA
PUBLICAT.MAC

HOLIDAYS.MAC

Add-on Clip Art:

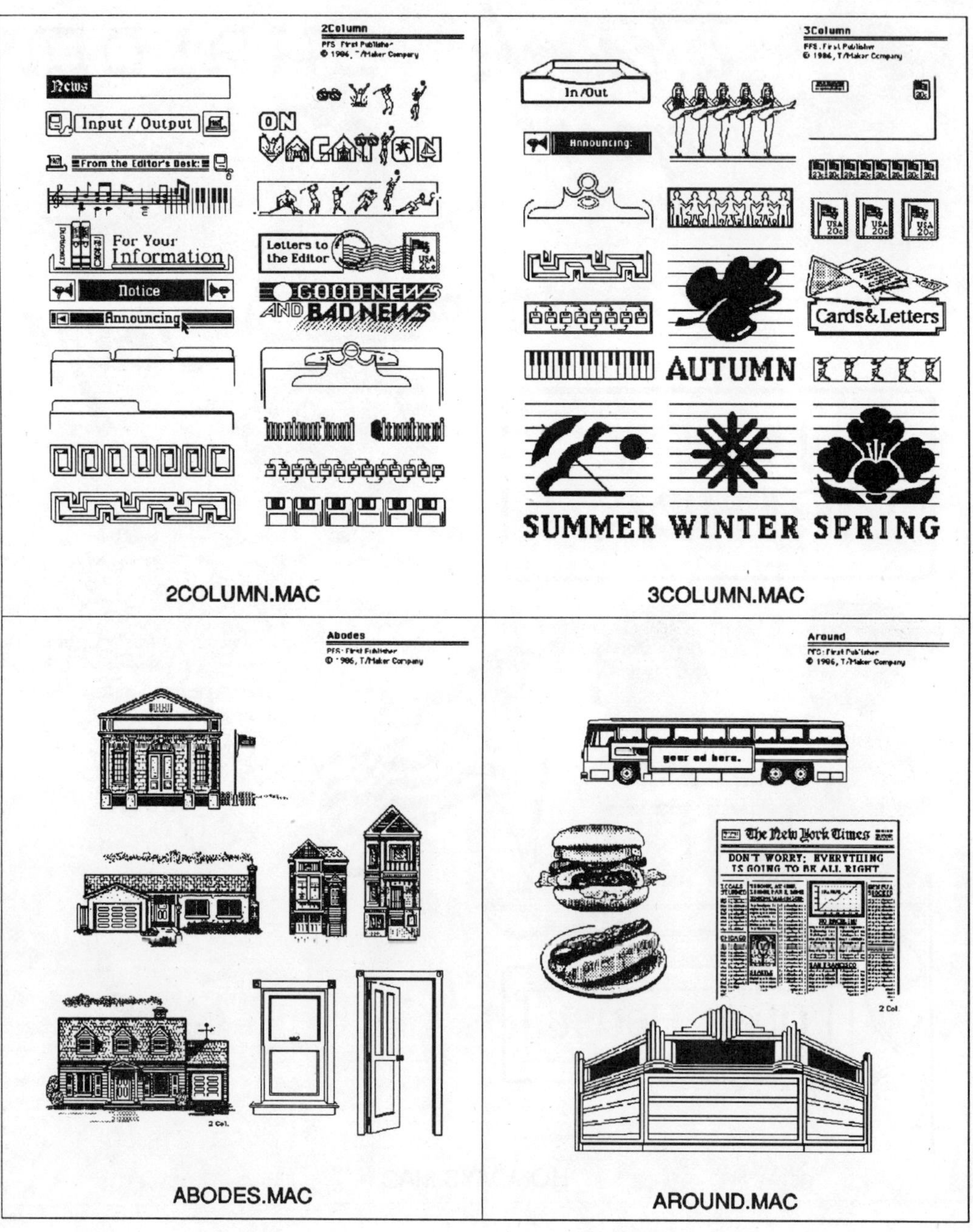

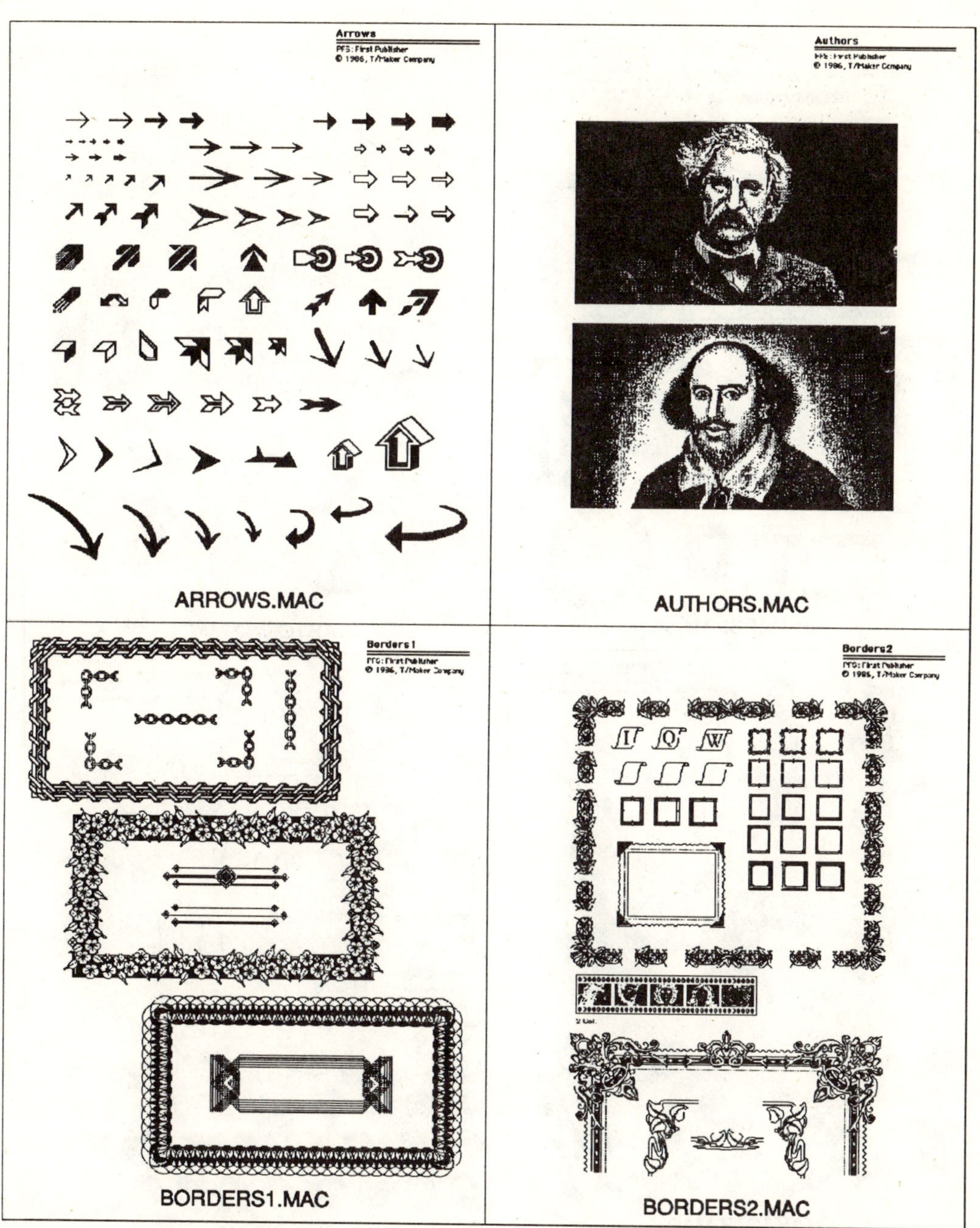
Arrows
PFS: First Publisher
© 1986, T/Maker Company
ARROWS.MAC
Authors
PFS: First Publisher
© 1986, T/Maker Company
AUTHORS.MAC
Borders1
PFS: First Publisher
© 1986, T/Maker Company
BORDERS1.MAC
Borders2
PFS: First Publisher
© 1986, T/Maker Company
BORDERS2.MAC

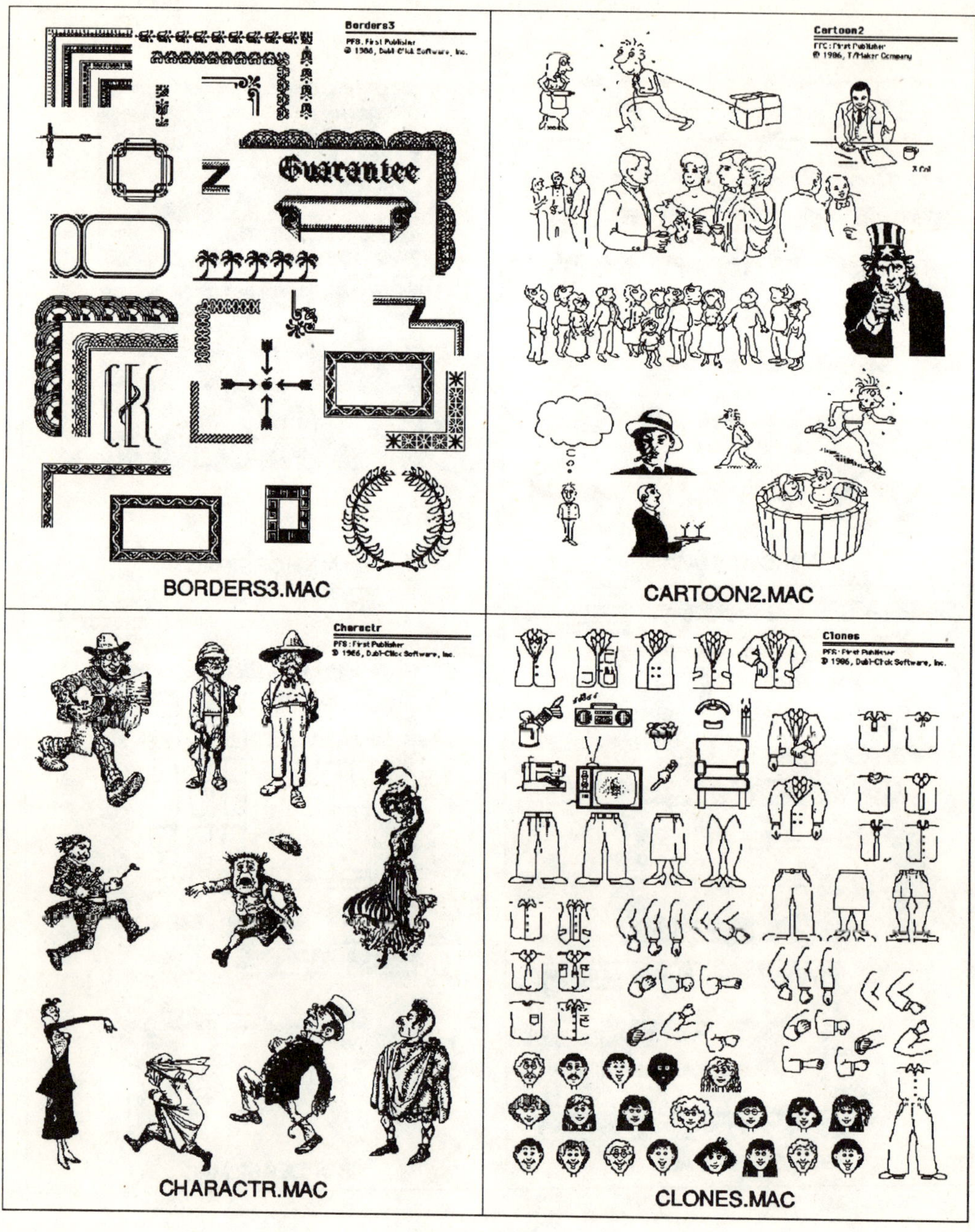
Borders3
PFS. First Publisher
© 1986, Dubl-Click Software, Inc.
Guarantee
BORDERS3.MAC
Cartoon2
© 1986, T/Maker Company
CARTOON2.MAC
Charactr
PFS : First Publisher
© 1986, Dubl-Click Software, Inc.
CHARACTR.MAC
Clones
© 1986, Dubl-Click Software, Inc.
CLONES.MAC

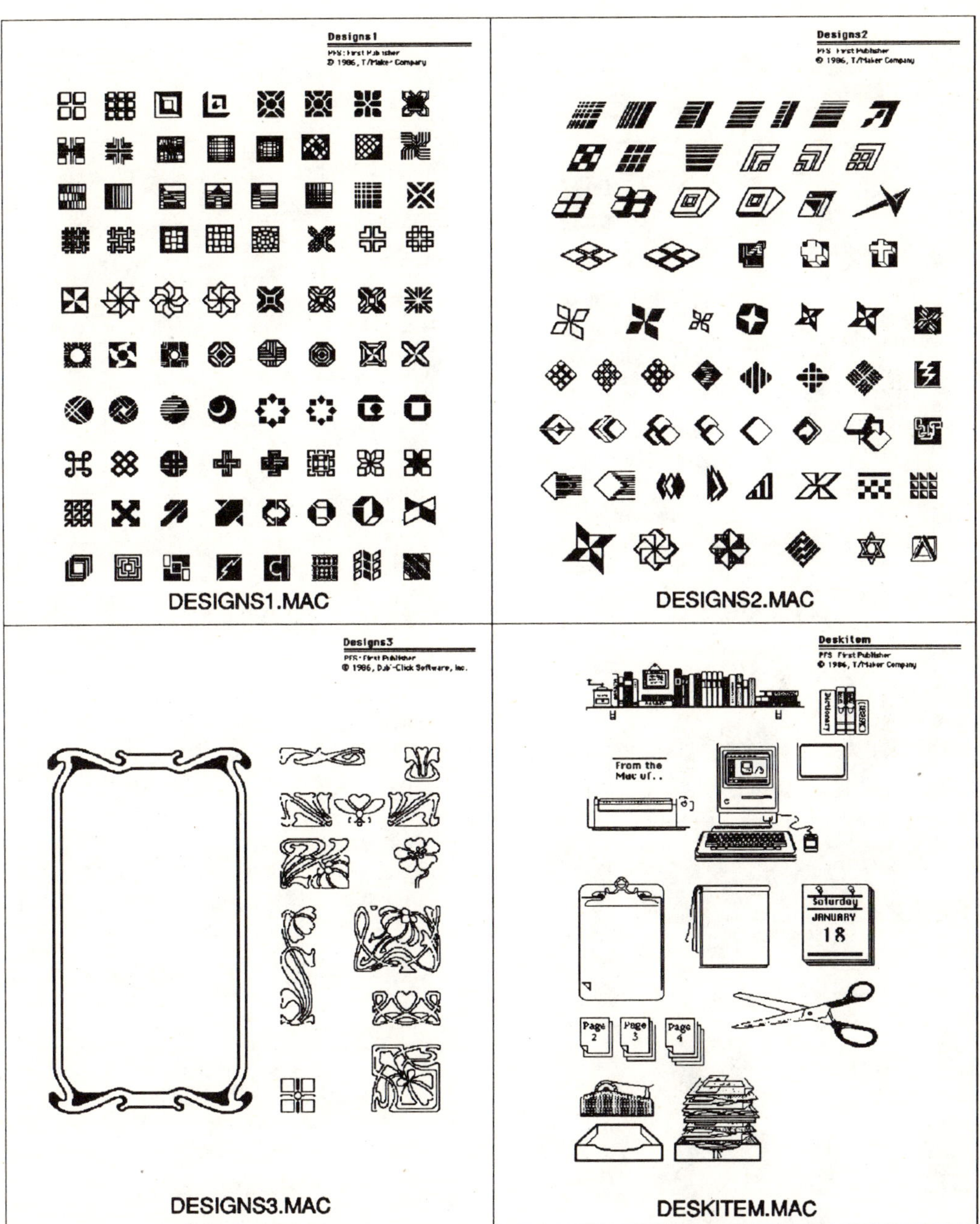
Designs1
PFS: First Publisher
© 1986, T/Maker Company
DESIGNS1.MAC
Designs2
PFS: First Publisher
© 1986, T/Maker Company
DESIGNS2.MAC
Designs3
PFS: First Publisher
© 1986, Dubl-Click Software, Inc.
DESIGNS3.MAC
Deskitem
PFS: First Publisher
© 1986, T/Maker Company
From the
Mac of..
Saturday
JANUARY
18
Page 2
Page 3
Page 4
DESKITEM.MAC

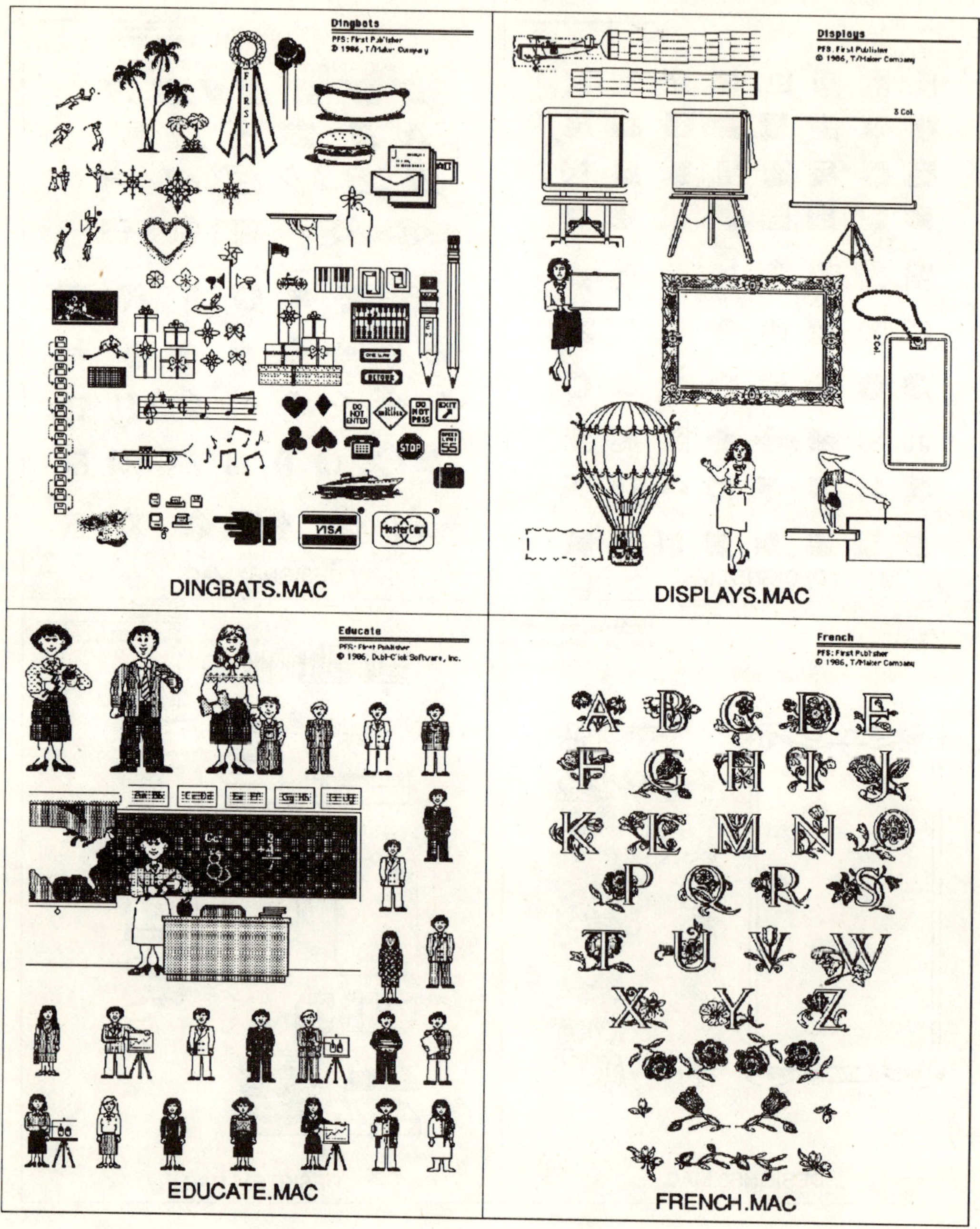
Dingbats
PFS: First Publisher
© 1986, T/Maker Company
FIRST
DO NOT ENTER
DO NOT PASS
EXIT
STOP
SPEED LIMIT 55
VISA
MasterCard
DINGBATS.MAC
Displays
PFS: First Publisher
© 1986, T/Maker Company
3 Col.
2 Col.
DISPLAYS.MAC
Educate
PFS: First Publisher
© 1986, Dubl-Click Software, Inc.
EDUCATE.MAC
French
PFS: First Publisher
© 1986, T/Maker Company
FRENCH.MAC

LOGO1.MAC

LOGO2.MAC

LOGO3.MAC

LOGO4.MAC

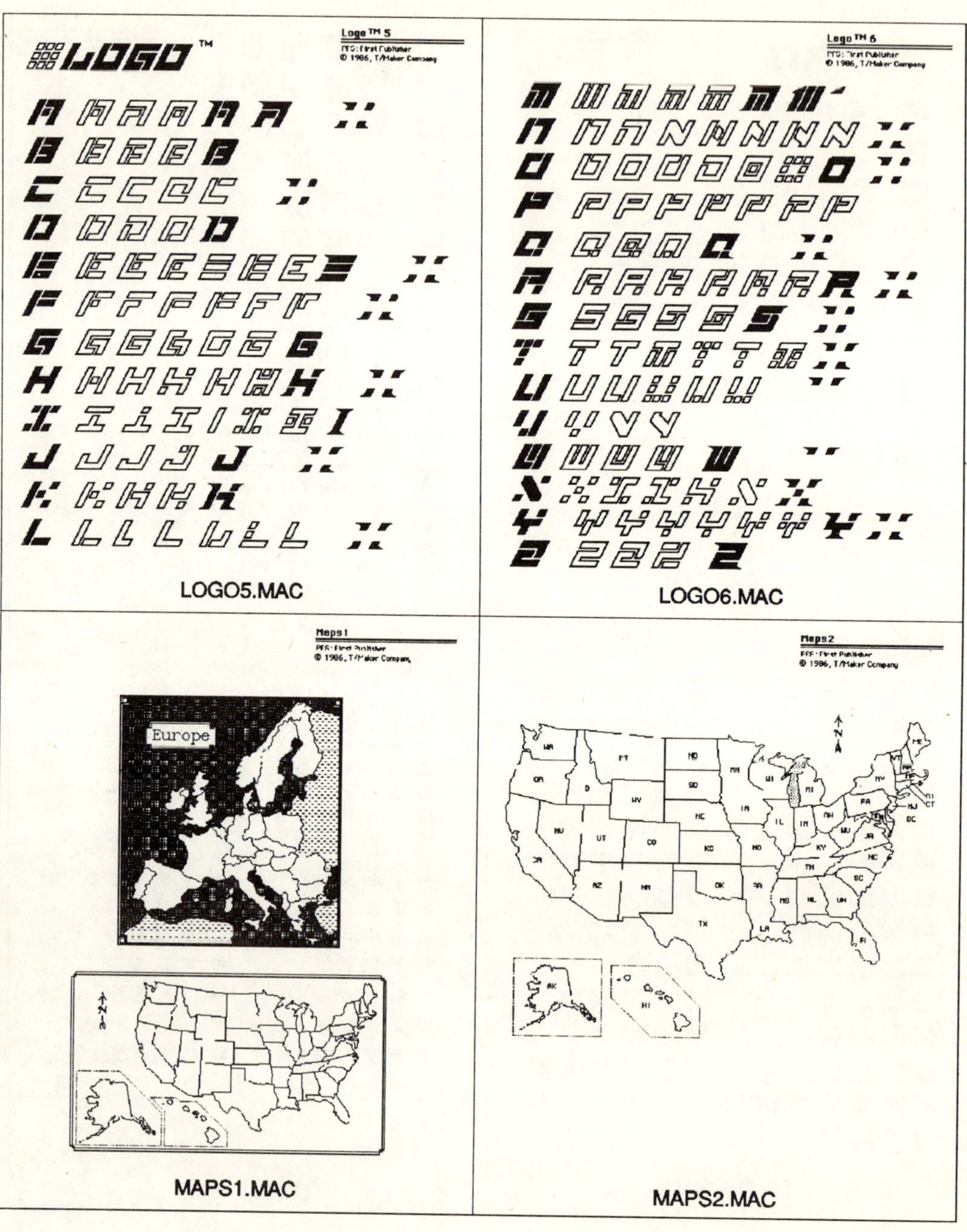

LOGO5.MAC

LOGO6.MAC

MAPS1.MAC

MAPS2.MAC

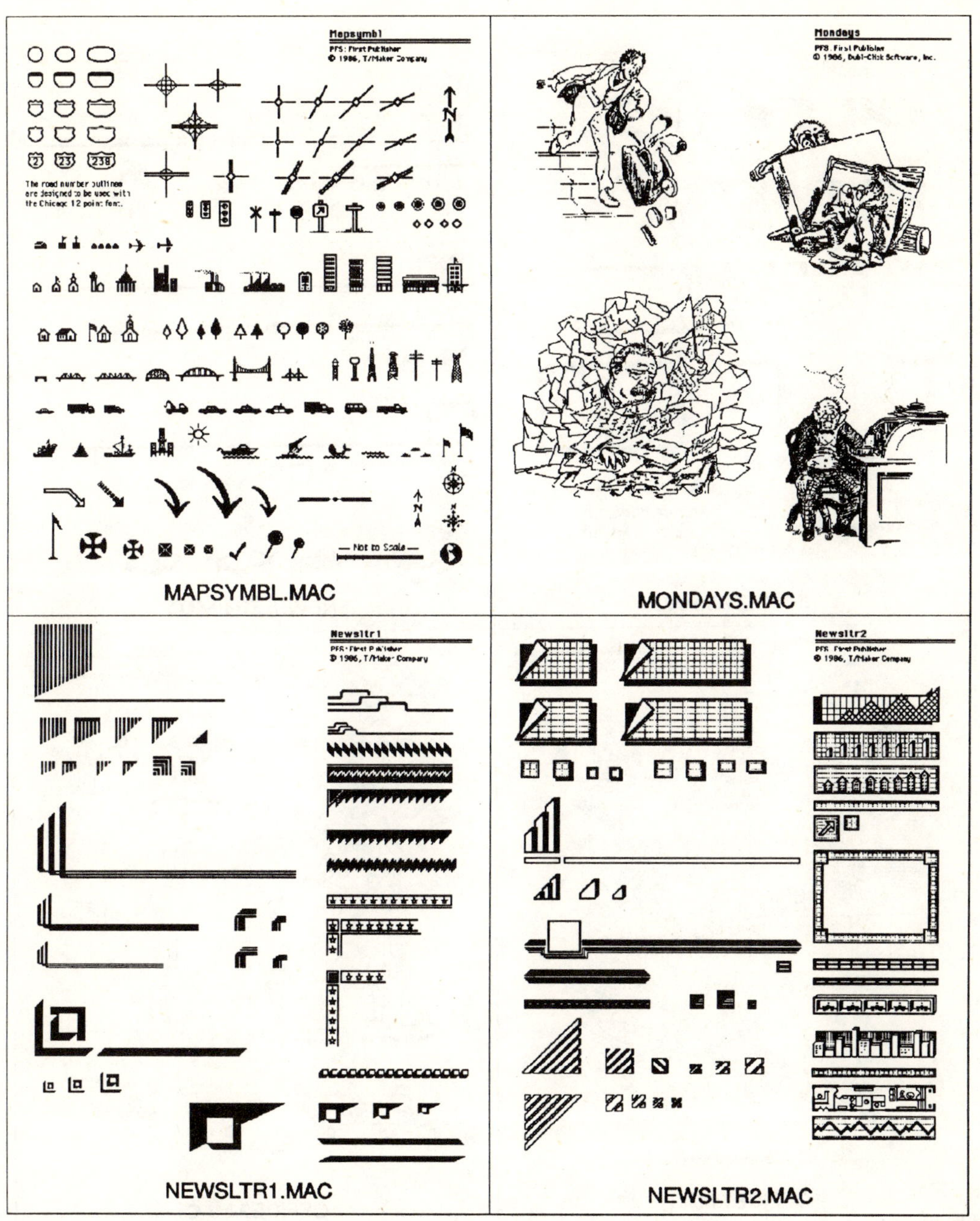

MAPSYMBL.MAC

MONDAYS.MAC

NEWSLTR1.MAC

NEWSLTR2.MAC

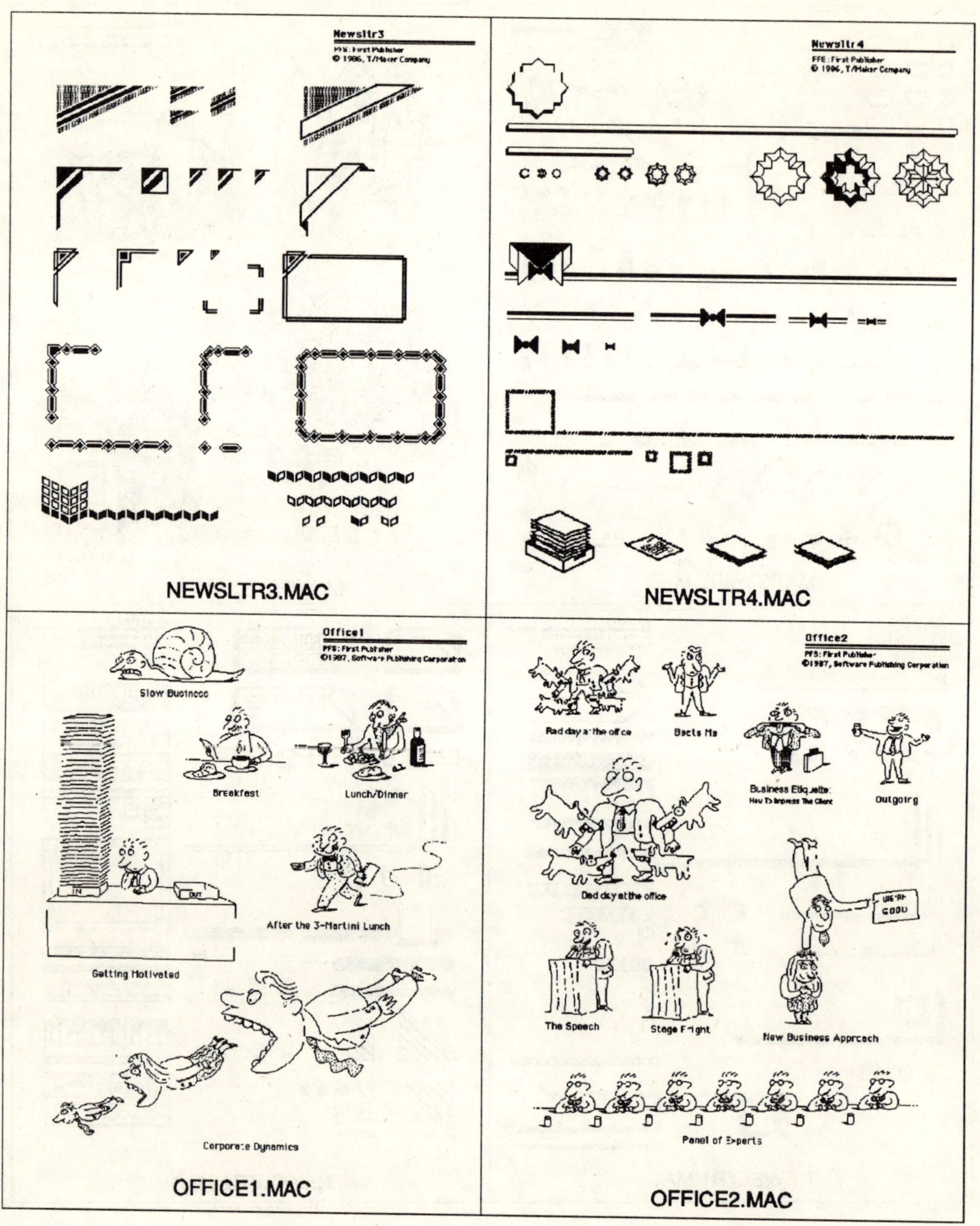
Newsltr3
PFS: First Publisher
© 1986, T/Maker Company
NEWSLTR3.MAC
Newsltr4
PFS: First Publisher
© 1986, T/Maker Company
NEWSLTR4.MAC
Office1
PFS: First Publisher
©1987, Software Publishing Corporation
Slow Business
Breakfast
Lunch/Dinner
After the 3-Martini Lunch
Getting Motivated
Corporate Dynamics
OFFICE1.MAC
Office2
PFS: First Publisher
©1987, Software Publishing Corporation
Bad day at the office
Beats Me
Business Etiquette:
How To Impress The Client
Outgoing
Bad day at the office
WE'RE GOOD
The Speech
Stage Fright
New Business Approach
Panel of Experts
OFFICE2.MAC

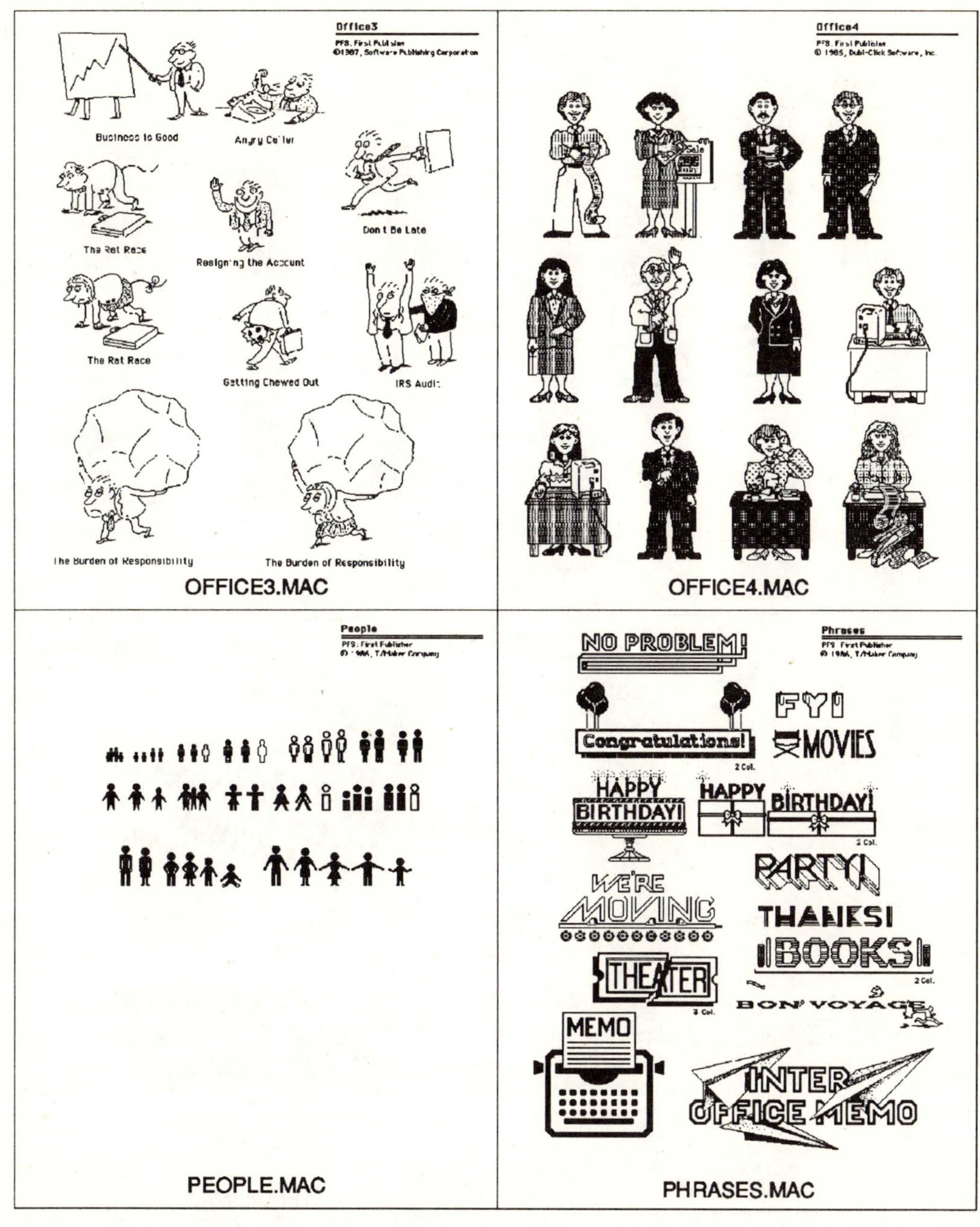
Office3
PFS: First Publisher
©1987, Software Publishing Corporation
Business Is Good
Angry Caller
The Rat Race
Resigning the Account
Don't Be Late
The Rat Race
Getting Chewed Out
IRS Audit
The Burden of Responsibility
The Burden of Responsibility
OFFICE3.MAC
Office4
PFS: First Publisher
© 1985, Dubl-Click Software, Inc.
OFFICE4.MAC
People
PFS: First Publisher
PEOPLE.MAC
Phrases
PFS: First Publisher
© 1986, T/Maker Company
NO PROBLEM!
FYI
Congratulations!
2 Col.
MOVIES
HAPPY BIRTHDAY!
HAPPY BIRTHDAY!
2 Col.
PARTY!
WE'RE MOVING
THANKS!
BOOKS
2 Col.
THEATER
3 Col.
BON VOYAGE
MEMO
INTER OFFICE MEMO
PHRASES.MAC

POSTERS.MAC

SERVICE.MAC

STATES.MAC

STENCIL.MAC

Symbols1
PFS: First Publisher
© 1986, T/Maker Company
SYMBOLS1.MAC
Symbols2
PFS First Publisher
© 1986, T/Maker Company
SYMBOLS2.MAC
TheBoss
PFS: First Publisher
©1987, Software Publishing Corporation
The Boss
Chairman of the Bored
Impressing The Boss
Boss
Bored Meeting
THEBOSS.MAC
Transprt
PFS First Publisher
© 1986, T/Maker Company
TRANSPRT.MAC

Whoswho1
PFS: First Publisher
©1987, Software Publishing Corporation
Spies
Gossip Columnist
Employee of the Month
Prima Donna
The Conductor
Violinist
Chef
Strength
Party Animal
Party Animal
WHOSWHO1.MAC

Al & Jim
PFS. First Publisher
© 1986, T/Maker Company
AL&JIM.MAC
American
PFS. First Publisher
© 1986, T/Maker Company
AMERICAN.MAC
Animal
PFS: First Publisher
© 1986, T/Maker Company
ANIMAL.MAC
Animal 1
PFS: First Publisher
© 1986, Dubl-Click Software, Inc.
ANIMAL1.MAC

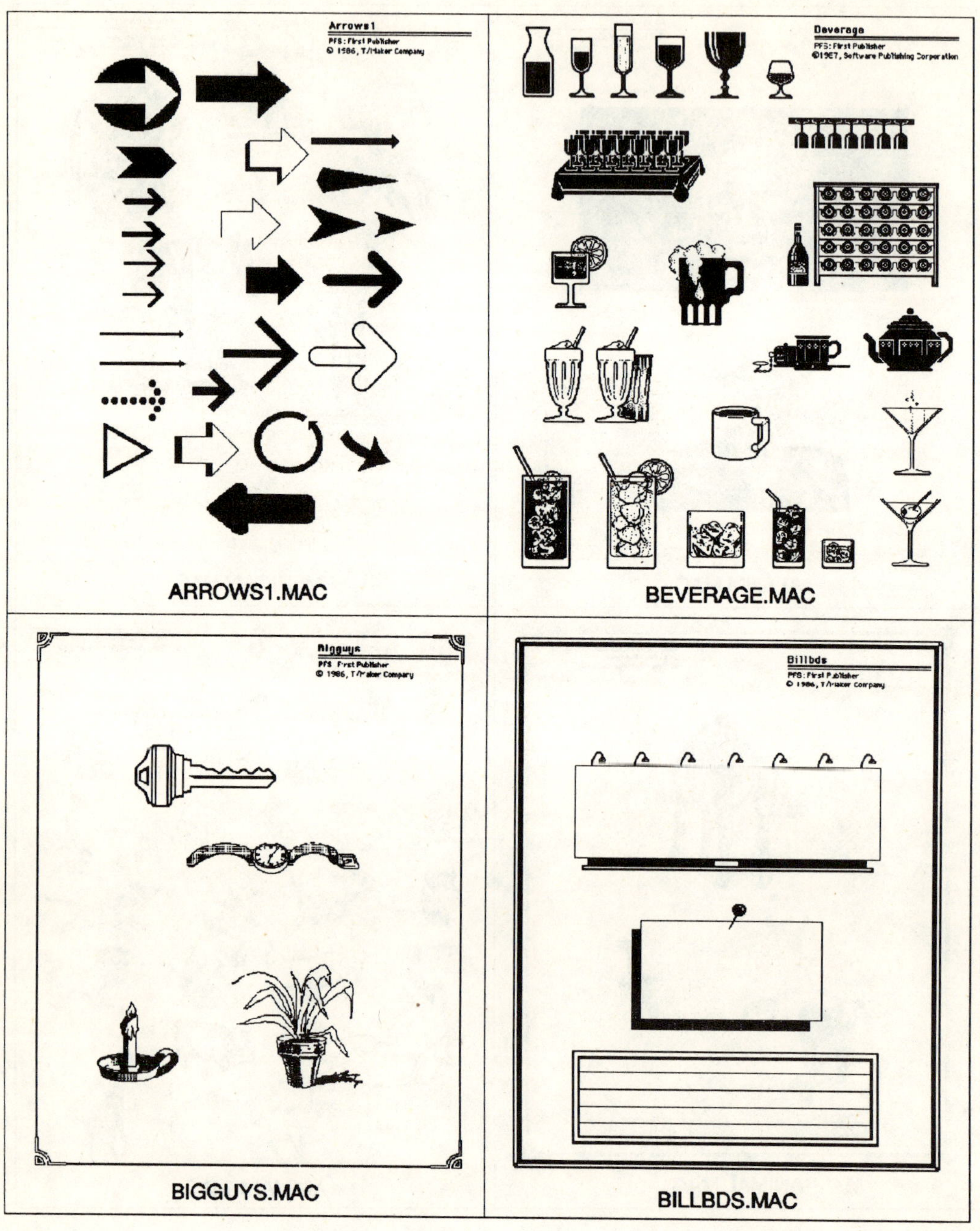

ARROWS1.MAC

BEVERAGE.MAC

BIGGUYS.MAC

BILLBDS.MAC

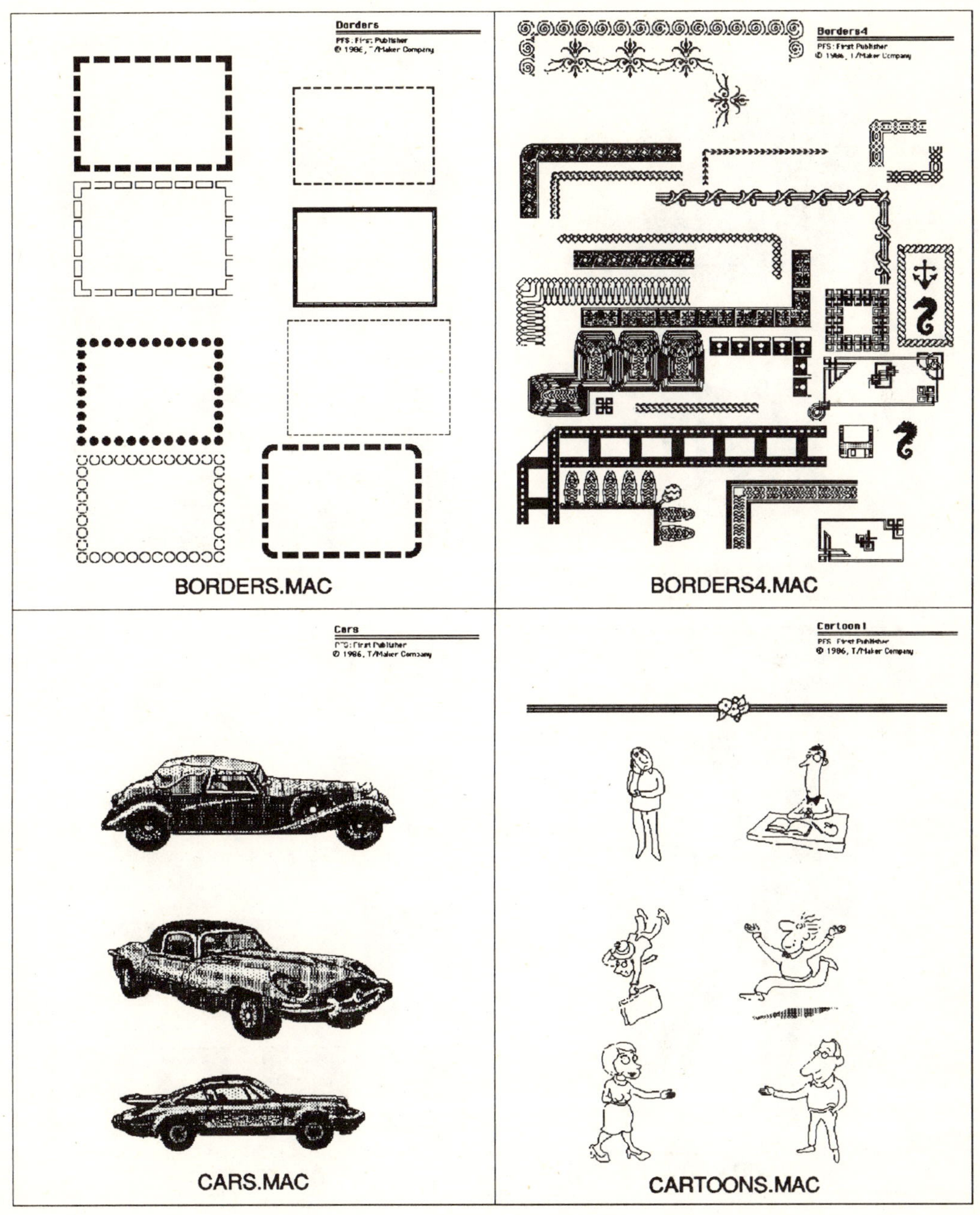
BORDERS.MAC
BORDERS4.MAC
CARS.MAC
CARTOONS.MAC

CATS.MAC

DANCE.MAC

DAVID.MAC

DINING1.MAC

Dining2
PFS: First Publisher
©1987, Software Publishing Corporation
Cafe
DINING2.MAC
Dogs
PFS: First Publisher
© 1986, Dubl-Click Software, Inc.
DOGS.MAC
Drama
PFS: First Publisher
© 1986, Dubl-Click Software, Inc.
DRAMA.MAC
Egret
PFS: First Publisher
© 1986, T/Maker Company
EGRET.MAC

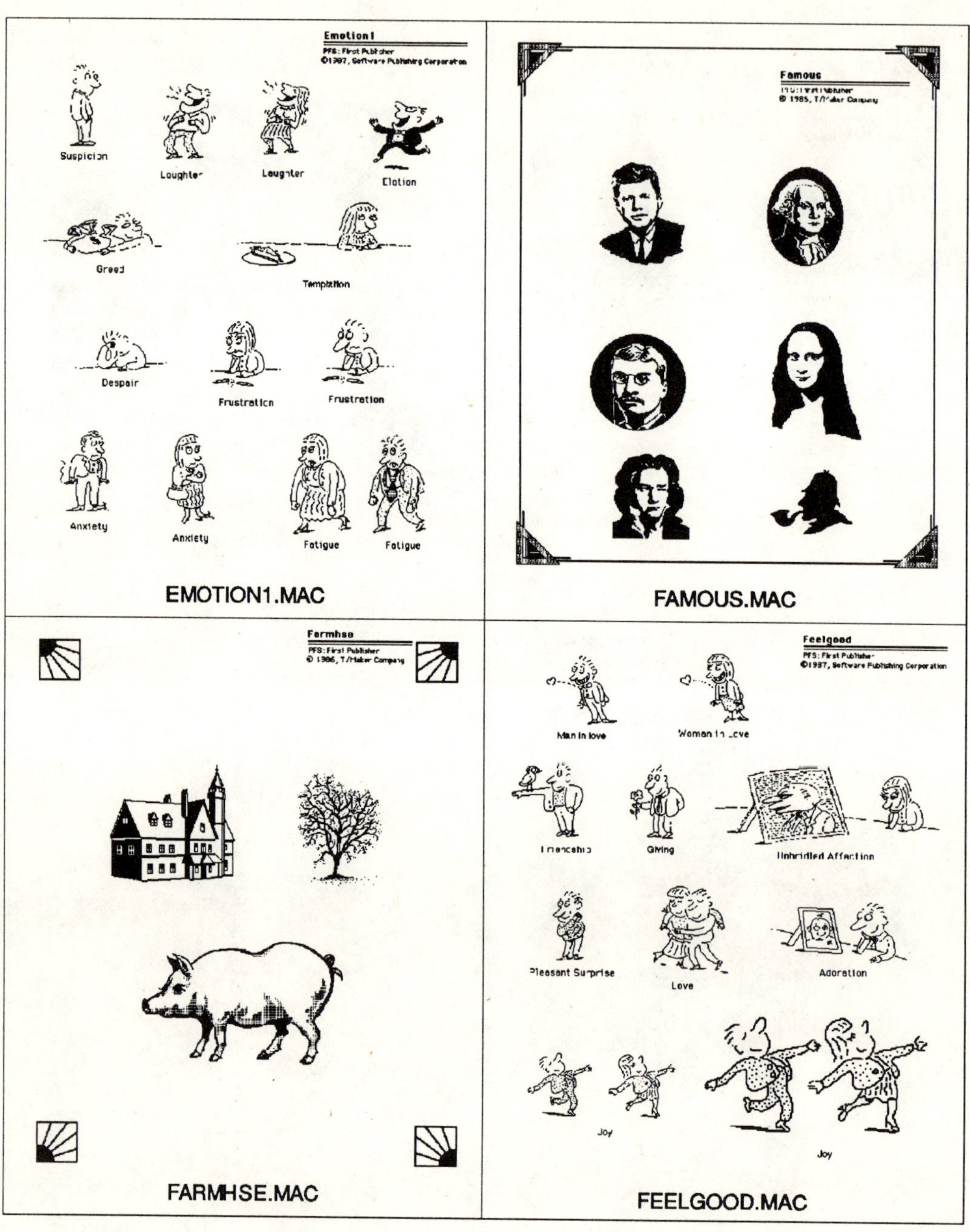
Emotion1
PFS: First Publisher
©1987, Software Publishing Corporation
Suspicion
Laughter
Laughter
Elation
Greed
Temptation
Despair
Frustration
Frustration
Anxiety
Anxiety
Fatigue
Fatigue
EMOTION1.MAC
Famous
© 1985, T/Maker Company
FAMOUS.MAC
Farmhse
PFS: First Publisher
© 1986, T/Maker Company
FARMHSE.MAC
Feelgood
PFS: First Publisher
©1987, Software Publishing Corporation
Man in love
Woman in Love
Friendship
Giving
Unbridled Affection
Pleasant Surprise
Love
Adoration
Joy
Joy
FEELGOOD.MAC

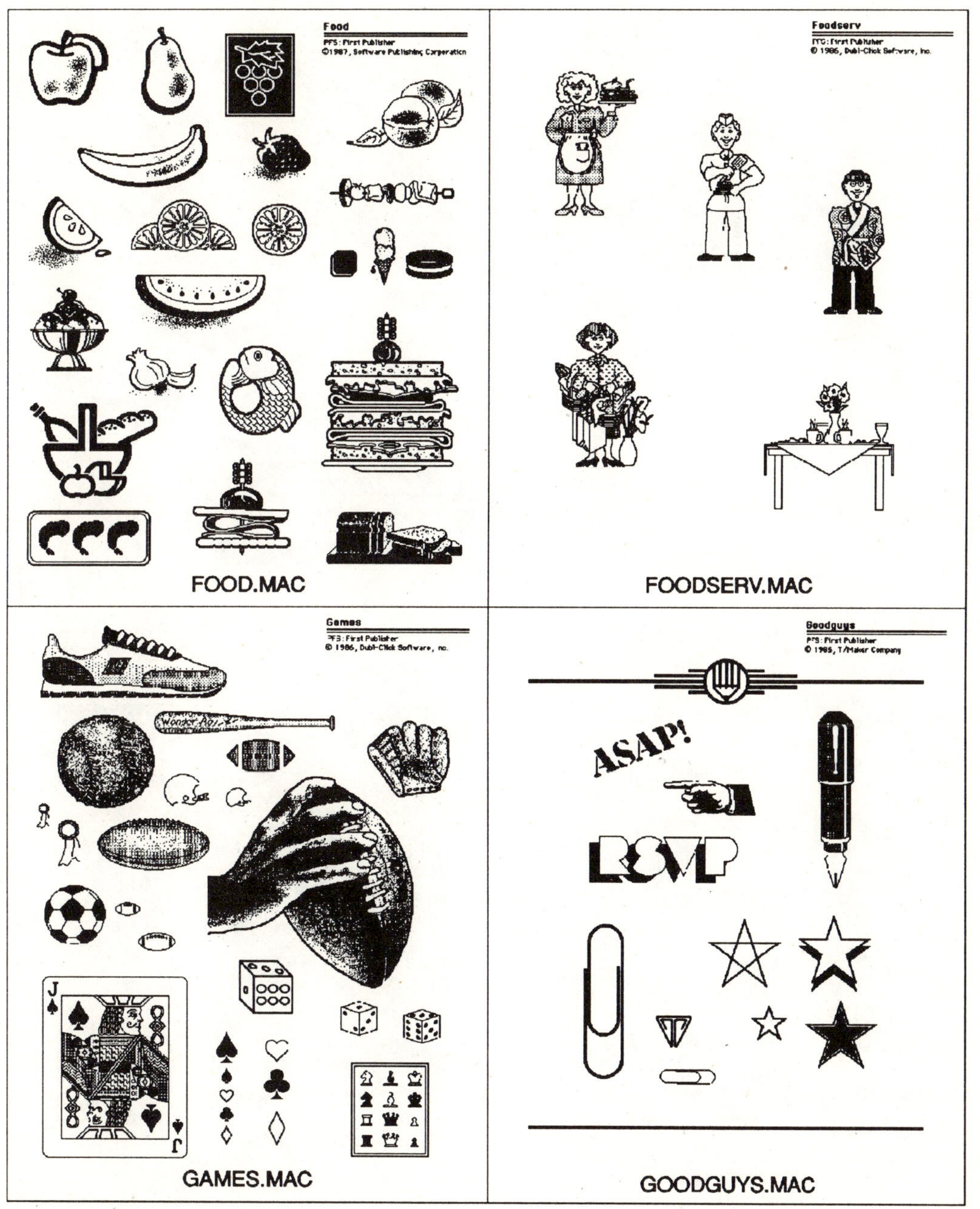
Food
PFS: First Publisher
©1987, Software Publishing Corporation
FOOD.MAC
Foodserv
PFS: First Publisher
© 1986, Dubl-Click Software, Inc.
FOODSERV.MAC
Games
PFS: First Publisher
© 1986, Dubl-Click Software, Inc.
GAMES.MAC
Goodguys
PFS: First Publisher
© 1985, T/Maker Company
ASAP!
RSVP
GOODGUYS.MAC

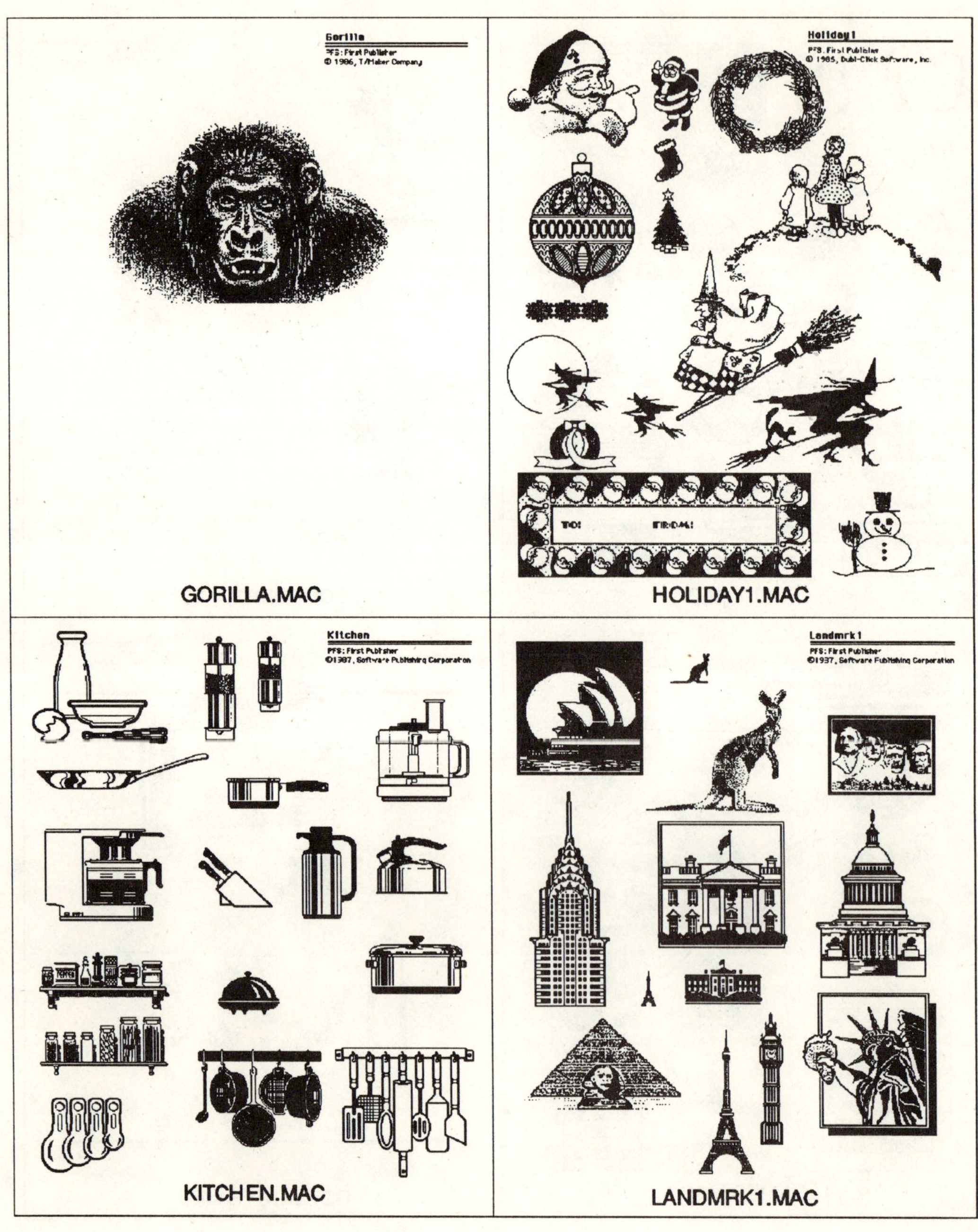

Gorilla
PFS: First Publisher
© 1986, T/Maker Company
GORILLA.MAC
Holiday1
PFS. First Publisher
© 1985, Dubl-Click Software, Inc.
TO:
FROM:
HOLIDAY1.MAC
Kitchen
PFS: First Publisher
©1987, Software Publishing Corporation
KITCHEN.MAC
Landmrk1
PFS: First Publisher
©1937, Software Publishing Corporation
LANDMRK1.MAC

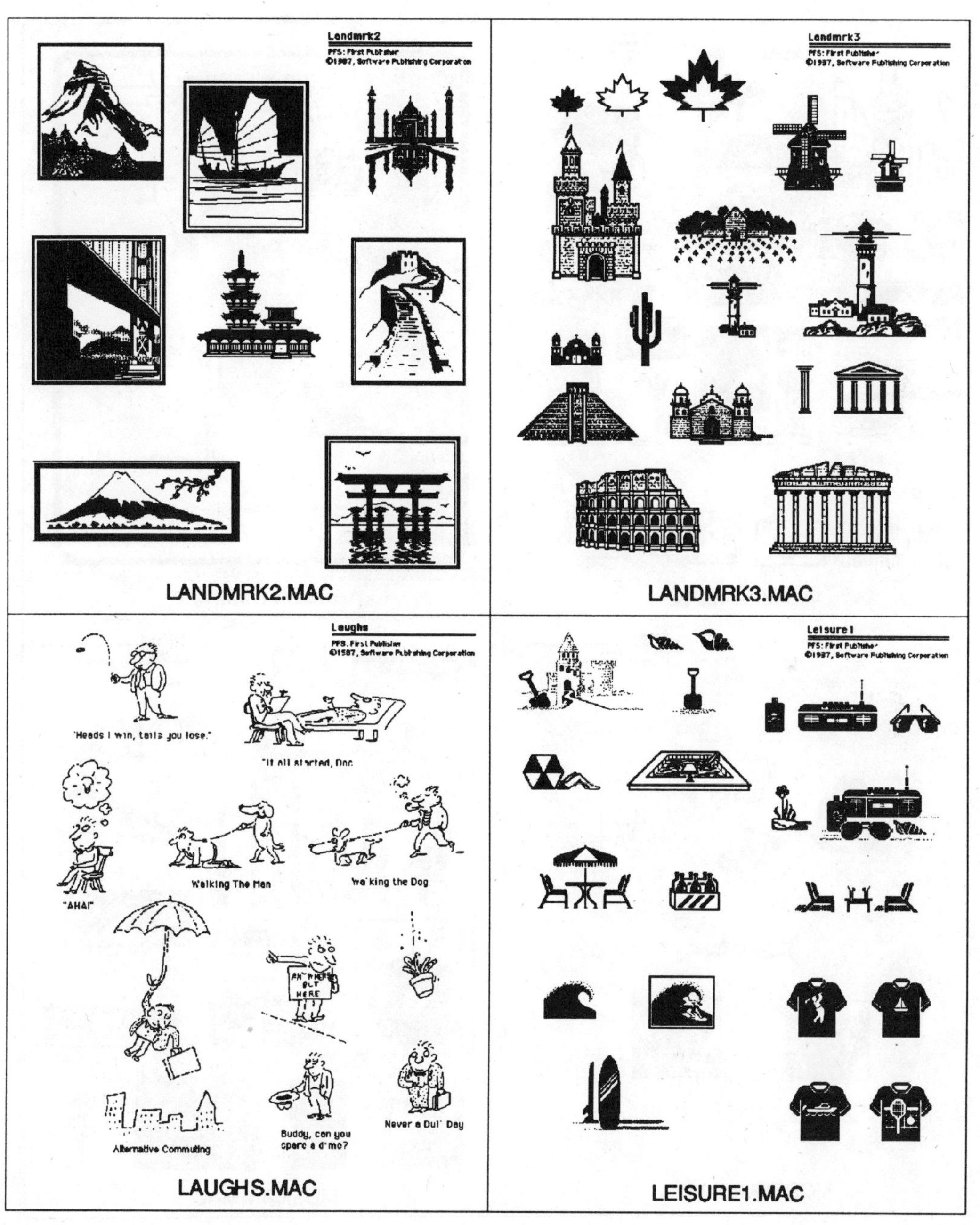
Landmrk2
PFS: First Publisher
©1987, Software Publishing Corporation
LANDMRK2.MAC
Landmrk3
PFS: First Publisher
©1987, Software Publishing Corporation
LANDMRK3.MAC
Laughs
PFS: First Publisher
©1987, Software Publishing Corporation
"Heads I win, tails you lose."
"It all started, Doc
"AHA!"
Walking The Man
Walking the Dog
Alternative Commuting
Buddy, can you spare a dime?
Never a Dull Day
LAUGHS.MAC
Leisure1
PFS: First Publisher
©1987, Software Publishing Corporation
LEISURE1.MAC

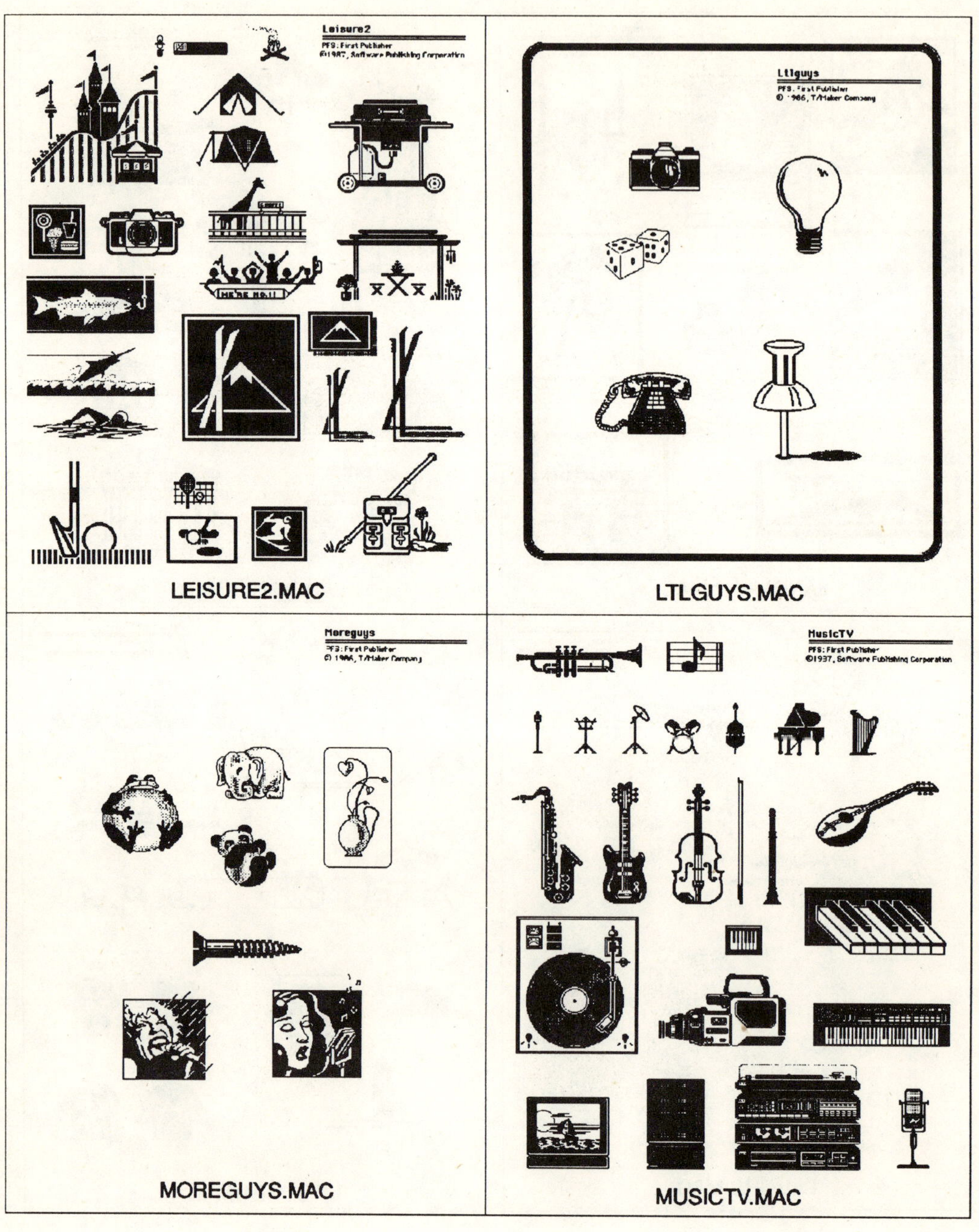
Leisure2
PFS: First Publisher
LEISURE2.MAC
Ltlguys
© 1986, T/Maker Company
LTLGUYS.MAC
Moreguys
MOREGUYS.MAC
MusicTV
PFS: First Publisher
MUSICTV.MAC

Outdoors
© 1986, T/Maker Company
OUTDOORS.MAC
Party 1
PFS: First Publisher
© 1986, Dubl-Click Software, Inc.
HAPPY NEW YEAR
PARTY1.MAC
Pets
© 1986, Dubl-Click Software
PETS.MAC
Rainy Day
PFS: First Publisher
RAINYDAY.MAC

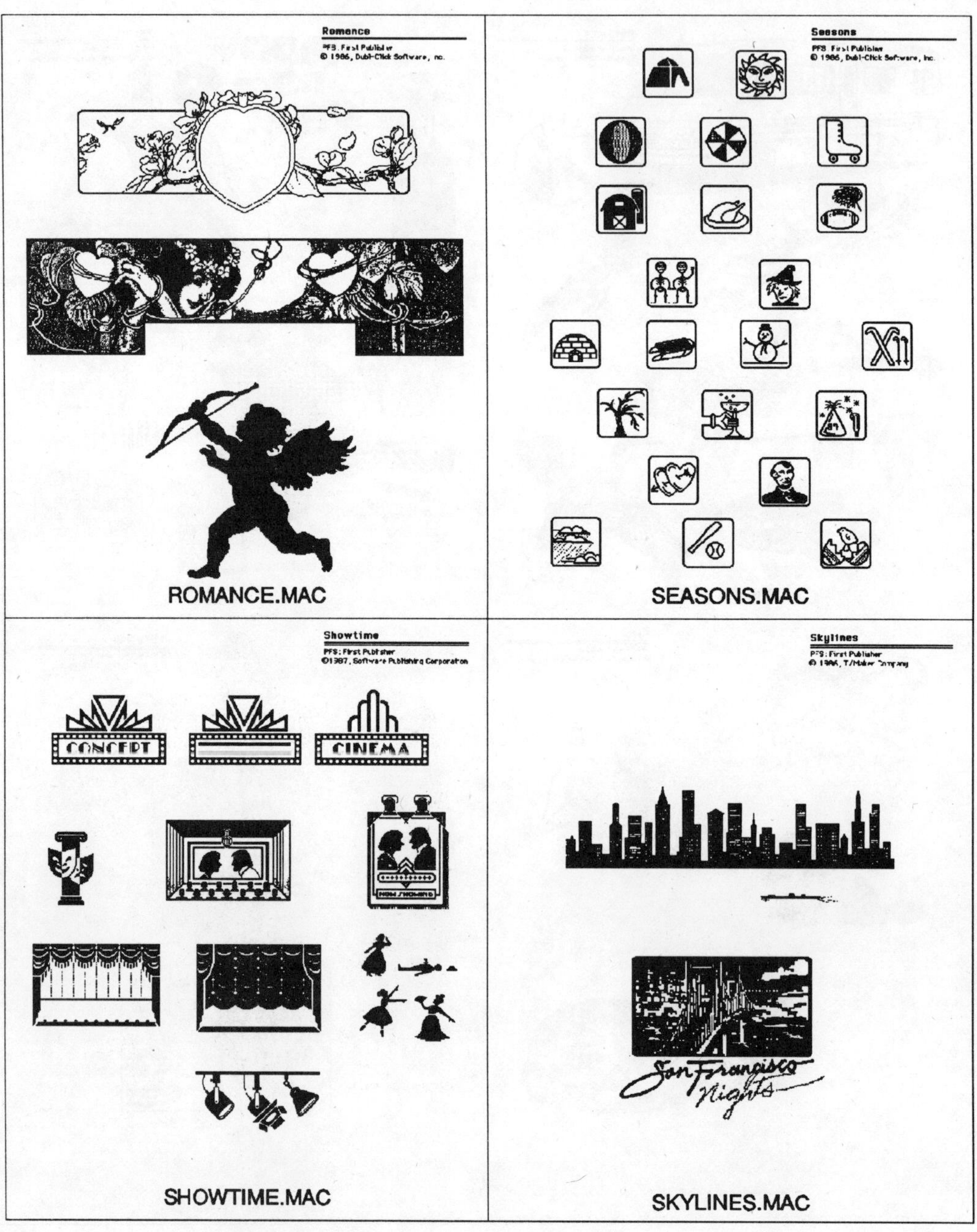
Romance
ROMANCE.MAC
Seasons
SEASONS.MAC
Showtime
CONCERT
CINEMA
SHOWTIME.MAC
Skylines
San Francisco
Nights
SKYLINES.MAC

Space
PFS: First Publisher
© 1986, T/Maker Company
SPACE.MAC
Sports1
PFS: First Publisher
© 1986, T/Maker Company
SPORTS1.MAC
Sports2
PFS: First Publisher
SPORTS2.MAC
Sports3
PFS: First Publisher
© 1985, Dubl-Click Software, Inc.
SPORTS3.MAC

Sports4
PFS: First Publisher
© 1986, Dubl-Click Software, Inc.
SPORTS4.MAC
Sportsmn
PFS: First Publisher
© 1985, Dubl-Click Software, Inc.
SPORTSMN.MAC
Statues
PFS: First Publisher
STATUES.MAC
Travel1
PFS: First Publisher
©1987, Software Publishing Corporation
TRAVEL1.MAC

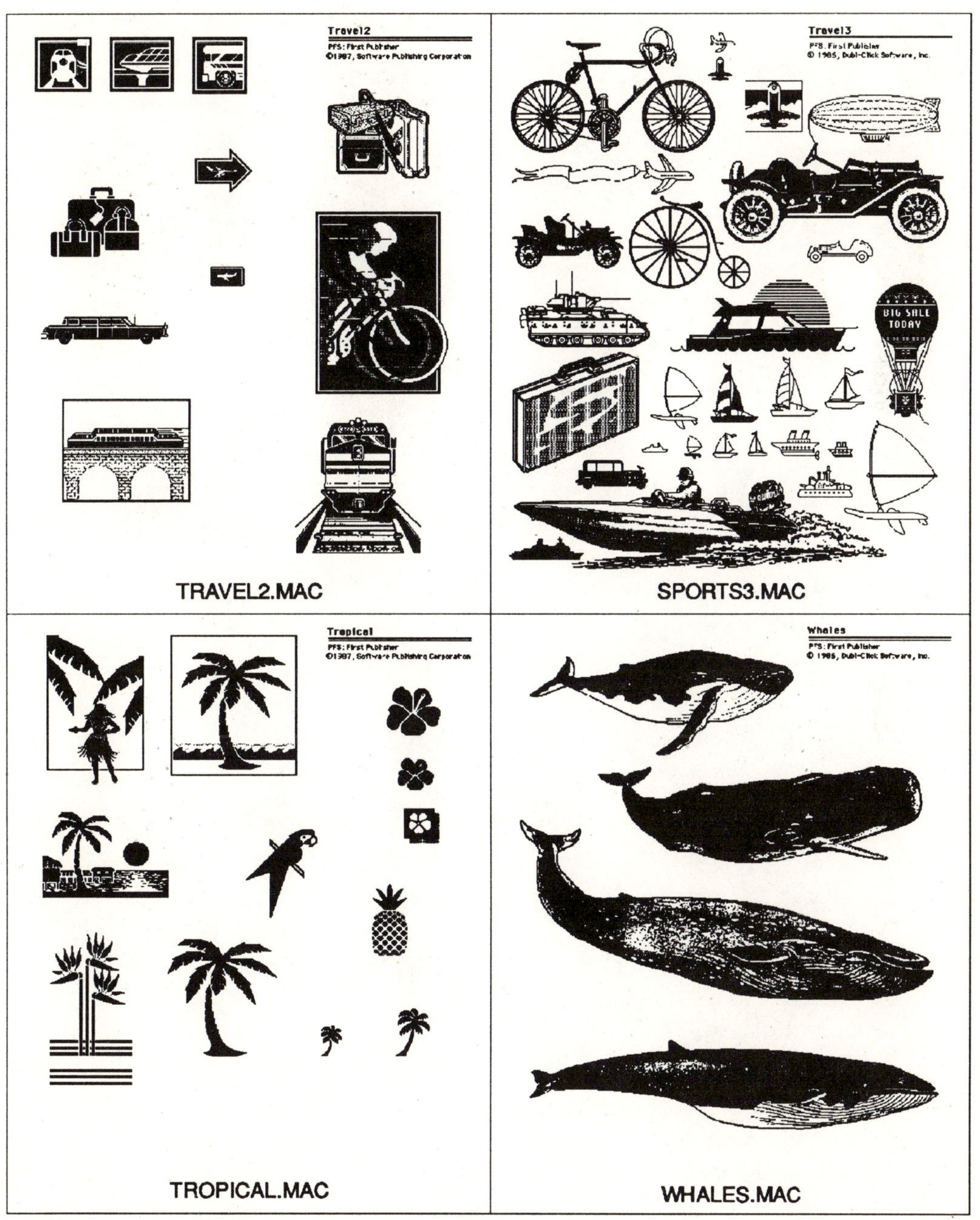
Travel2
PFS: First Publisher
©1987, Software Publishing Corporation
TRAVEL2.MAC
Travel3
PFS: First Publisher
© 1985, Dubl-Click Software, Inc.
BIG SALE TODAY
SPORTS3.MAC
Tropical
PFS: First Publisher
©1987, Software Publishing Corporation
TROPICAL.MAC
Whales
PFS: First Publisher
© 1985, Dubl-Click Software, Inc.
WHALES.MAC

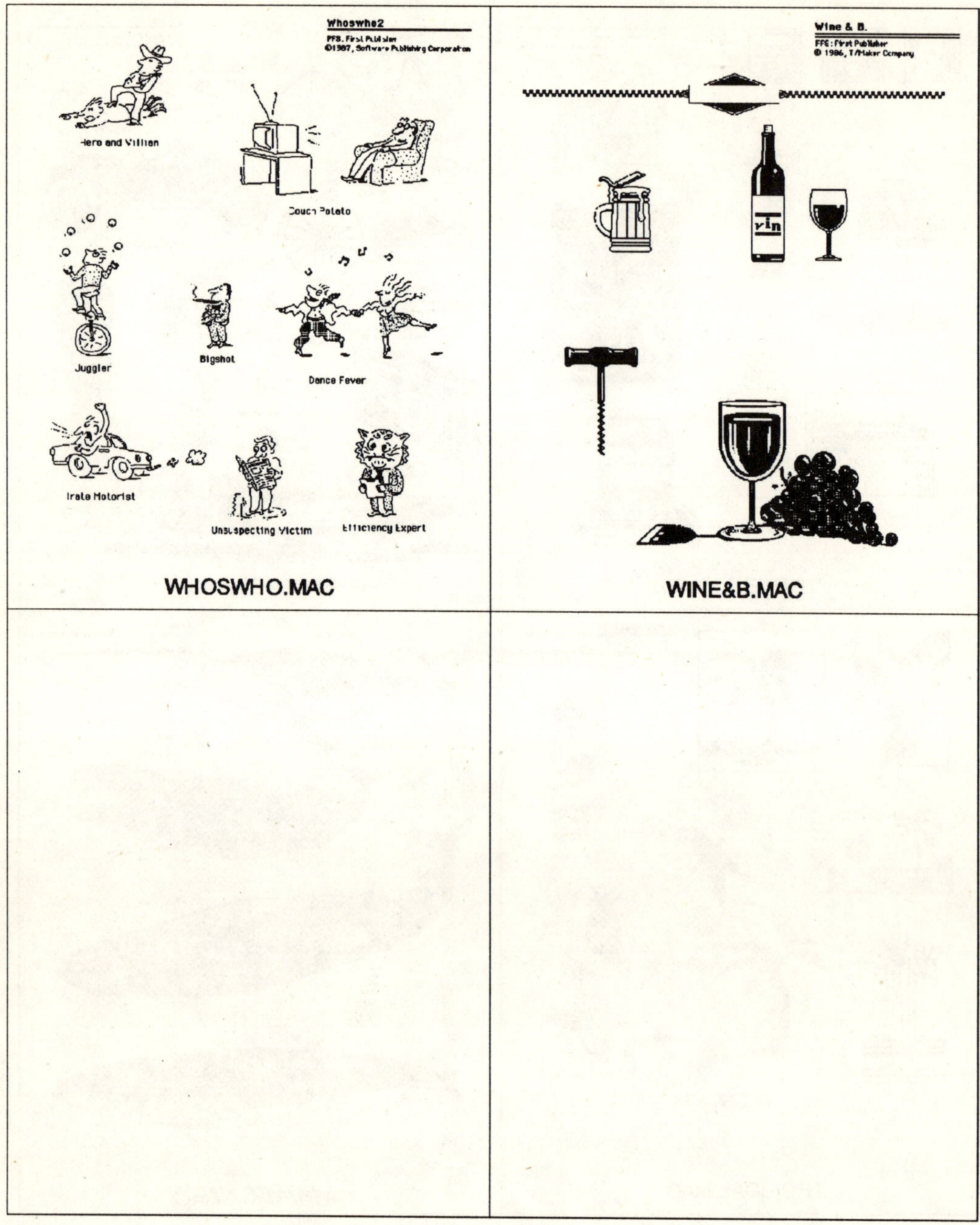

WHOSWHO.MAC

WINE&B.MAC

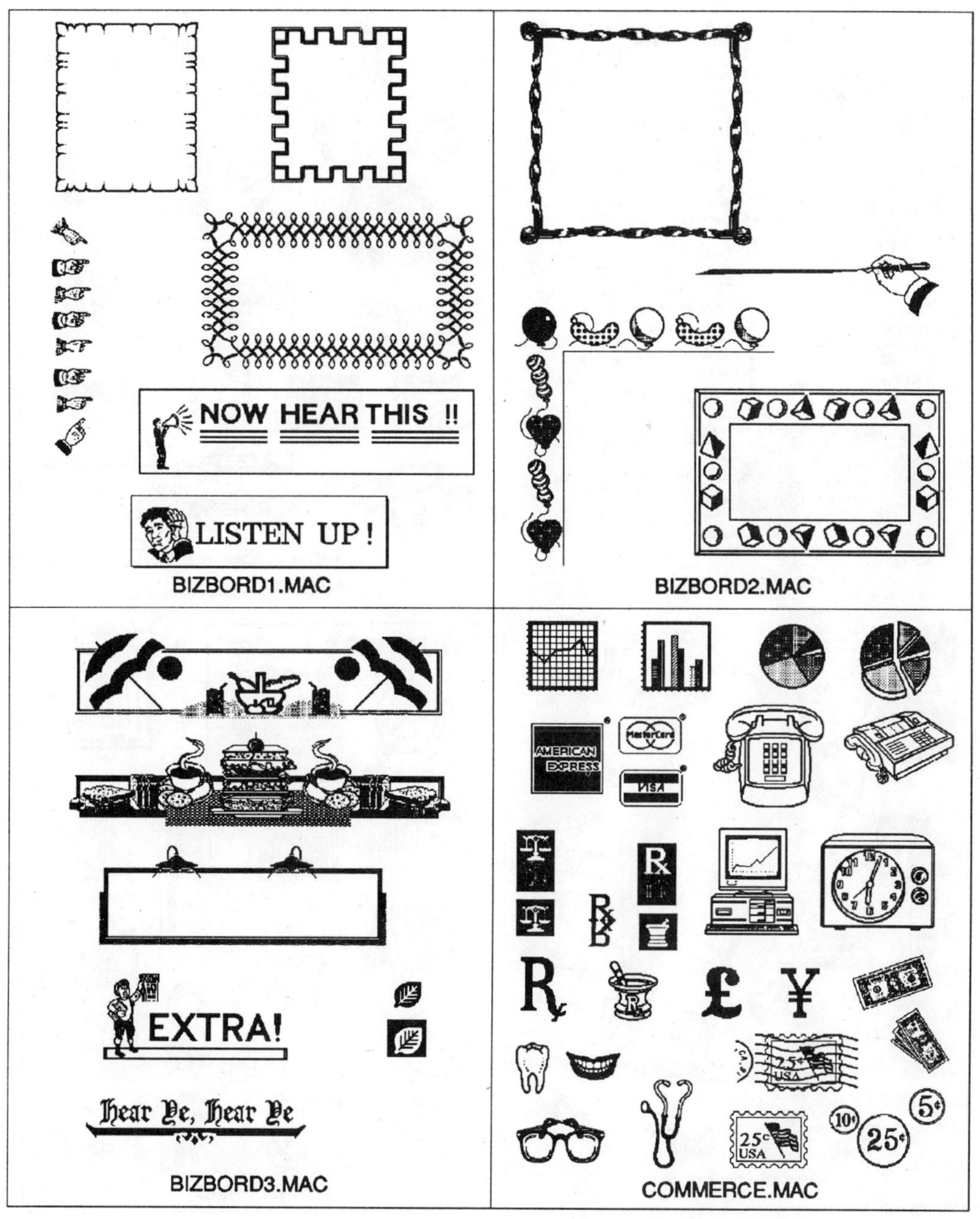
NOW HEAR THIS !!
LISTEN UP!
BIZBORD1.MAC
BIZBORD2.MAC
EXTRA!
Hear Ye, Hear Ye
BIZBORD3.MAC
AMERICAN EXPRESS
MasterCard
VISA
25¢ USA
10¢
25¢
5¢
COMMERCE.MAC

Business Name
1/2 off on
Banana Split
with this coupon ! expires:
Business Name
Rent 10
Videos
Get ONE
Rental FREE
Business Name
ONE
Regular Size
Yogurt
FREE !
with this coupon expires:
Business Name
Buy 5
slices . . .
Get one
slice
FREE !
Business
Name
One Shirt
Dry Cleaned
FREE
with this coupon expires:
Business Name
INTRODUCTORY
OFFER
Mailbox Rental
First Month
FREE !
COUPON
Save
25-50%
on marked
items
with this coupon.
COME SAVE
at all
Business Name
locations.
VALUE-SAVING
COUPONS.MAC
SUBURBAN.MAC
IMPORTANT
RECEIVED
CONFIDENTIAL
PAID
SUPPLIES.MAC
Business Hours
Open: 9:00
Close: 6:30
Come in, WE'RE
OPEN
FOR
RENT
FOR
SALE
OPEN
HOUSE
Meadow Heights
VARIETY.MAC

Appendix L
USING THE BUSINESS TEMPLATE KIT

DESCRIPTION

The Business Template Kit provides your business with a selection of predefined publication templates, fonts, and clip art. These templates cover a wide range of business application needs including: awards, signs, posters, and newsletters. The fonts add extra capability to the fonts you already receive with First Publisher. Finally, the clip art provides you with art appropriate for the business setting. You could easily use this kit for school and church activities as well as general business needs.

The following paragraphs describe some essential differences between the way you use the business templates with older versions of First Publisher and version 3.0. The major differences come not from a lack of compatibility, but from the new features that you will want to use to create your publication. Rather than repeat all the valuable information contained in the booklet that accompanies the kit, this appendix tells you how to make the best use of these templates with version 3.0. Appendix K shows you a reduced version of each piece of clip art provided in the kit. Please refer to the booklet for specific ideas on using each template, font, or piece of clip art.

APPLICATIONS

Each template, font, and piece of clip art in the Business Template Kit allows you to create enticing publications with a minimum of effort. Use these templates to reduce the work required to create a professional-looking document. Each template addresses a specific business need. For example, you would use MEMO.PUB to create a memorandum. As you use the templates, you will want to modify them to meet your company's specific needs. For example, you may want to place your logo at the top of each document. The different fonts allow you to create professional-looking headlines. Finally, the clip art can add the final polish that differentiates a professionally created document from a mediocre attempt.

NOTE

> Make certain that you do not modify the original copy of the template. Create a copy of the template and modify it instead. This allows you to modify the template with minimal risk. (You can retrieve the original copy if your modifications do not work correctly.)

TYPICAL OPERATION

The kit you receive from Software Publishing Corporation contains instructions that cover a variety of versions of PFS:First Publisher. However, you need to refer to the instructions below to make fullest use of the business template kit with version 3.0 of First Publisher. You can still use the original instructions as a guideline; these additional instructions make it easier for you to use the package. There are two basic additions to the instructions you receive in the kit. First, you need to add fonts to the new version of First Publisher in a different way than previous versions. Second, version 3.0 of First Publisher provides you with greater capabilities than older versions; therefore, you may need to modify some of the techniques used with this kit.

ADDING NEW FONTS

In this example you learn how to add fonts from the Business Template Kit to your standard font file. Begin at the Main menu with nothing loaded. This procedure assumes you installed the template file in the directory D:\FIRSTPUB\TEMPLATE. Please make any appropriate changes in the directory entries to reflect your particular configuration.

1. Press **F4** to select the Font menu. Highlight the Setup Fonts options using the arrow keys or mouse as shown in the following.

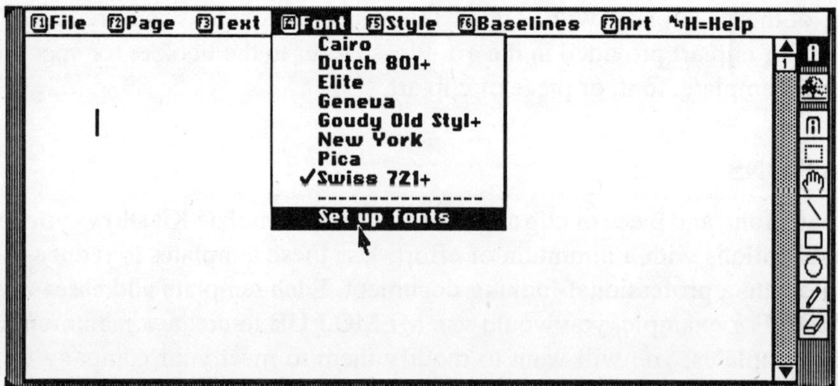

2. Press **Enter** or the left mouse button. The Set Up Fonts menu appears.

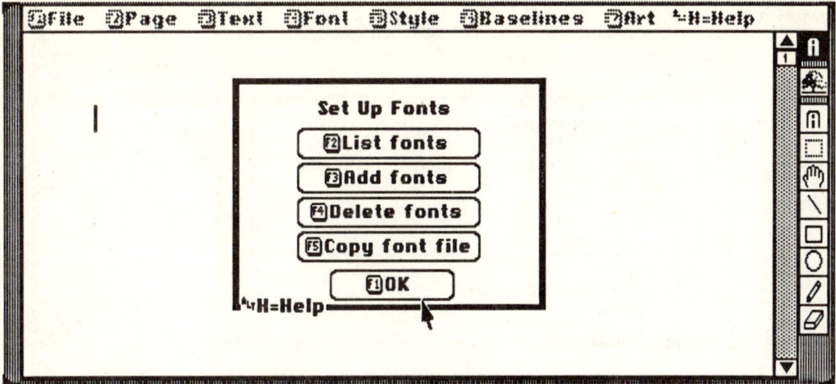

3. Press **F3** or click on the Add Fonts entry to select the Add Fonts option. First Publisher displays the following dialogue box.

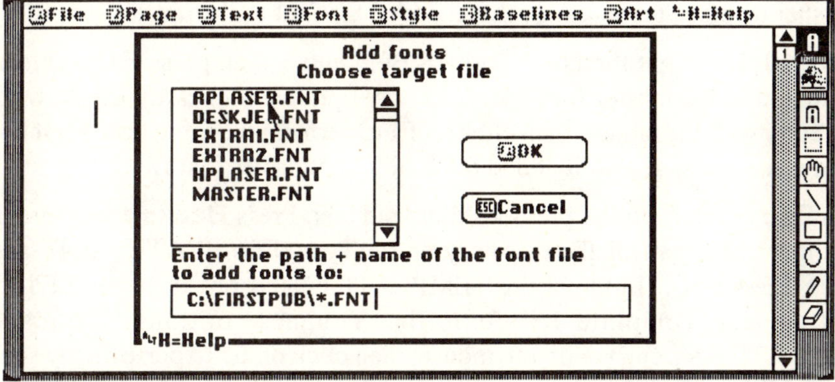

4. Press **F10**. Highlight the MASTER.FNT entry, then press **F1** to select the master font file. You may optionally click on the MASTER.FNT entry with the mouse, then click on F1 to perform the same task. First Publisher displays another dialogue box similar to the one shown above.

5. Press **F10**. Highlight the EXTRA1.FNT entry, then press **F1** to select the extra font file. You may optionally click on the EXTRA1.FNT entry with the mouse, then click on F1 to perform the same task. First Publisher displays the following dialogue box.

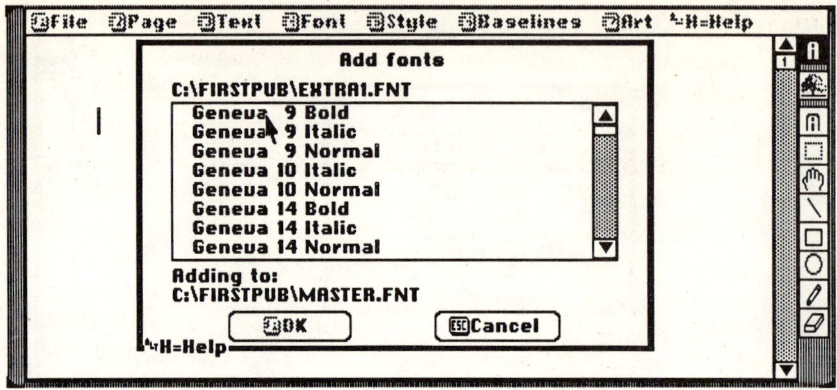

6. Press **F10**. Highlight the New York 12 Normal entry, then press **F1** to select a new font to add to the master font file. You may optionally click on the New York 12 Normal entry with the mouse, then click on F1 to perform the same task. First Publisher displays the message that it added the font to the master font file.

7. Press **F10**. Highlight the New York 18 Bold entry, then press **F1** to select a new font to add to the master font file. You may optionally click on the New York 18 Bold entry with the mouse, then click on F1 to perform the same task. First Publisher displays the message that it added the font to the master font file.

8. Press **Esc** to return to the previous dialogue box. Press **Backspace** five times to erase the *.FN? part of the directory entry. Type **TEMPLATE*.FNT** and press **Enter**. Press **F10**. Highlight the TEMPLATE.FNT entry, then press **F1** to select the Business Template Kit font file. You may optionally click on the TEMPLATE.FNT entry with the mouse, then click on F1 to perform the same task. First Publisher displays the dialogue box shown above.

9. Press **F10**. Highlight the Detroit 24 Normal entry, then press **F1** to select a new font to add to the master font file. You may optionally click on the Detroit 24 Normal entry with the mouse, then click on F1 to perform the same task. First Publisher displays the message that it added the font to the master font file.

10. Press **Esc** twice to return to the Set Up Fonts menu. You may optionally point to the Esc button and click the left mouse button to perform the same task. Press **F1** or click on the F1 button to return to the Main menu. First Publisher displays a message saying that it is reinitializing the font file, then returns you to the Main menu. The MASTER.FNT file now contains three new fonts taken from two different sources. You may use this same procedure to add any number of new fonts to the master font file.

USING THE TEMPLATES

In this example you use one of the templates to create a business mailing. Many businesses must rely on in-house capabilities to perform this task on a regular basis. In addition, both schools and churches use this technique to provide information to people involved in their activities. This procedure assumes that you added the necessary fonts to the master font file. The previous procedure tells you how to add these fonts. Begin at the Main menu with nothing loaded. This procedure also assumes you installed the template file in the directory D:\FIRSTPUB\TEMPLATE. Please make any appropriate changes in the directory entries to reflect your particular configuration.

1. Press **F1** to select the File menu. Highlight the Get Publication option using the arrow keys and press **Enter**. You may optionally use the mouse to point and click on each item. First Publisher displays the following dialogue box.

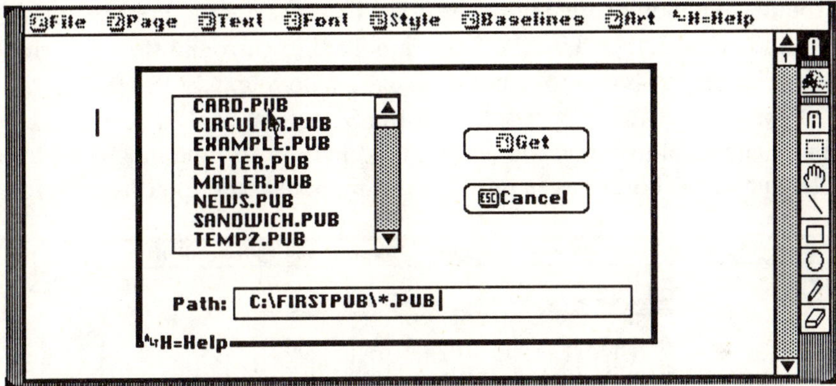

2. Press **Backspace** five times to erase the *.PUB part of the directory entry. Type **TEMPLATE*.PUB** and press **Enter**. Press **F10**. Highlight the MAILER1.PUB entry, then press **F1** to select the mailer file. You may optionally click on the MAILER1.PUB entry with the mouse, then click on F1 to perform the same task. First Publisher displays a getting document message, then displays the document on-screen. Notice that each text entry contains notes as to its size and font. Also note that the cursor automatically positions itself on the first line of your text. This allows you to begin typing the message immediately.

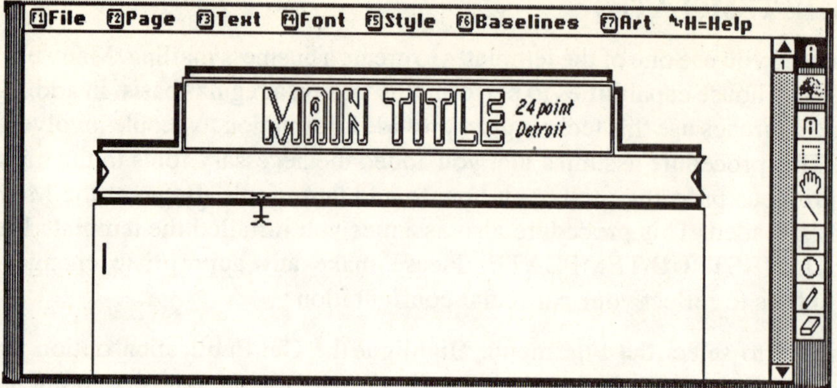

3. Press **Alt-S** to display the Save dialogue box. Type **MAILER1A** and press **F1** to save the new version of the template. Press **F4** to select the Font menu. Highlight Detroit and press **Enter**. Use the Selection Tool to surround the main title and its type description. Press **Del** to remove the explanatory text. Select the Graphics Text Tool. Type **A Chance for More**. Use the Selection Tool to select the new text. Use the Hand Tool to center the text within the box. Use the magnifier to perform any cleanup of the border as required. Your mailer should look like the following.

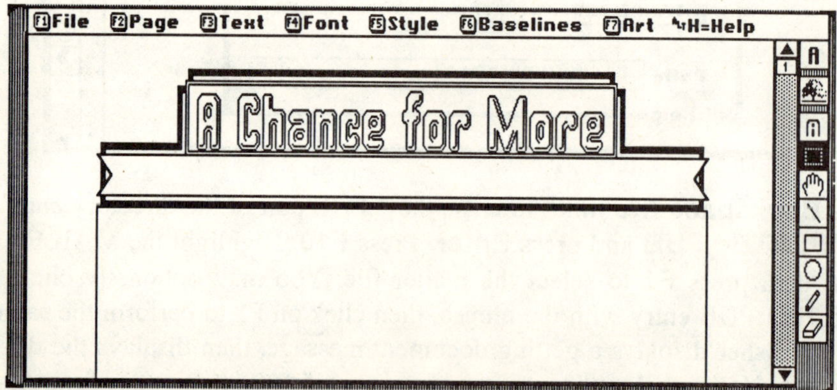

4. Press **F4** to select the Font menu. Highlight New York and press **Enter**. Press **F5** to select the Style menu. Highlight Bold and press **Enter**. Press **F5** to select the Style menu. Highlight 18 and press **Enter**. Use the Selection Tool to surround the header and its type description. Press **Del** to remove the explanatory text. Select the Graphics Text Tool. Type **Georges' Restaurant Offers More**. Use the Selection Tool to select the new text. Use the Hand Tool to place the text within the upper left corner of the box.

5. Save your mailer by pressing **Alt-S**, then **F1** twice. Press **Alt-Y** to clear the display. Press **F7**, highlight the Get Art option, and press **Enter**. Press **Backspace** five time to remove the *.ART part of the directory entry. Type **\TEMPLATE*.MAC** and **Enter**. Highlight COUPONS.MAC and press **F1**. First Publisher displays a warning message. Press **F1** to continue. Press **F10** twice to display the art. Select the pizza coupon using the Selection Tool. Press **F7**, highlight the Save Art option, and press **Enter**. Type **COUPON** and press **F1** to save the coupon to an art file.
6. Press **Alt-G**, then **F2** to display the Get Publication dialogue box. Press **Backspace** five times to erase the *.PUB part of the directory entry. Type **TEMPLATE*.PUB** and press **Enter**. Press **F10**. Highlight the MAILER1A.PUB entry, then press **F1** to select the mailer file. Press **F7**, highlight the Get Art option, and press **Enter**. Press **Backspace** three times. Type **ART** and press **Enter**. Highlight COUPON.ART and press **F1**. First Publisher displays the Hand Tool.
7. Use the Resize option of the Art menu and the Hand Tool to size and center the clip art in the center section of the mailer. Use the Selection Tool to select the restaurant name in the center of the coupon. Press **Del**. Type **Georges' Restaurant**. Center the clip art using the Hand Tool. Your mailer should look like the following.

8. Press **F5** to select the Style menu. Highlight Normal and press **Enter**. Press **F5**, highlight 12, and press **Enter**. Select the Text Tool and type **You place your sales pitch here. As you can tell, this is a very versatile template. You could use it to produce just about any type of mailer.** Your mailer should look like the following.

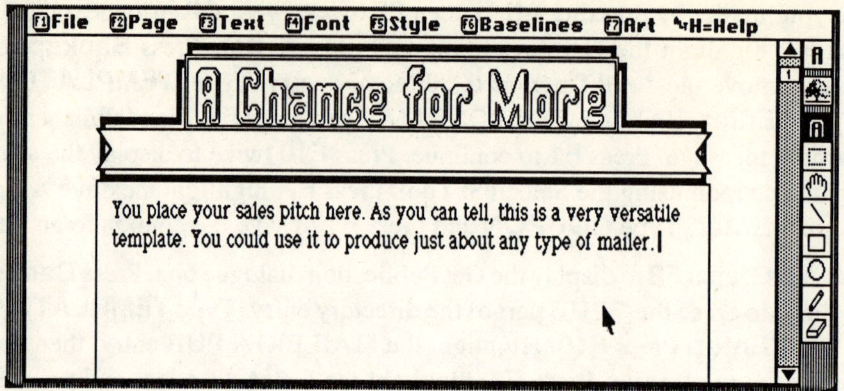

9. Finishing touches include adding a logo and company address at the bottom of the mailer. Refer to Module 27 for instructions on printing the final mailer. As you can see, the Business Template Kit allows you to create complex, professional-looking documents in a short time.

Appendix M
EXERCISES

1. About This Book
   a. How does a desktop publishing program like First Publisher differ from a word processor or painting program?
   b. How can you use the examples in this book?
   c. What are some of the features offered by First Publisher?
   d. What is the minimum hardware needed to run First Publisher?
2. PFS: First Publisher Overview
   a. Describe desktop publishing in your own words.
   b. How can you choose a menu from withing the First Publisher program?
   c. How can you use alternate keystroke combinations to choose menu commands?
   d. What does the tool bar contain?
   e. How do you use the page scroll bar?
3. A Sample Session with PFS: First Publisher
   a. How do you start First Publisher?
   b. How can you import a graphics image into a document?
   c. Which key can you press to get help at any time?
   d. How can you choose a different tool from the tool bar?
   e. Name the three print quality settings that First Publisher provides.
4. Adjust Single, Adjust Column, Adjust Above, Adjust Below
   a. How do these four commands differ?
   b. What is the shortcut key for choosing the Adjust Single command?
   c. Name the three ways you can adjust the baseline.
5. Center, Left Justify, Right Justify, Full Justify
   a. When would you want to right-justify text?
   b. How does the full justify command affect the appearance of text?
   c. How does the center command affect the right and left margins of text?
6. Change Leading
   a. Explain what leading does.
   b. When would you want to adjust the leading of a document?

7. Cut, Copy, Paste (Art)
   a. How do these commands differ when applied to graphics instead of text?
   b. When would you use the Cut command instead of the Copy command?
   c. When would you use the Paste command?

8. Cut, Copy, Paste (Text)
   a. What must you do first before cutting or copying text?
   b. How do these commands differ when applied to text instead of graphics?
   c. What can you use the Copy command for?

9. Define Page, Choose Layout, Adjust Layout
   a. In which menu does the Define Page command appear?
   b. What characteristics can you define with this command?
   c. Define the gutter of a page.
   d. Define what leading is.

10. Delete File
    a. Why would you want to delete a file from within First Publisher?
    b. Explain how you can delete a file using MS-DOS.
    c. In which menu does this command appear?

11. Delete Page
    a. How many pages will this command delete?
    b. In which menu does this command appear?
    c. What happens to the numbering of other pages when you choose this command to delete a page?

12. Drawing Tools
    a. How many different types of drawing tools does First Publisher provide?
    b. How can you choose a drawing tool with the keyboard?
    c. Which tool can move graphic images?
    d. Give three uses for the drawing tools.

13. Duplicate
    a. How does this command differ from the Copy command?
    b. What is the shortcut keystroke to choose this command?

14. Exit
    a. In which menu does this command appear?
    b. What is the shortcut keystroke to choose this command?
    c. What happens if you exit a document without saving it first?

15. Flip Horizontal, Flip Vertical, Rotate
    a. How many degrees do these command rotate graphic images?
    b. How can you reverse the effect of these commands?
    c. What is the shortcut keystroke to choose this command?
16. Font Menu
    a. What do fonts do?
    b. In which disk file does First Publisher store fonts?
    c. What are the two methods for using fonts stored in other files?
17. Get Art
    a. What does this command do?
    b. Name the two ways First Publisher can produce art files.
    c. What is the file extension needed to store graphic images that First Publisher can use?
18. Get Graphics
    a. In which menu does this command appear?
    b. How can you use this command to import graphic images from other programs?
19. Get Publication
    a. What is the shortcut keystroke to choose this command?
    b. In which menu does this command appear?
    c. How can you retrieve a file stored on a different drive?
20. Get Text
    a. How can this command help you import word processor files from another program?
    b. Name three different word processor file formats that First Publisher can use.
    c. How do ASCII files differ from regular word processor files such as WordStar or WordPerfect files?
21. Help, Help Topics, Customer Info
    a. Name two ways you can choose the Help command.
    b. When would you use this command instead of the manual?
    c. How do you exit from this command?
22. Insert Page
    a. In which menu does this command appear?
    b. Does this command insert a new page before or after an existing page that you specify?

23. Invert
    a. In which menu does this command appear?
    b. How does this command affect the colors of graphic images?
    c. Why would you want to use this command?
    d. How can you add a new page to the end of a document?

24. Jump To Page
    a. In which menu does this command appear?
    b. What happens if you ask First Publisher to jump to a page higher that exists in your document?
    c. Describe another way to move between pages. Explain the advantages of the Jump To Page command.

25. Magnify, Crop
    a. In which menu does this command appear?
    b. What can the Magnify command display?
    c. What is the shortcut keystroke to choose this command?
    d. Why would you use this command for graphic images?

26. Picturewrap
    a. In which menu does this command appear?
    b. What is the shortcut keystroke to choose this command?
    c. How does this command affect text?

27. Print
    a. Besides sending a file to a printer, where else can First Publisher print a file?
    b. Name the three levels of print quality First Publisher provides.
    c. Which print quality option provides the best appearance?
    d. Which print quality option prints the fastest?

28. Realign Text
    a. When should you use this command?
    b. How does this command work when you adjust a baseline?

29. Resize
    a. In which menu does this command appear?
    b. What is the shortcut keystroke to choose this command?
    c. When you choose the Resize command, how does First Publisher show you the edges of a selected graphic image?
    d. Why would you want to resize a graphic image?

30. Save
    a. Why should you use this command periodically?
    b. Name two ways to choose this command.
    c. Name the three ways First Publisher can store a file on disk.
    d. How can First Publisher convert graphics from different programs?
31. Save Art
    a. In which menu does this command appear?
    b. Why would you want to save only protions of a graphic image?
    c. How can you save a graphic image on a different drive?
32. Save Text
    a. In what format does this command save text?
    b. Why would you want to save a file with this command?
    c. What are the drawbacks to saving files with this command?
    d. In which menu does this command appear?
33. Set Grid Size
    a. How does this command affect grid points?
    b. What are the options that the Grid Size dialogue box displays?
    c. When would you choose small increments in the Grid Size dialogue box? Large increments?
34. Show Page
    a. How does this command display a page?
    b. Why would you want to use this command?
    c. What happens to the appearance of text when you choose this command?
    d. What is the shortcut keystroke to choose this command?
    e. In which menu does this command appear?
35. Show Rulers
    a. Where do the rulers appear when you choose this command?
    b. What is the unit of measurement that the rulers display?
    c. What can you use the rulers for?
    d. What is the shortcut keystroke to choose this command?
    e. In which menu does this command appear?
36. Start Over
    a. How does this command affect text and graphics on a page?
    b. What are the drawbacks to using this command?
    c. Why would you want to use this command?

37. Status, Customize
    a. What are the parameters that this command displays?
    b. What happens to the overflow characters if you exit a file?
    c. How can you change the printer port that First Publisher will use?
    d. What can you use the version number for?

38. Style Menu
    a. What are the four styles normally supplied with font packages?
    b. How can you use styles to enhance the appearance of text?
    c. Why should you limit the different number of styles on a page?

39. Use Grid
    a. What does this command display on the screen?
    b. When do the grid dots disappear from the screen?
    c. How can the grid help you design pages?
    d. What is the shortcut keystroke to choose this command?

40. Width Selections, Set Line Width
    a. How does this command affect the lines on a page?
    b. What is the shortcut keystroke for changing the thickness of a line?
    c. How many line thicknesses does First Publisher provide?
    d. Name three applications for lines on a page.

Index